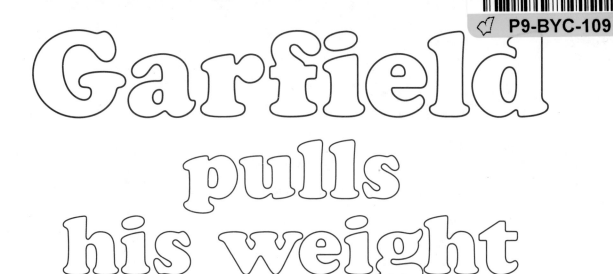

Garfield pulls his weight

BY: JIM DAVIS

belongs:
Jim Qi
Mrs. zarcone

Ballantine Books • New York

Copyright © 1994 United Feature Syndicate, Inc.
GARFIELD Comic Strips © 1993 United Feature Syndicate, Inc.

All rights reserved under International and Pan-American Copyright
Conventions. Published in the United States by Ballantine Books, a
division of Random House, Inc., New York, and simultaneously in
Canada by Random House of Canada Limited, Toronto.

Library of Congress Catalog Card Number: 93-90469

ISBN: 0-345-38666-3

Manufactured in the United States of America

First Edition: October 1994

10 9 8 7 6 5 4 3 2 1

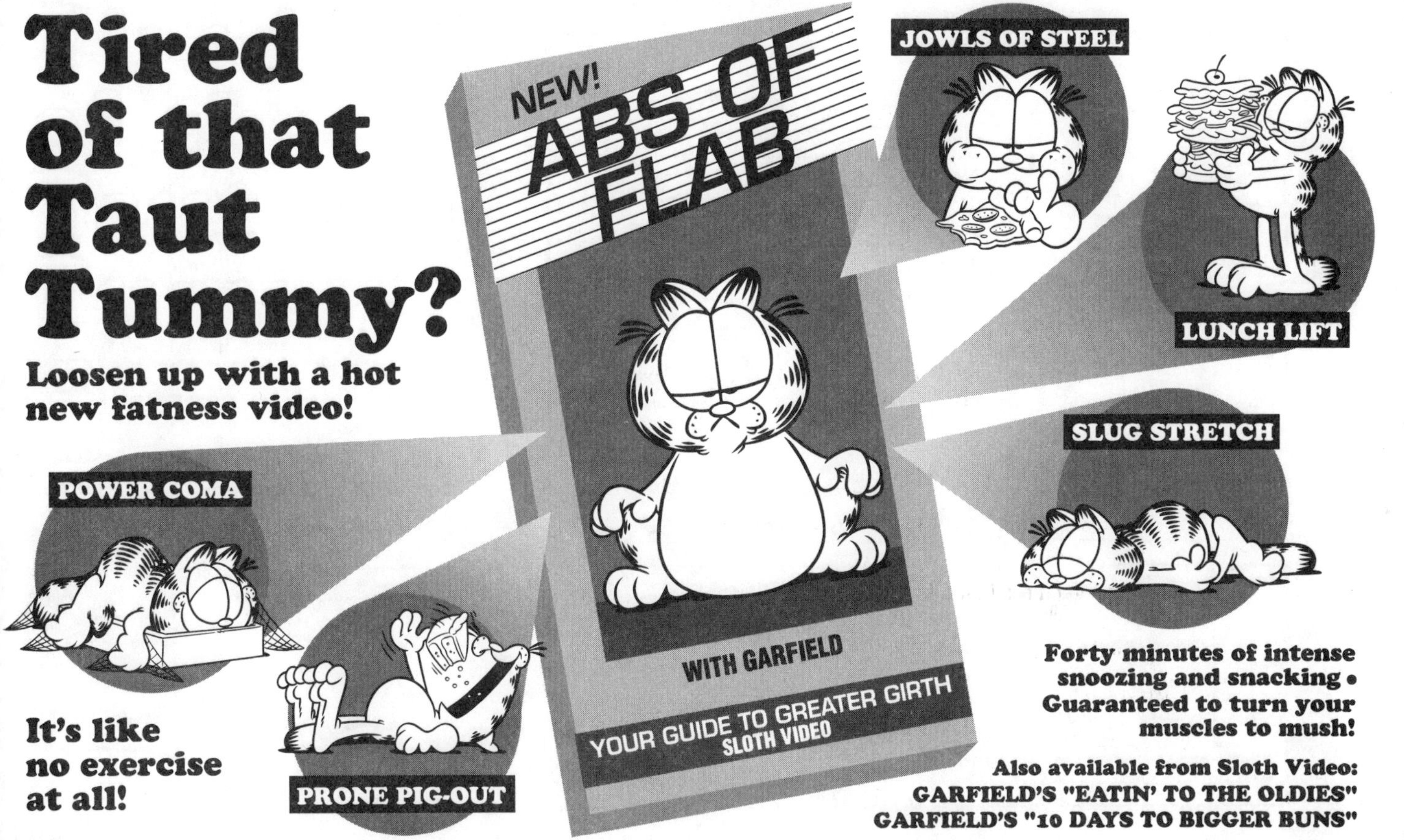
Tired of that Taut Tummy?
Loosen up with a hot new fatness video!
NEW!
ABS OF FLAB
WITH GARFIELD
YOUR GUIDE TO GREATER GIRTH
SLOTH VIDEO
JOWLS OF STEEL
LUNCH LIFT
SLUG STRETCH
POWER COMA
PRONE PIG-OUT
It's like no exercise at all!
Forty minutes of intense snoozing and snacking • Guaranteed to turn your muscles to mush!
Also available from Sloth Video:
GARFIELD'S "EATIN' TO THE OLDIES"
GARFIELD'S "10 DAYS TO BIGGER BUNS"

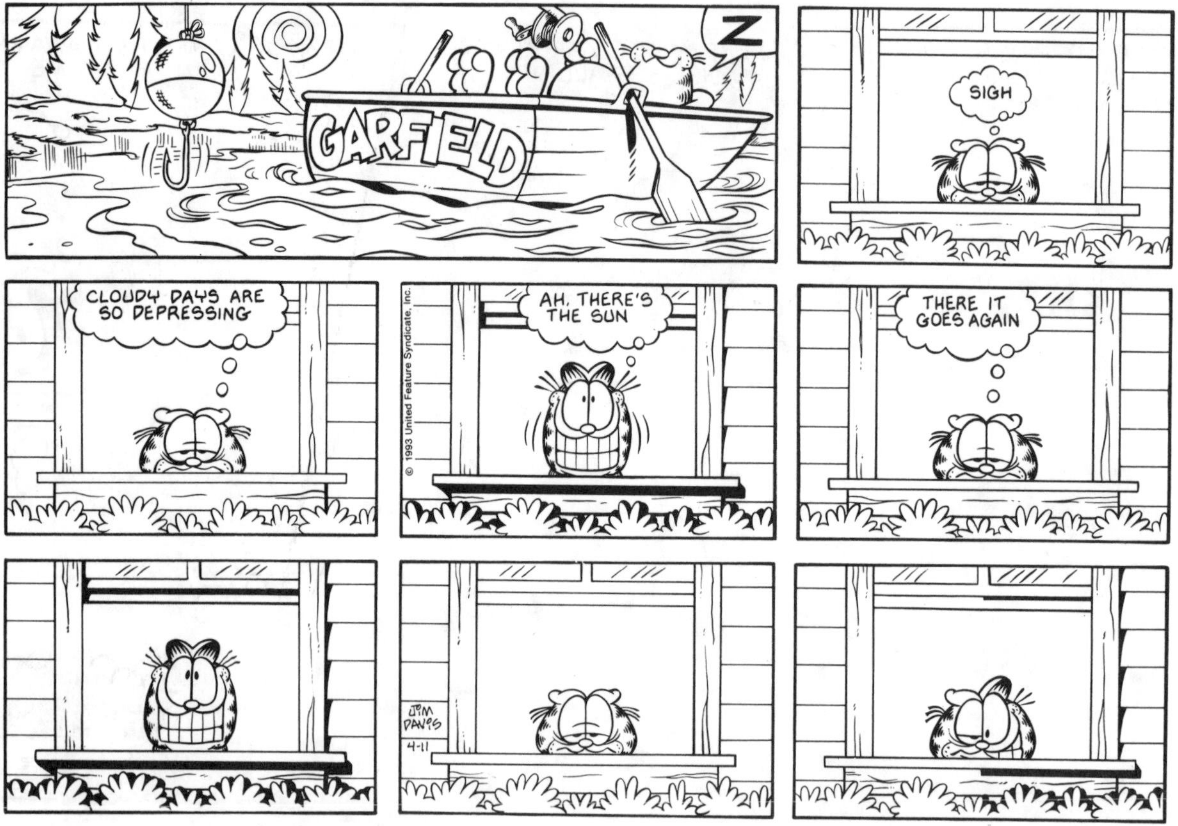
GARFIELD
Z
SIGH
CLOUDY DAYS ARE SO DEPRESSING
© 1993 United Feature Syndicate, Inc.
AH, THERE'S THE SUN
THERE IT GOES AGAIN
JIM DAVIS
4-11

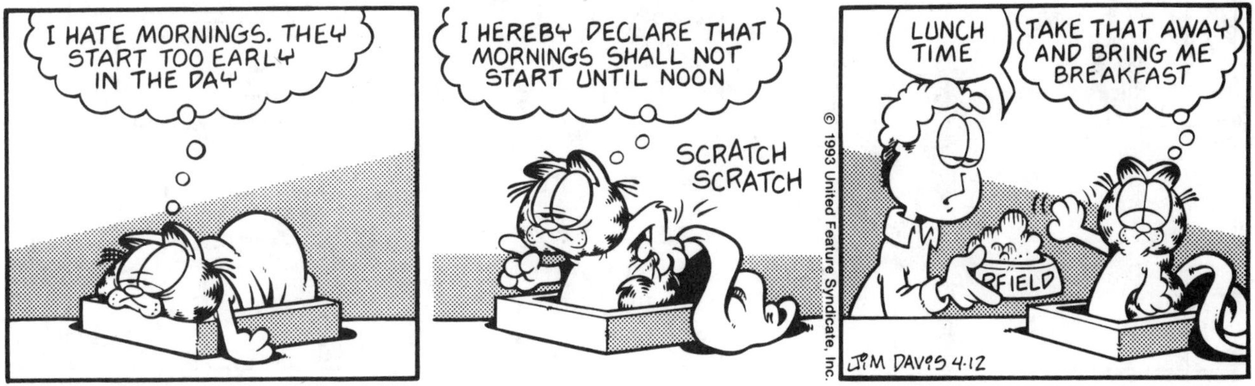

I HATE MORNINGS. THEY START TOO EARLY IN THE DAY
I HEREBY DECLARE THAT MORNINGS SHALL NOT START UNTIL NOON
SCRATCH SCRATCH
LUNCH TIME
TAKE THAT AWAY AND BRING ME BREAKFAST
JIM DAVIS 4.12

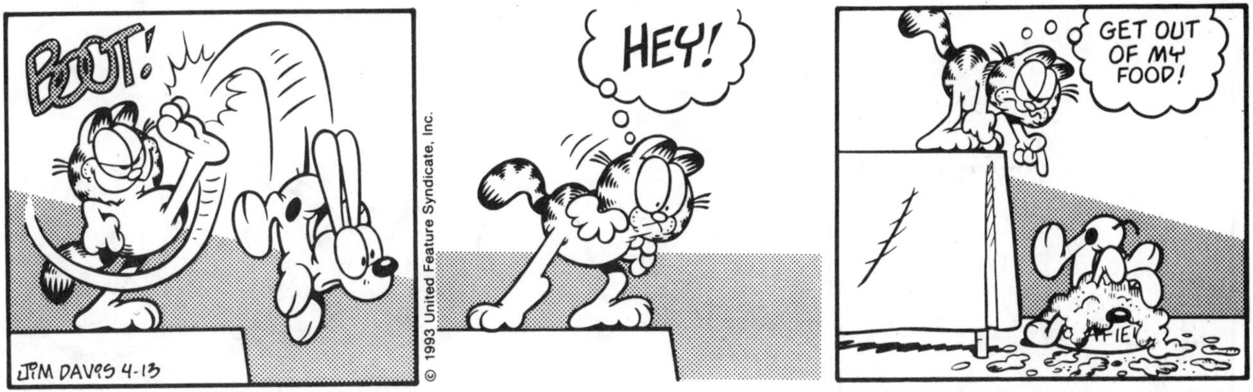

BOOT!
HEY!
GET OUT OF MY FOOD!
JIM DAVIS 4-13

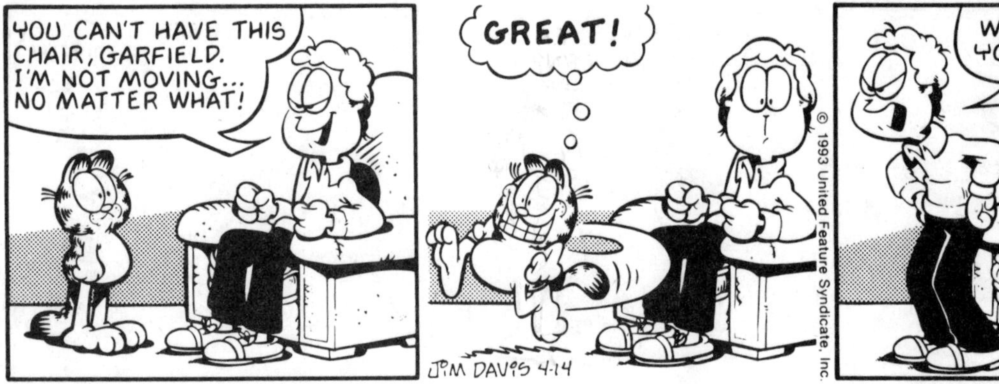
YOU CAN'T HAVE THIS CHAIR, GARFIELD. I'M NOT MOVING... NO MATTER WHAT!
GREAT!
JIM DAVIS 4-14
© 1993 United Feature Syndicate, Inc.
WHAT ARE YOU UP TO?!

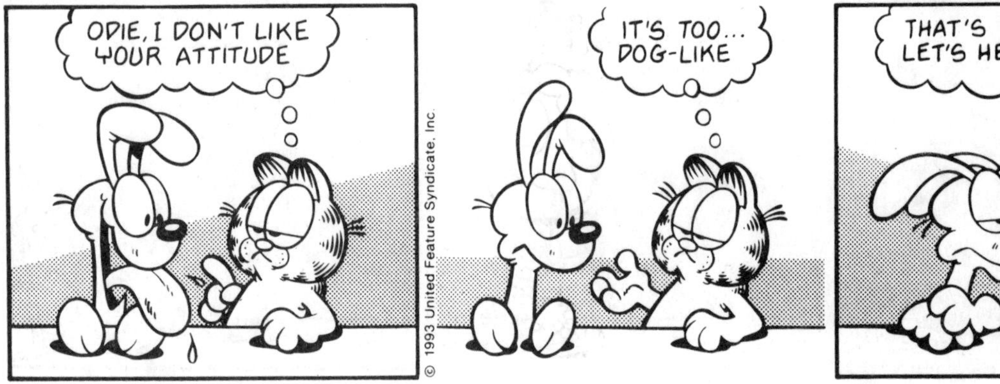
ODIE, I DON'T LIKE YOUR ATTITUDE
© 1993 United Feature Syndicate, Inc.
IT'S TOO... DOG-LIKE
THAT'S BETTER, NOW LET'S HEAR YOU MEOW
JIM DAVIS 4-15

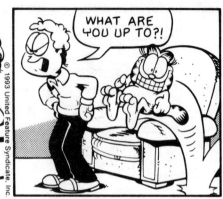

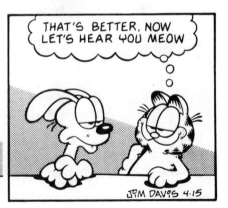

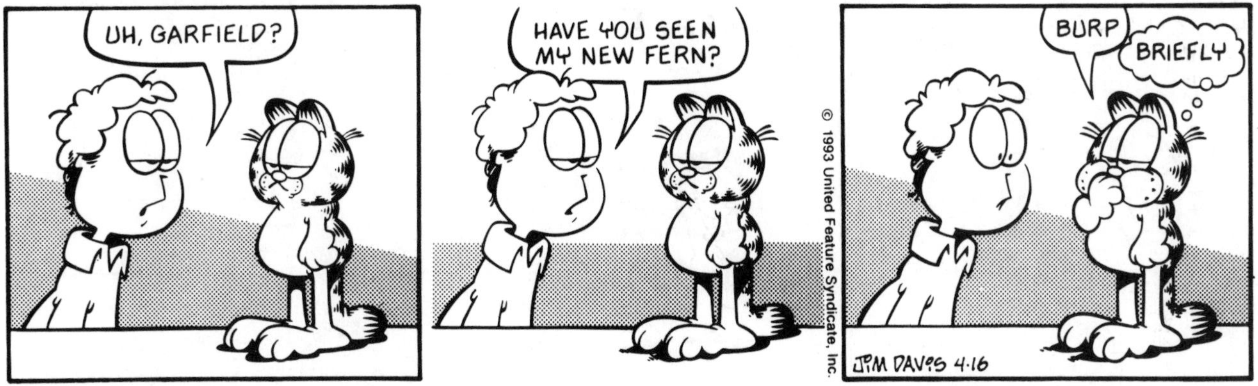
UH, GARFIELD?
HAVE YOU SEEN MY NEW FERN?
BURP
BRIEFLY
© 1993 United Feature Syndicate, Inc.
JIM DAVIS 4·16

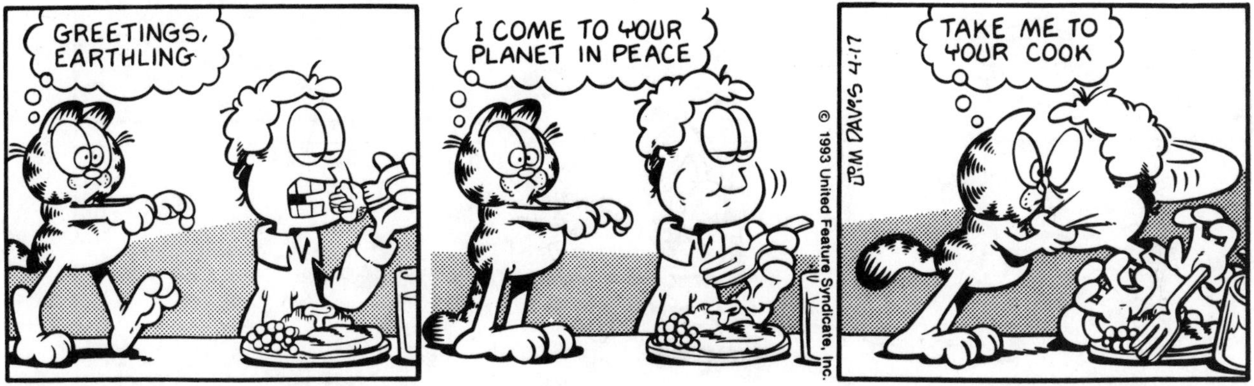
GREETINGS, EARTHLING
I COME TO YOUR PLANET IN PEACE
TAKE ME TO YOUR COOK
© 1993 United Feature Syndicate, Inc.
JIM DAVIS 4·17

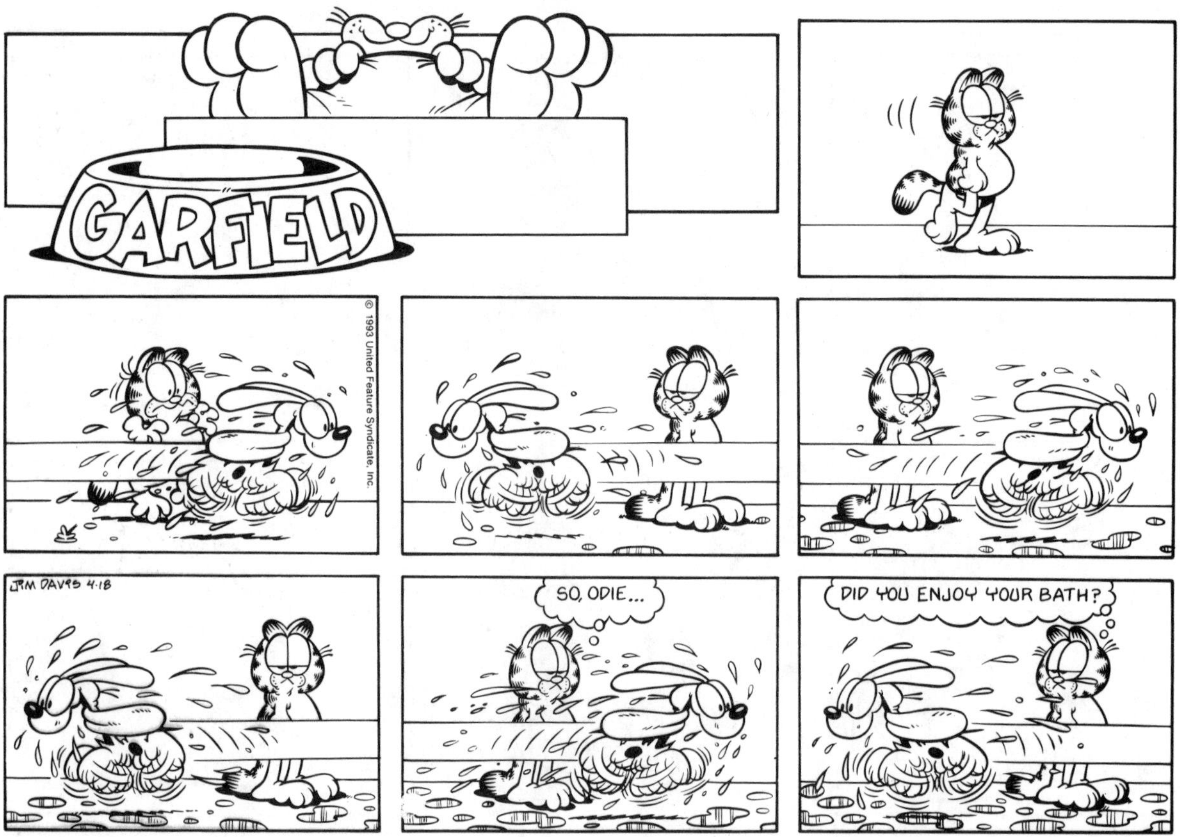

GARFIELD
© 1993 United Feature Syndicate, Inc.
JIM DAVIS 4-18
SO, ODIE...
DID YOU ENJOY YOUR BATH?

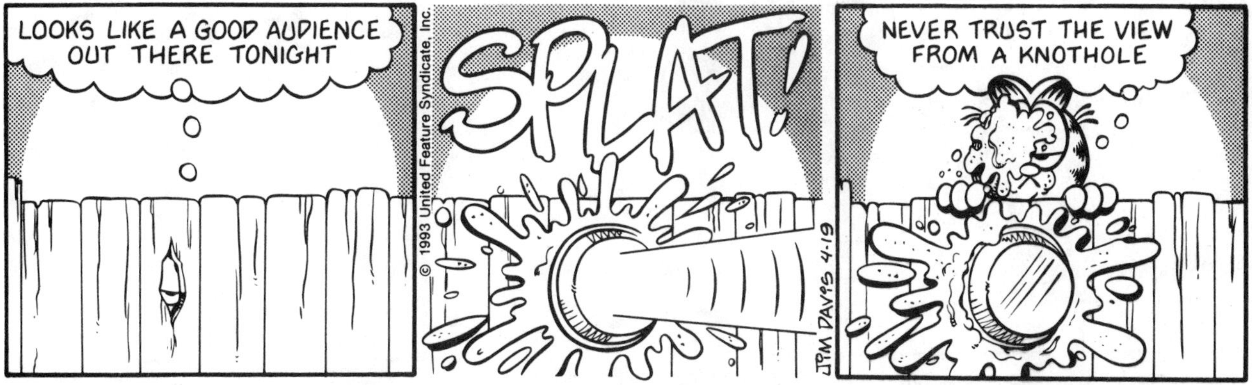
LOOKS LIKE A GOOD AUDIENCE OUT THERE TONIGHT
SPLAT!
NEVER TRUST THE VIEW FROM A KNOTHOLE
© 1993 United Feature Syndicate, Inc.
JIM DAVIS 4-19

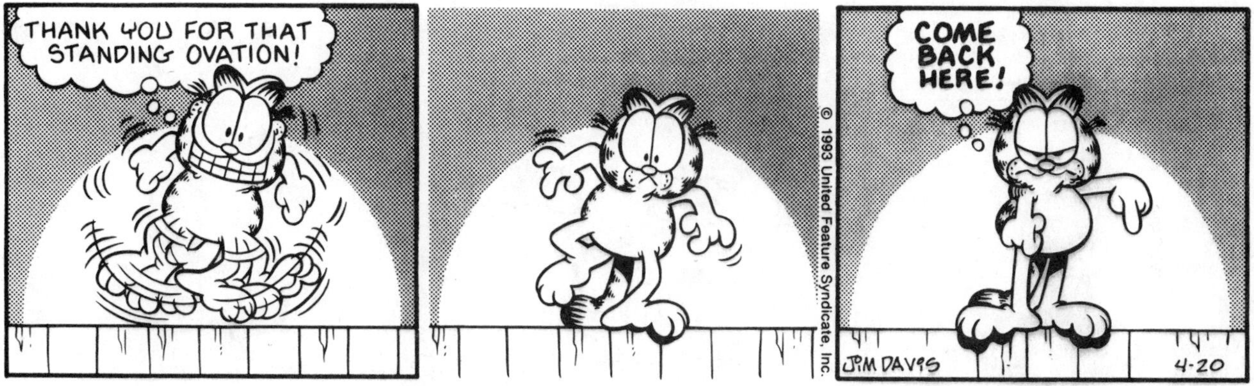
THANK YOU FOR THAT STANDING OVATION!
COME BACK HERE!
© 1993 United Feature Syndicate, Inc.
JIM DAVIS
4-20

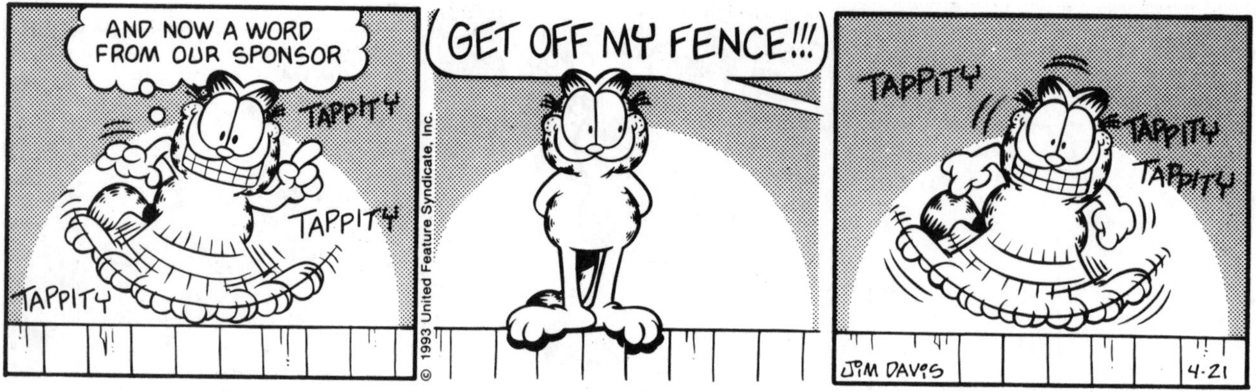
AND NOW A WORD FROM OUR SPONSOR
TAPPITY
TAPPITY
TAPPITY
GET OFF MY FENCE!!!
TAPPITY
TAPPITY
TAPPITY
© 1993 United Feature Syndicate, Inc.
JIM DAVIS
4-21

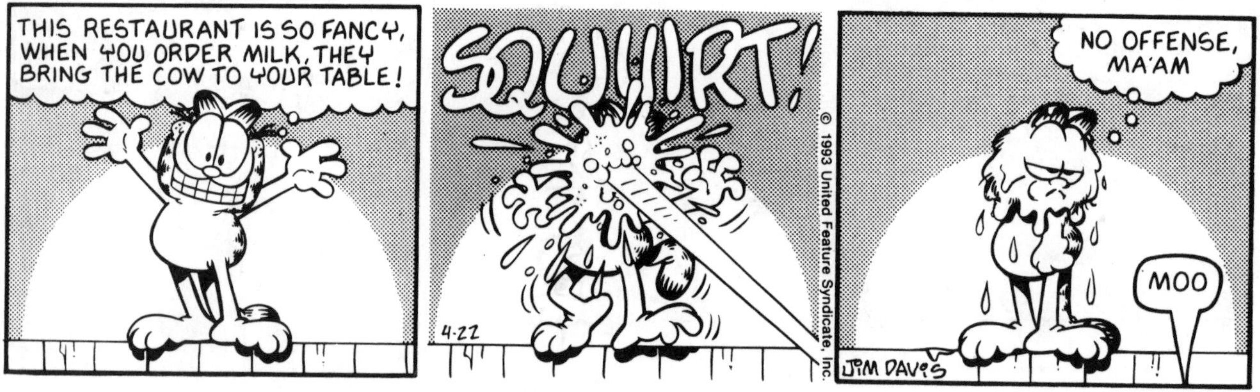
THIS RESTAURANT IS SO FANCY, WHEN YOU ORDER MILK, THEY BRING THE COW TO YOUR TABLE!
SQUIIIRT!
4-22
© 1993 United Feature Syndicate, Inc.
NO OFFENSE, MA'AM
MOO
JIM DAVIS

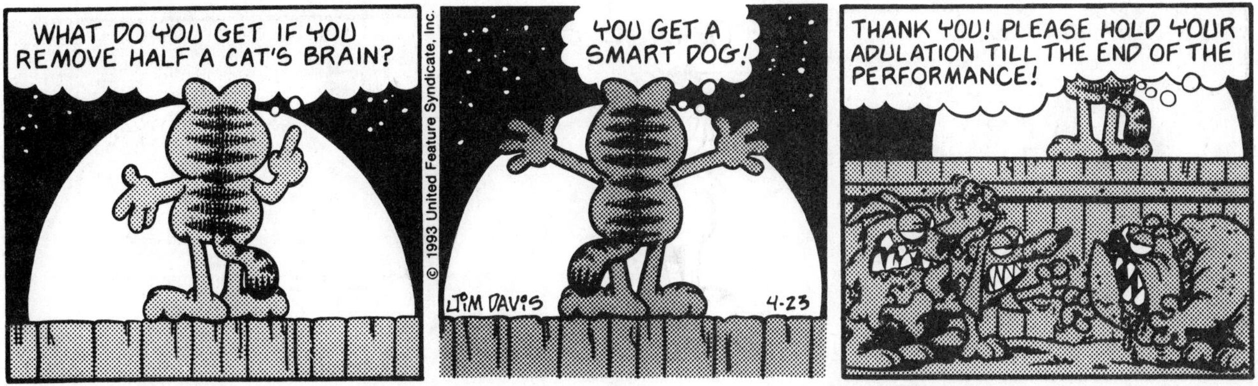
WHAT DO YOU GET IF YOU REMOVE HALF A CAT'S BRAIN?
YOU GET A SMART DOG!
THANK YOU! PLEASE HOLD YOUR ADULATION TILL THE END OF THE PERFORMANCE!
JIM DAVIS 4-23
© 1993 United Feature Syndicate, Inc.

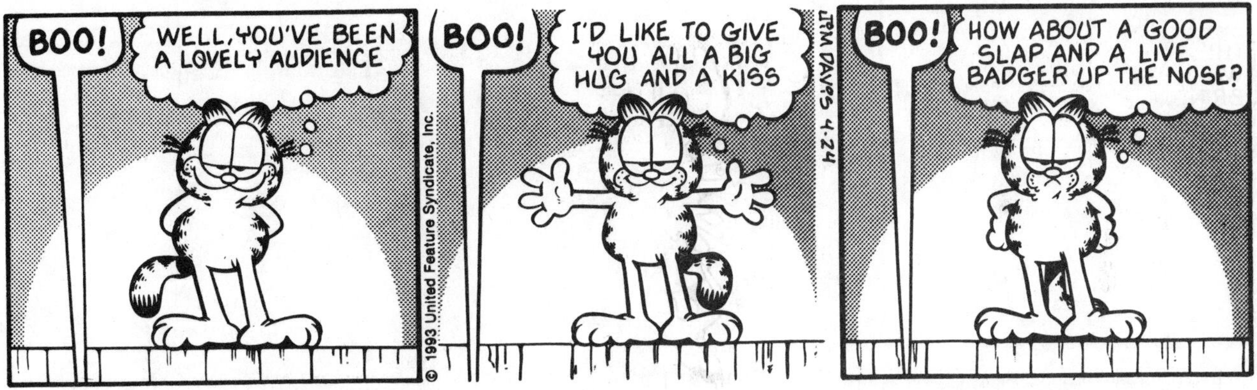
BOO!
WELL, YOU'VE BEEN A LOVELY AUDIENCE
BOO!
I'D LIKE TO GIVE YOU ALL A BIG HUG AND A KISS
BOO!
HOW ABOUT A GOOD SLAP AND A LIVE BADGER UP THE NOSE?
JIM DAVIS 4-24
© 1993 United Feature Syndicate, Inc.

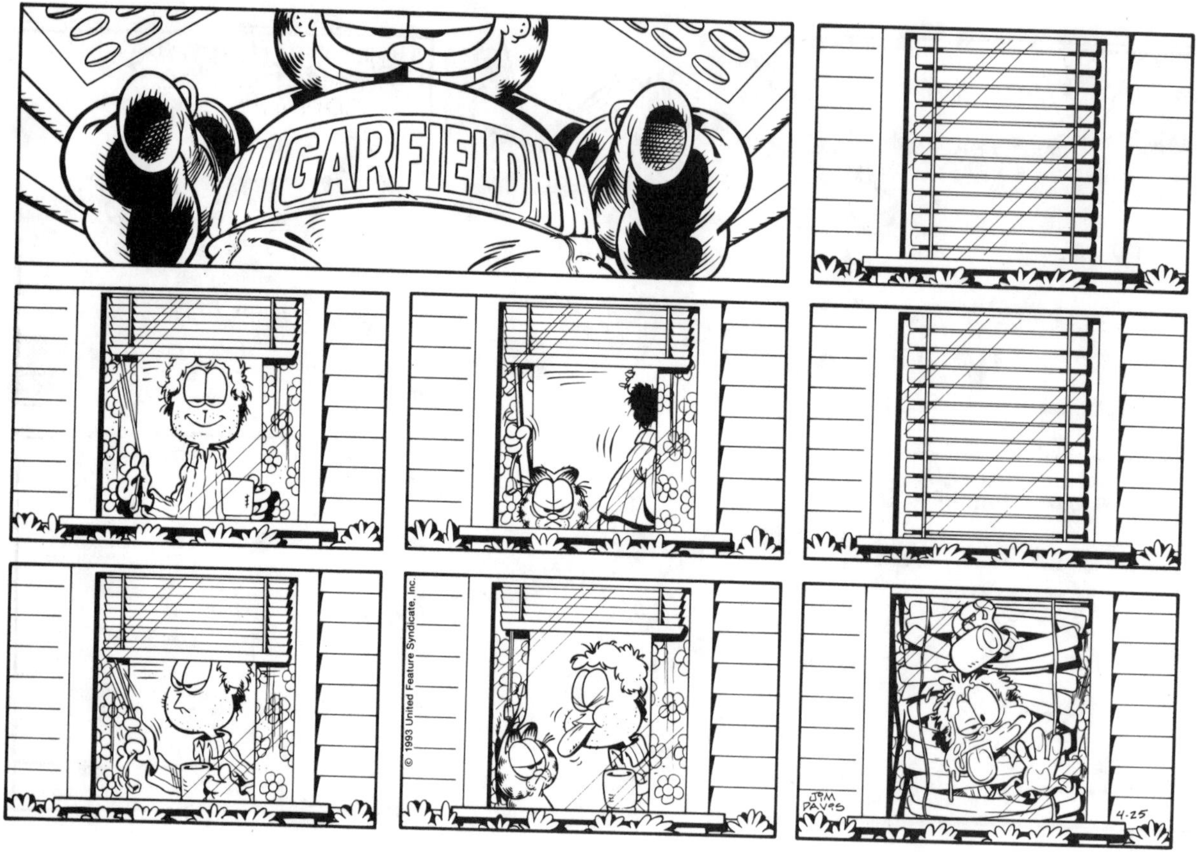
GARFIELD
© 1993 United Feature Syndicate, Inc.
JIM DAVIS
4-25

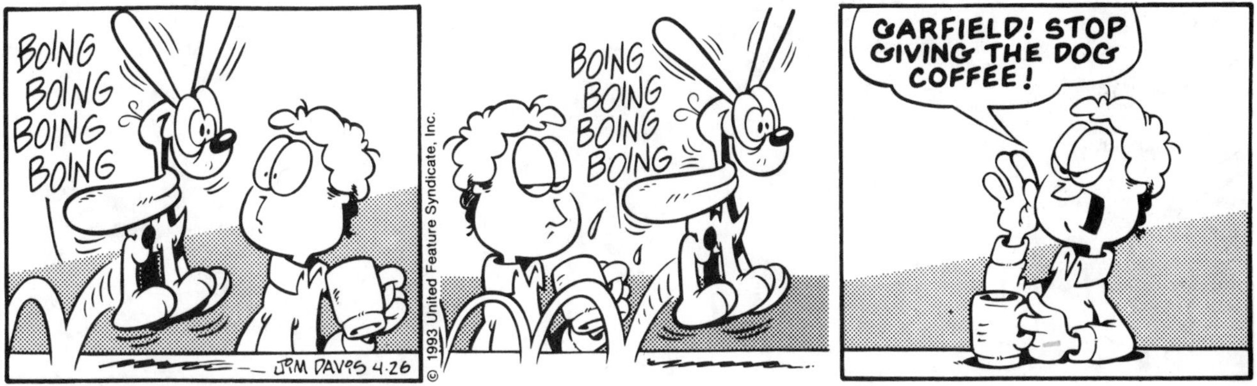
BOING BOING BOING BOING
JIM DAVIS 4-26
© 1993 United Feature Syndicate, Inc.
BOING BOING BOING BOING
GARFIELD! STOP GIVING THE DOG COFFEE!

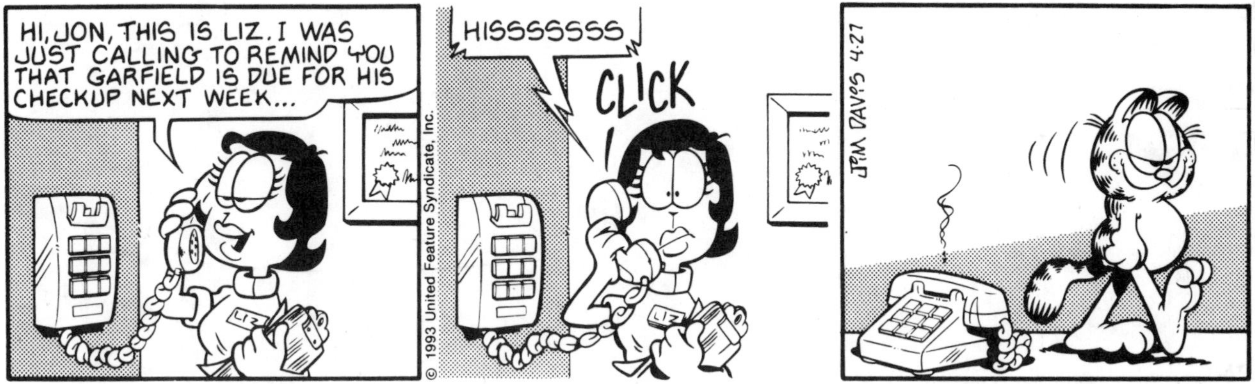
HI, JON, THIS IS LIZ. I WAS JUST CALLING TO REMIND YOU THAT GARFIELD IS DUE FOR HIS CHECKUP NEXT WEEK...
LIZ
© 1993 United Feature Syndicate, Inc.
HISSSSSSS
CLICK
LIZ
JIM DAVIS 4-27

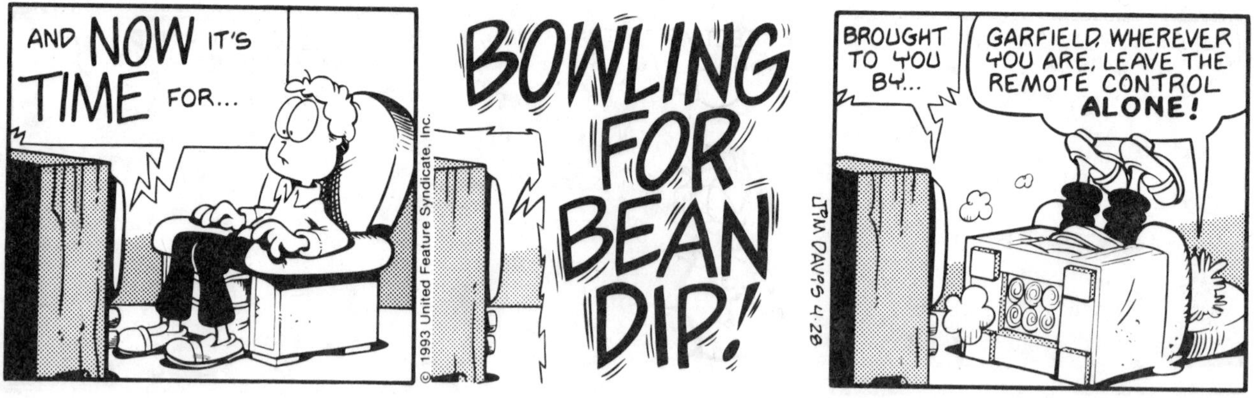
AND NOW IT'S TIME FOR...
BOWLING FOR BEAN DIP!
BROUGHT TO YOU BY...
GARFIELD, WHEREVER YOU ARE, LEAVE THE REMOTE CONTROL ALONE!
© 1993 United Feature Syndicate, Inc.
JIM DAVIS 4·28

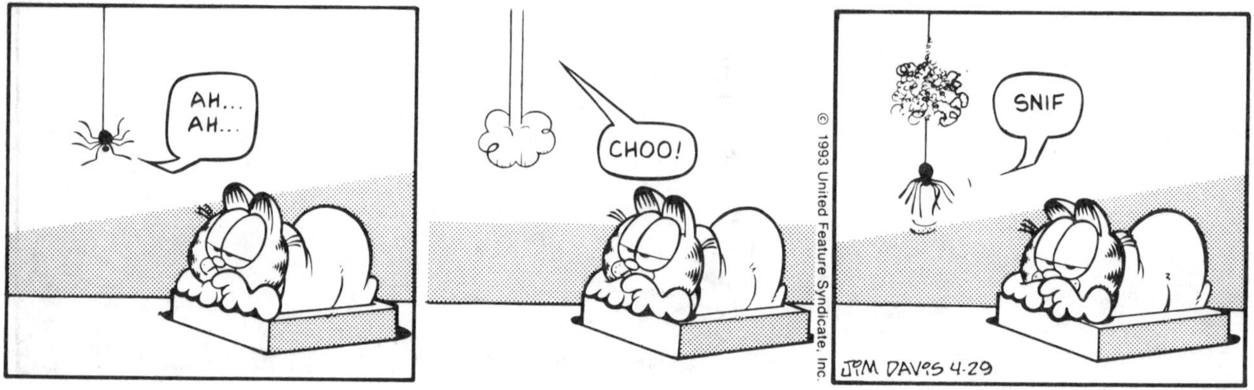
AH... AH...
CHOO!
SNIF
© 1993 United Feature Syndicate, Inc.
JIM DAVIS 4·29

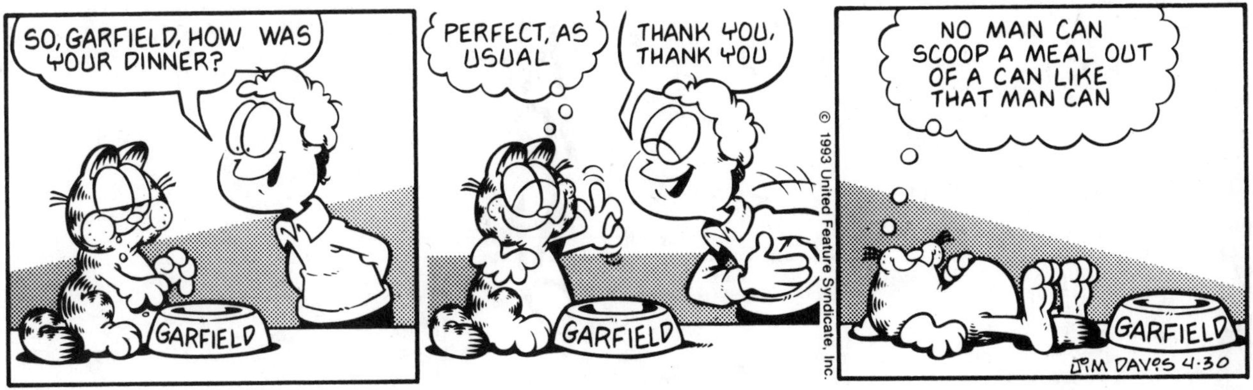
SO, GARFIELD, HOW WAS YOUR DINNER?
GARFIELD
PERFECT, AS USUAL
THANK YOU, THANK YOU
GARFIELD
© 1993 United Feature Syndicate, Inc.
NO MAN CAN SCOOP A MEAL OUT OF A CAN LIKE THAT MAN CAN
GARFIELD
JIM DAVIS 4-30

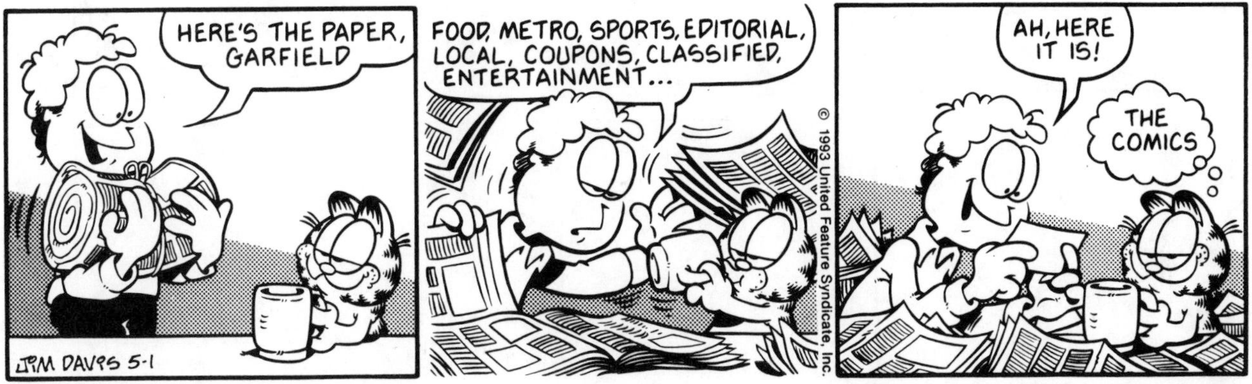
HERE'S THE PAPER, GARFIELD
JIM DAVIS 5-1
FOOD, METRO, SPORTS, EDITORIAL, LOCAL, COUPONS, CLASSIFIED, ENTERTAINMENT...
© 1993 United Feature Syndicate, Inc.
AH, HERE IT IS!
THE COMICS

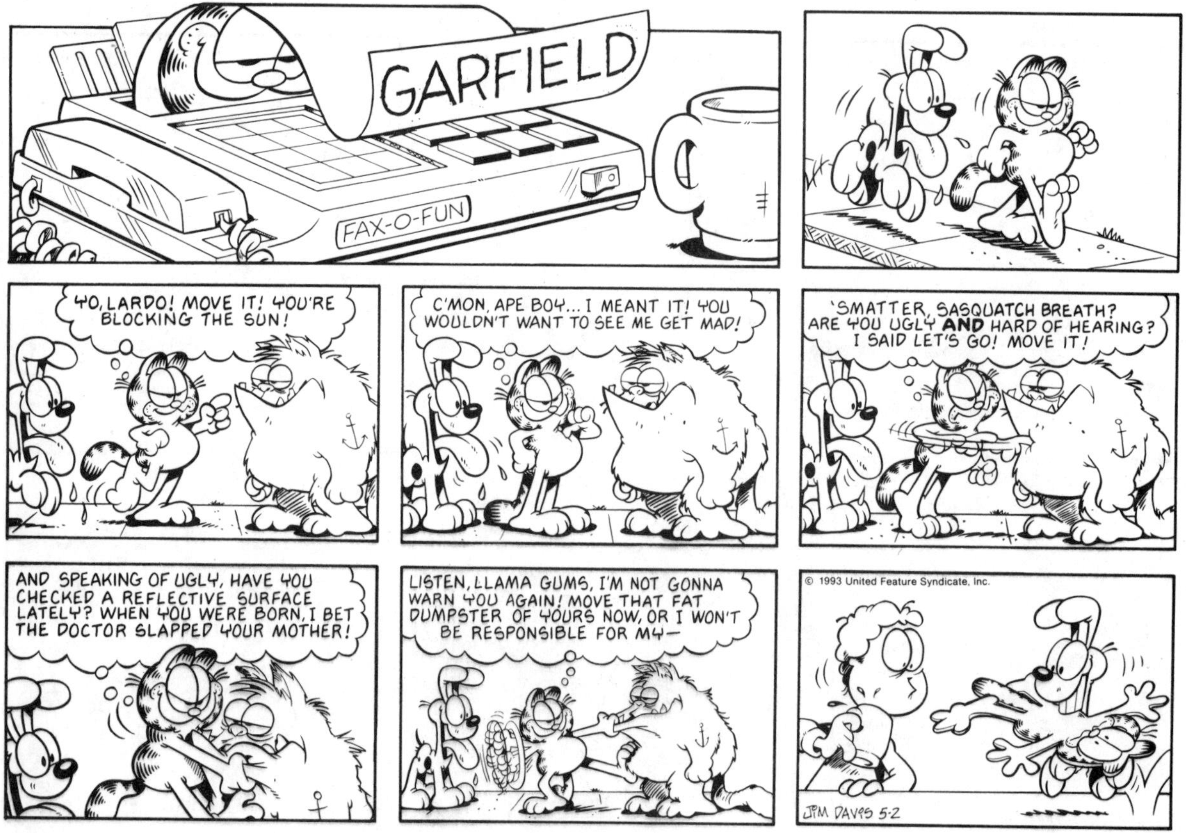
GARFIELD
FAX-O-FUN
YO, LARDO! MOVE IT! YOU'RE BLOCKING THE SUN!
C'MON, APE BOY... I MEANT IT! YOU WOULDN'T WANT TO SEE ME GET MAD!
'SMATTER, SASQUATCH BREATH? ARE YOU UGLY **AND** HARD OF HEARING? I SAID LET'S GO! MOVE IT!
AND SPEAKING OF UGLY, HAVE YOU CHECKED A REFLECTIVE SURFACE LATELY? WHEN YOU WERE BORN, I BET THE DOCTOR SLAPPED YOUR MOTHER!
LISTEN, LLAMA GUMS, I'M NOT GONNA WARN YOU AGAIN! MOVE THAT FAT DUMPSTER OF YOURS NOW, OR I WON'T BE RESPONSIBLE FOR MY—
© 1993 United Feature Syndicate, Inc.
JIM DAVIS 5-2

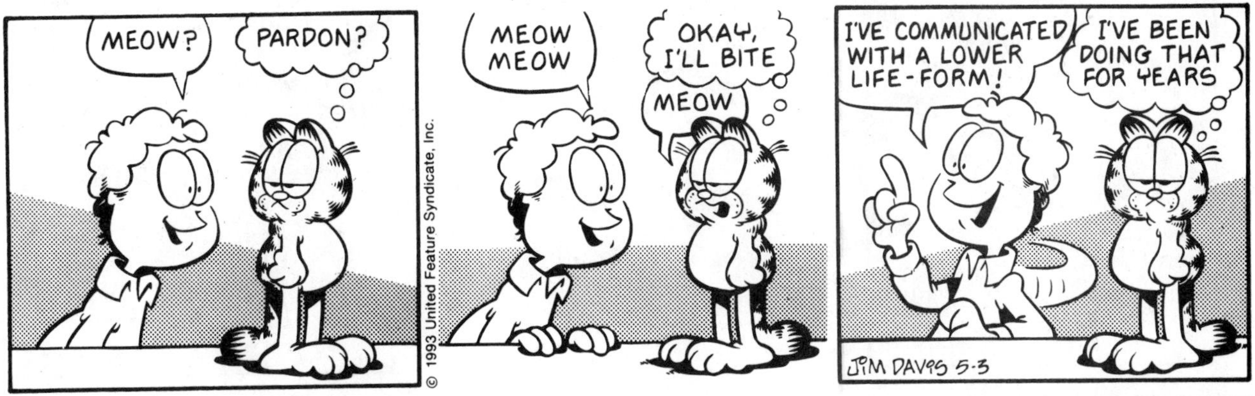
MEOW?
PARDON?
MEOW MEOW
OKAY, I'LL BITE
MEOW
I'VE COMMUNICATED WITH A LOWER LIFE-FORM!
I'VE BEEN DOING THAT FOR YEARS
JIM DAVIS 5-3
© 1993 United Feature Syndicate, Inc.

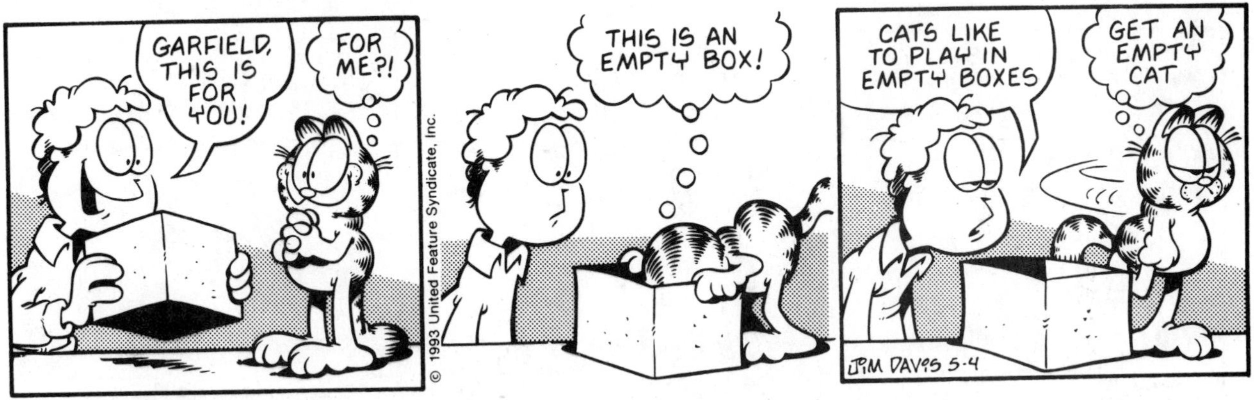
GARFIELD, THIS IS FOR YOU!
FOR ME?!
THIS IS AN EMPTY BOX!
CATS LIKE TO PLAY IN EMPTY BOXES
GET AN EMPTY CAT
JIM DAVIS 5-4
© 1993 United Feature Syndicate, Inc.

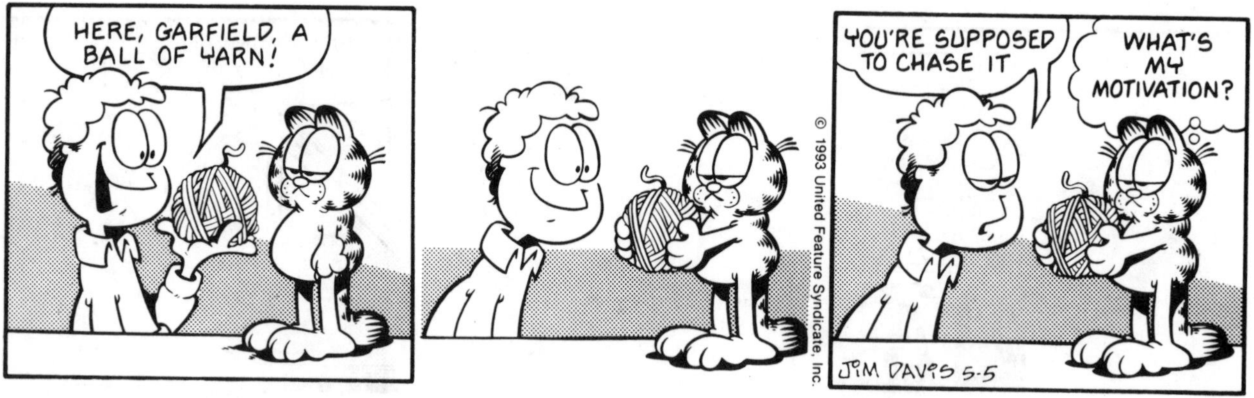
HERE, GARFIELD, A BALL OF YARN!
YOU'RE SUPPOSED TO CHASE IT
WHAT'S MY MOTIVATION?
JIM DAVIS 5-5
© 1993 United Feature Syndicate, Inc.

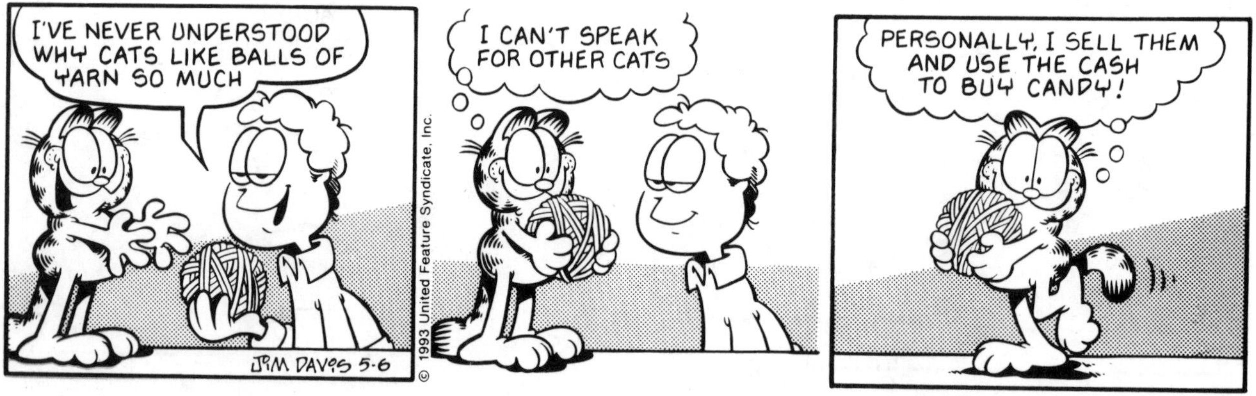
I'VE NEVER UNDERSTOOD WHY CATS LIKE BALLS OF YARN SO MUCH
JIM DAVIS 5-6
© 1993 United Feature Syndicate, Inc.
I CAN'T SPEAK FOR OTHER CATS
PERSONALLY, I SELL THEM AND USE THE CASH TO BUY CANDY!

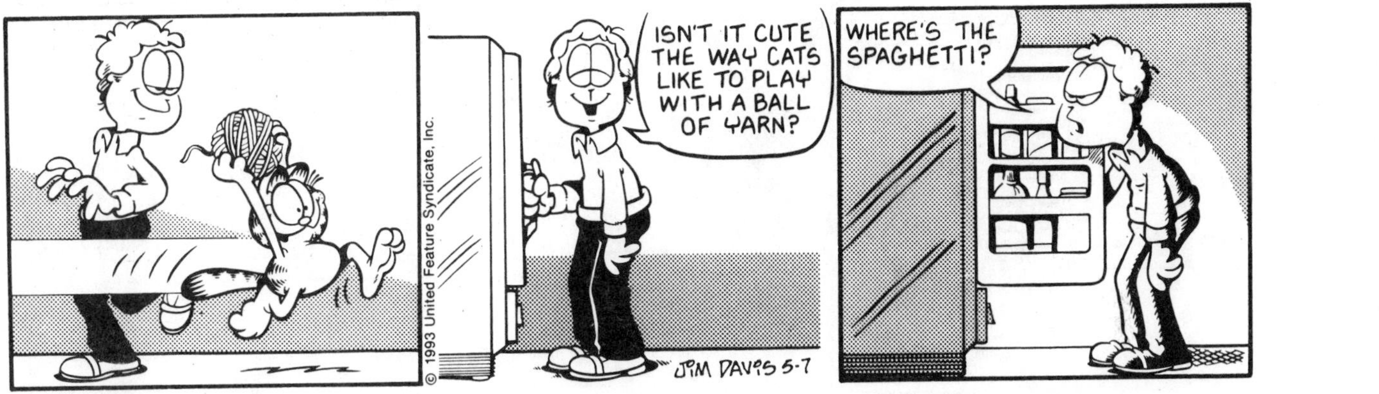
© 1993 United Feature Syndicate, Inc.
ISN'T IT CUTE THE WAY CATS LIKE TO PLAY WITH A BALL OF YARN?
JIM DAVIS 5-7
WHERE'S THE SPAGHETTI?

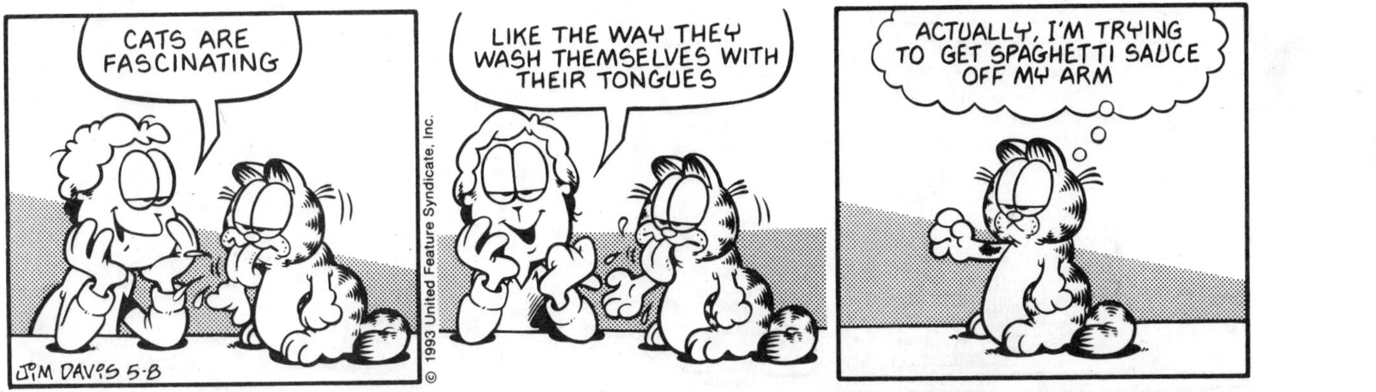
CATS ARE FASCINATING
JIM DAVIS 5-8
© 1993 United Feature Syndicate, Inc.
LIKE THE WAY THEY WASH THEMSELVES WITH THEIR TONGUES
ACTUALLY, I'M TRYING TO GET SPAGHETTI SAUCE OFF MY ARM

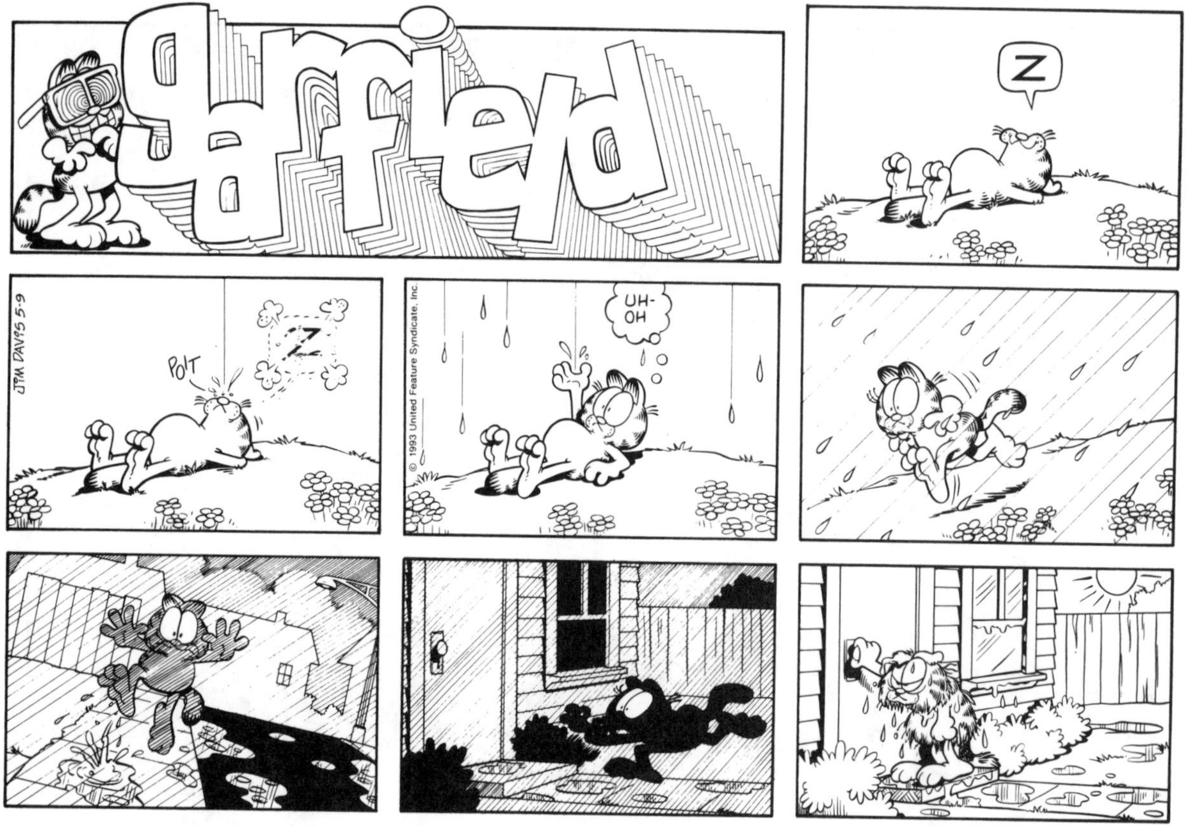
garfield
Z
JIM DAVIS 5-9
POIT
Z
© 1993 United Feature Syndicate, Inc.
UH-OH

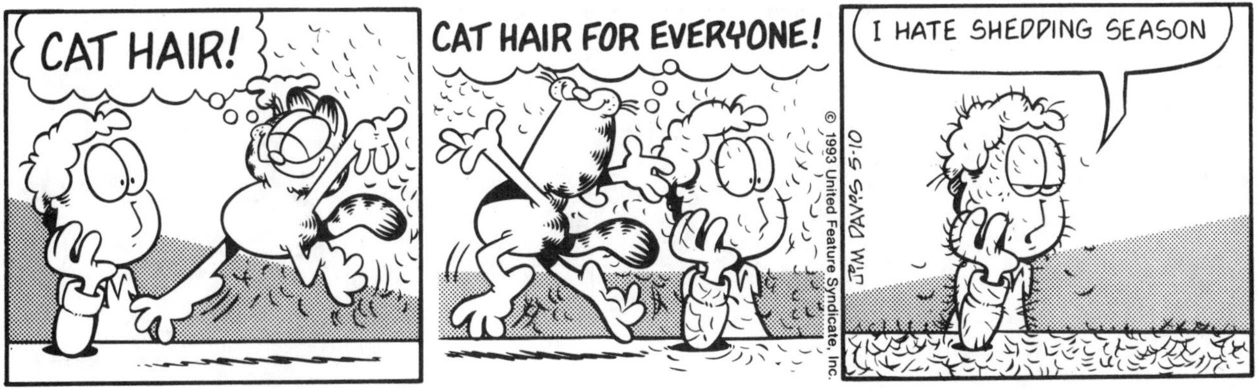
CAT HAIR!
CAT HAIR FOR EVERYONE!
I HATE SHEDDING SEASON
© 1993 United Feature Syndicate, Inc.
JIM DAVIS 5-10

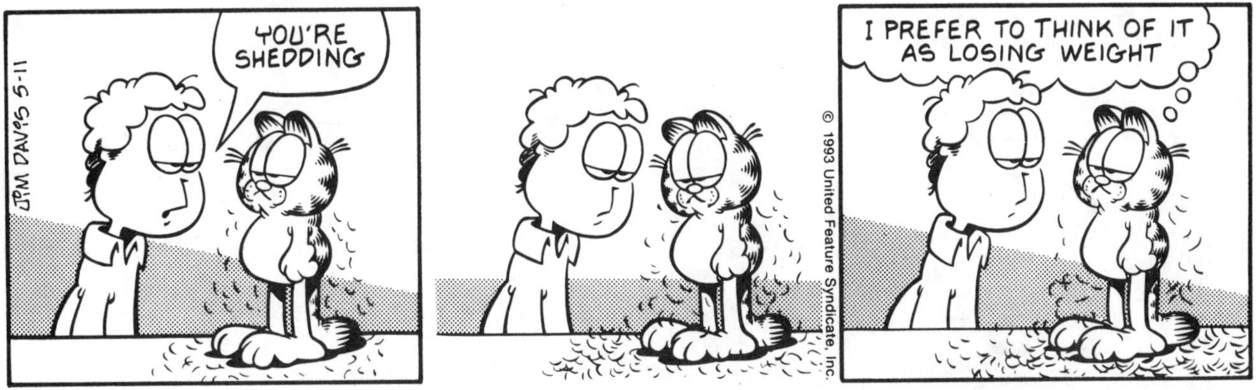
JIM DAVIS 5-11
YOU'RE SHEDDING
I PREFER TO THINK OF IT AS LOSING WEIGHT
© 1993 United Feature Syndicate, Inc.

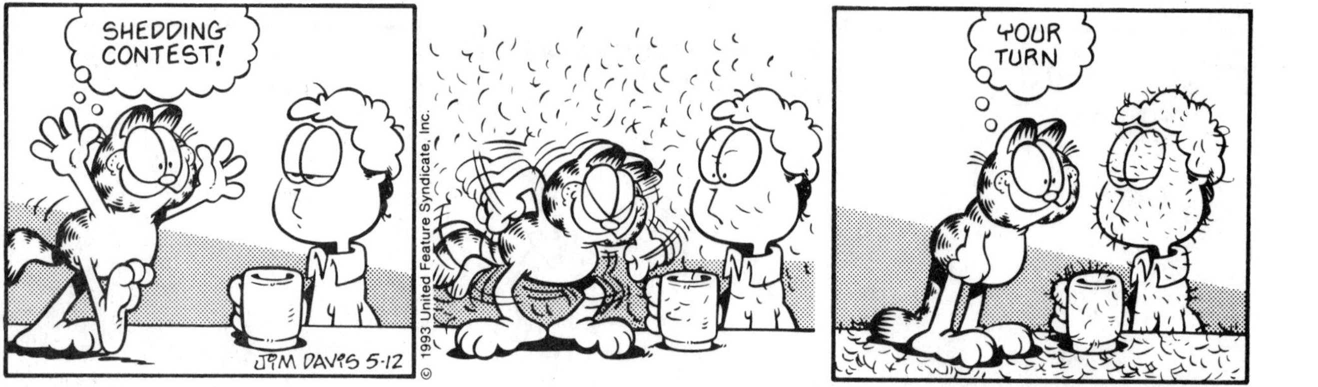
SHEDDING CONTEST!
JIM DAVIS 5-12
© 1993 United Feature Syndicate, Inc.
YOUR TURN

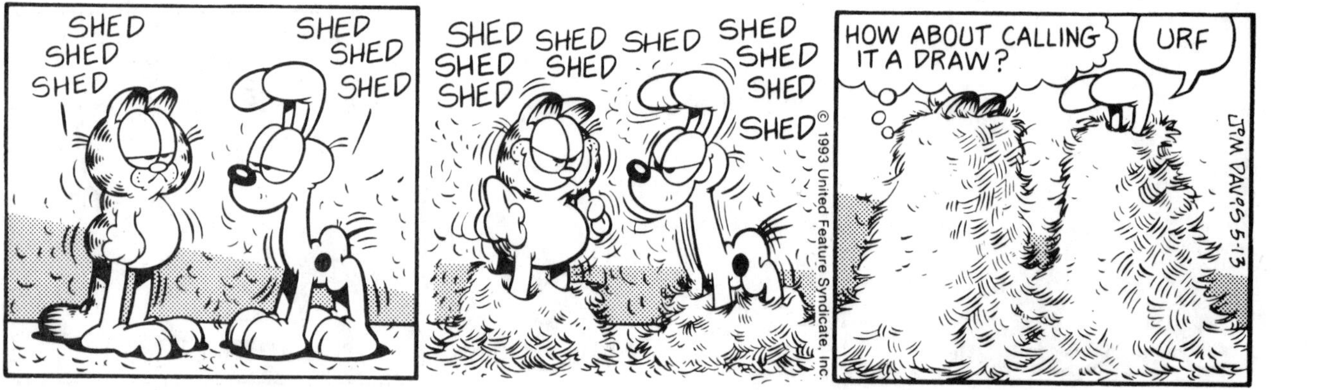
SHED SHED SHED
SHED SHED SHED
SHED SHED SHED
SHED SHED
SHED
SHED SHED SHED SHED
© 1993 United Feature Syndicate, Inc.
HOW ABOUT CALLING IT A DRAW?
URF
JIM DAVIS 5-13

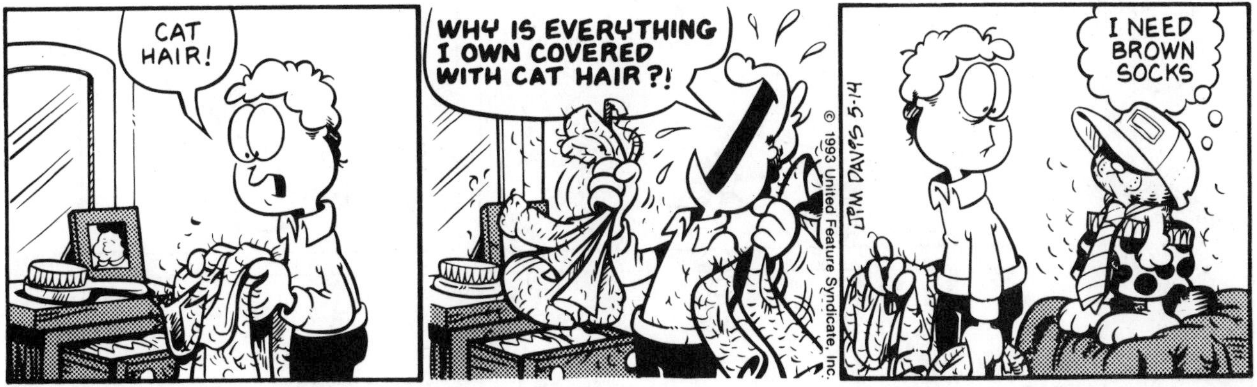
CAT HAIR!
WHY IS EVERYTHING I OWN COVERED WITH CAT HAIR?!
© 1993 United Feature Syndicate, Inc.
JIM DAVIS 5-14
I NEED BROWN SOCKS

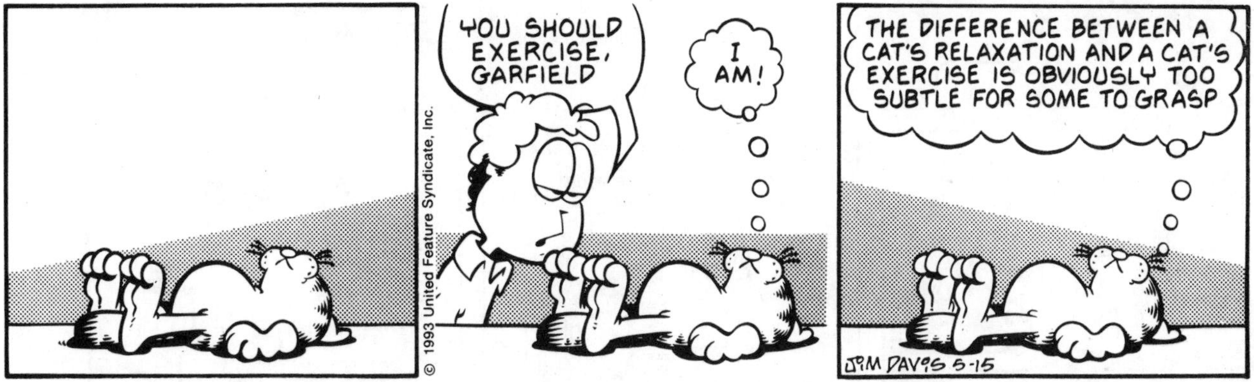
© 1993 United Feature Syndicate, Inc.
YOU SHOULD EXERCISE, GARFIELD
I AM!
THE DIFFERENCE BETWEEN A CAT'S RELAXATION AND A CAT'S EXERCISE IS OBVIOUSLY TOO SUBTLE FOR SOME TO GRASP
JIM DAVIS 5-15

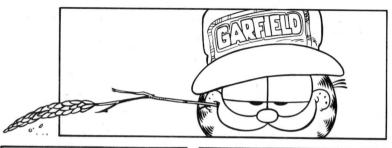

© 1993 United Feature Syndicate, Inc.

SIGH

DOESN'T IT BUG YOU WHEN DOGS GET IN FRONT OF YOU JUST BECAUSE THEY WANT YOUR

ATTENTION

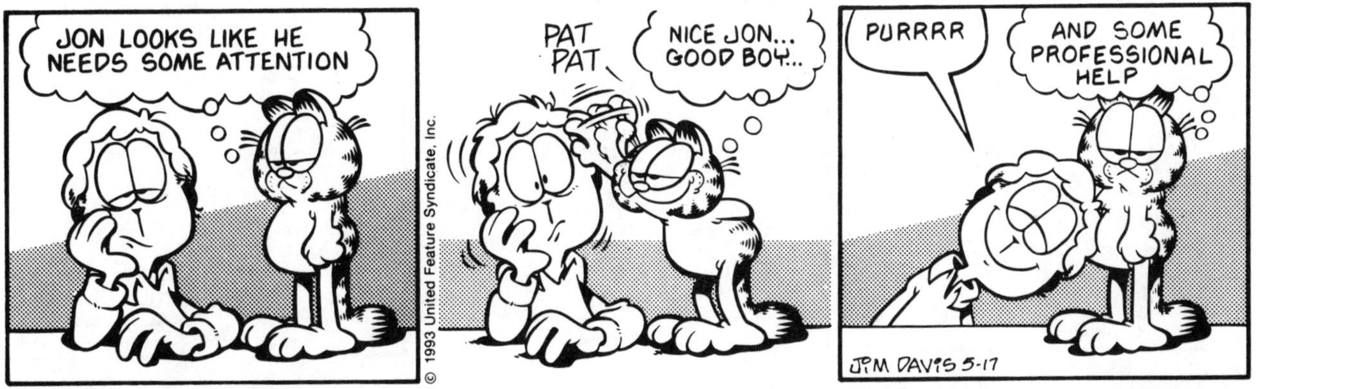
JON LOOKS LIKE HE NEEDS SOME ATTENTION
PAT PAT
NICE JON... GOOD BOY...
PURRRR
AND SOME PROFESSIONAL HELP
JIM DAVIS 5-17
© 1993 United Feature Syndicate, Inc.

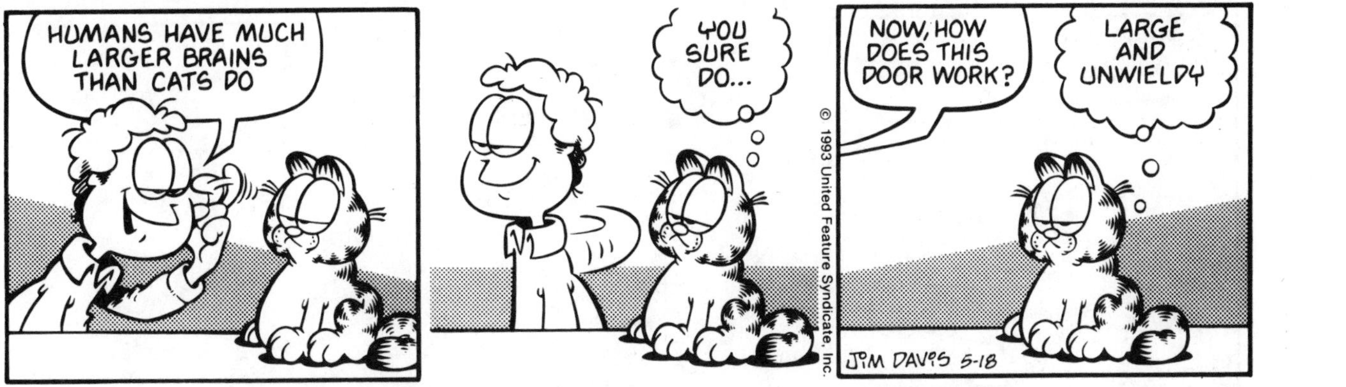
HUMANS HAVE MUCH LARGER BRAINS THAN CATS DO
YOU SURE DO...
NOW, HOW DOES THIS DOOR WORK?
LARGE AND UNWIELDY
JIM DAVIS 5-18
© 1993 United Feature Syndicate, Inc.

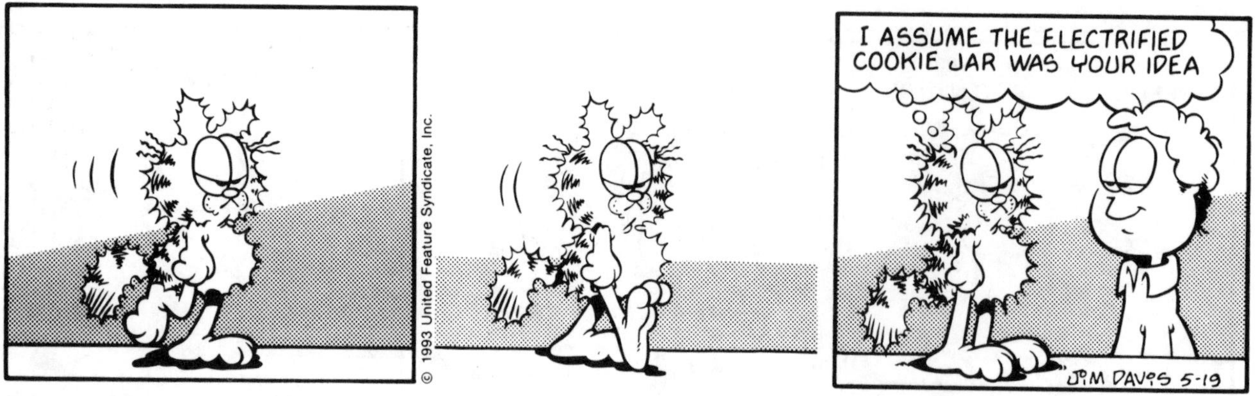
I ASSUME THE ELECTRIFIED COOKIE JAR WAS YOUR IDEA
JIM DAVIS 5-19

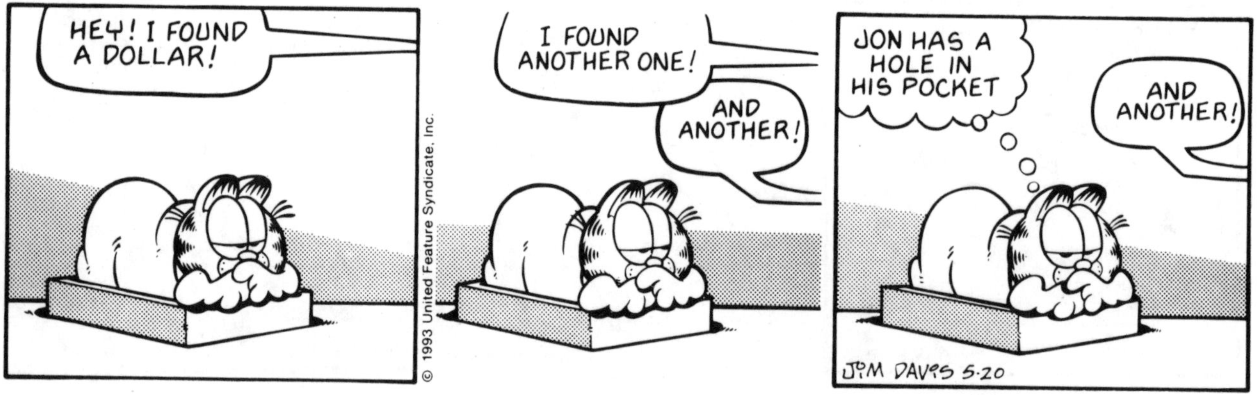
HEY! I FOUND A DOLLAR!
I FOUND ANOTHER ONE!
AND ANOTHER!
JON HAS A HOLE IN HIS POCKET
AND ANOTHER!
JIM DAVIS 5-20

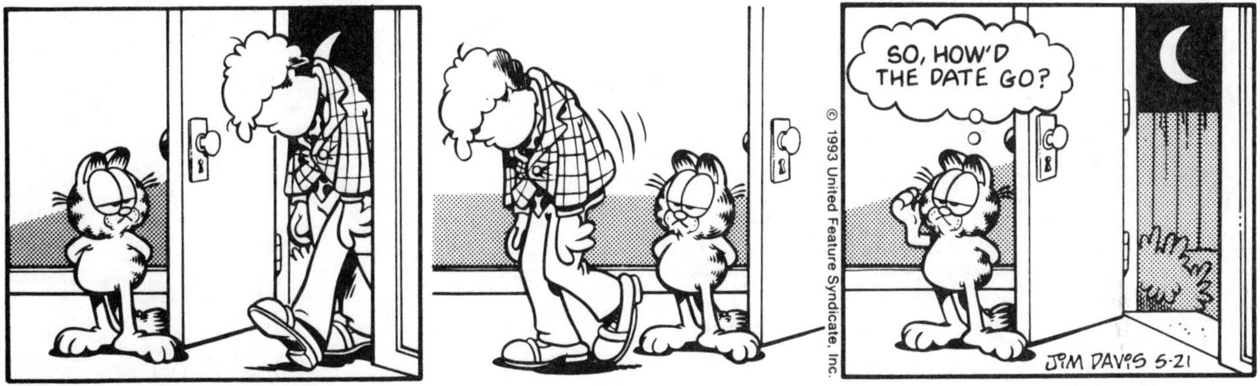
SO, HOW'D THE DATE GO?
JIM DAVIS 5-21

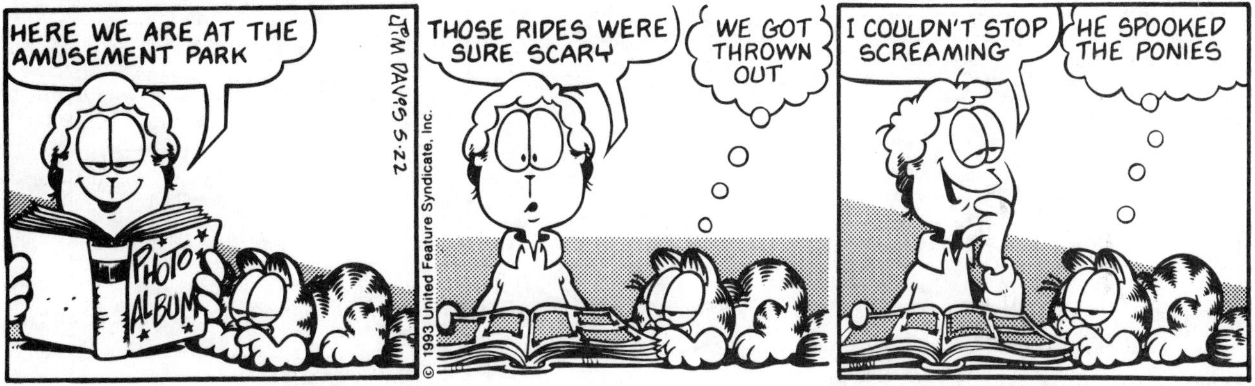
HERE WE ARE AT THE AMUSEMENT PARK
PHOTO ALBUM
JIM DAVIS 5-22
THOSE RIDES WERE SURE SCARY
WE GOT THROWN OUT
I COULDN'T STOP SCREAMING
HE SPOOKED THE PONIES

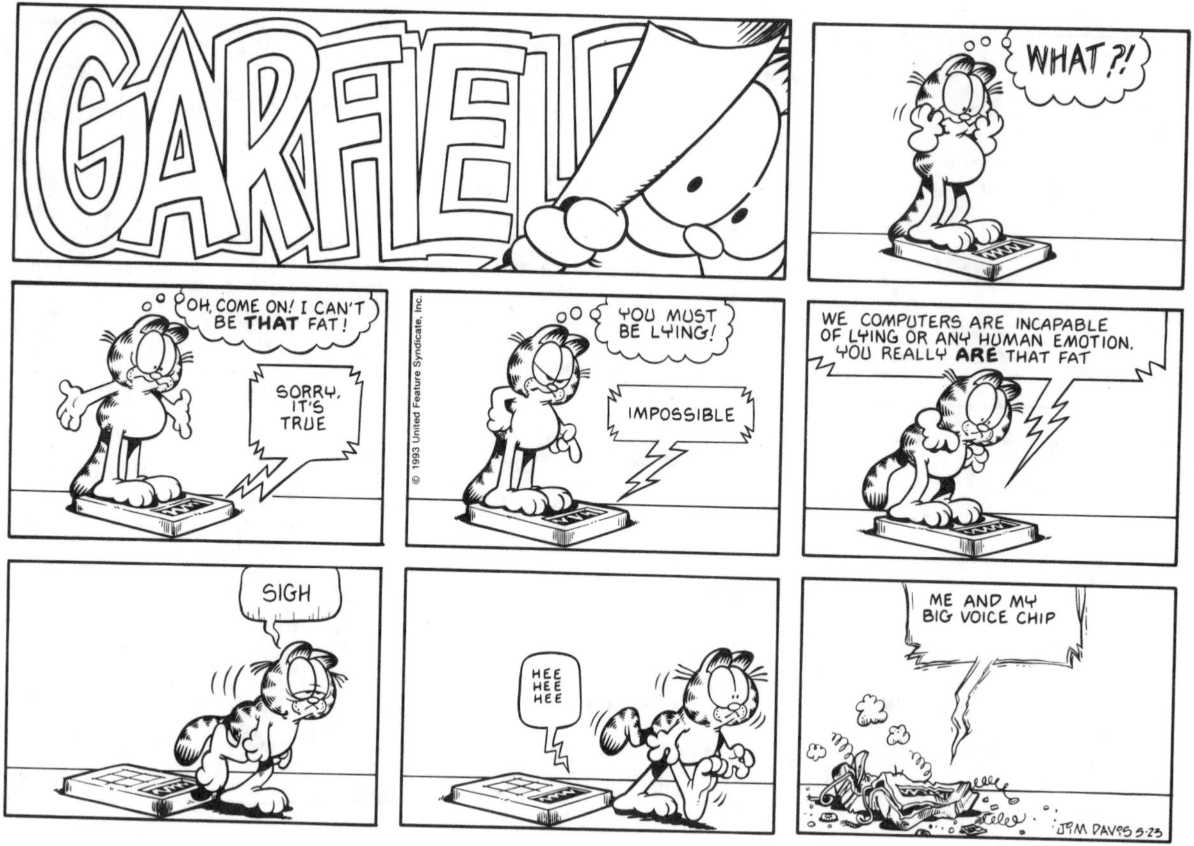
GARFIELD
WHAT?!
OH, COME ON! I CAN'T BE **THAT** FAT!
SORRY, IT'S TRUE
© 1993 United Feature Syndicate, Inc.
YOU MUST BE LYING!
IMPOSSIBLE
WE COMPUTERS ARE INCAPABLE OF LYING OR ANY HUMAN EMOTION. YOU REALLY **ARE** THAT FAT
SIGH
HEE HEE HEE
ME AND MY BIG VOICE CHIP
JIM DAVIS 5-23

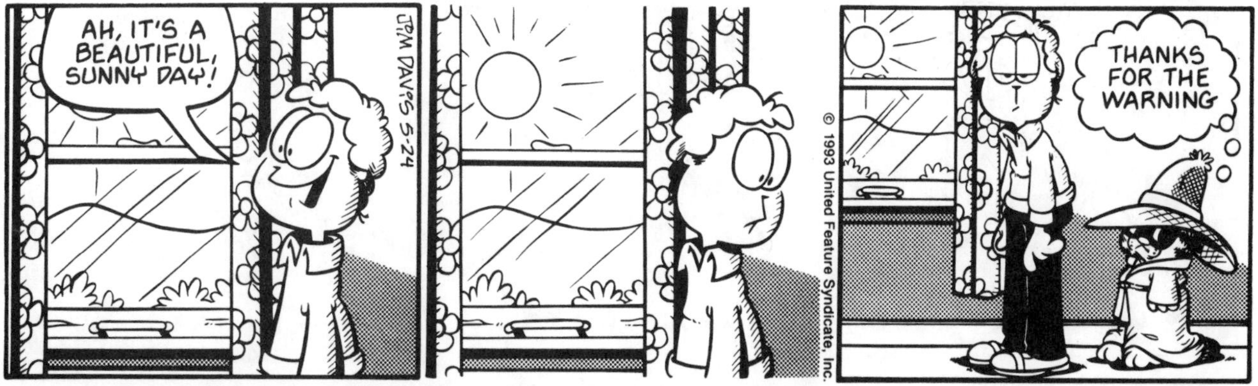
AH, IT'S A BEAUTIFUL, SUNNY DAY!
JIM DAVIS 5-24
© 1993 United Feature Syndicate, Inc.
THANKS FOR THE WARNING

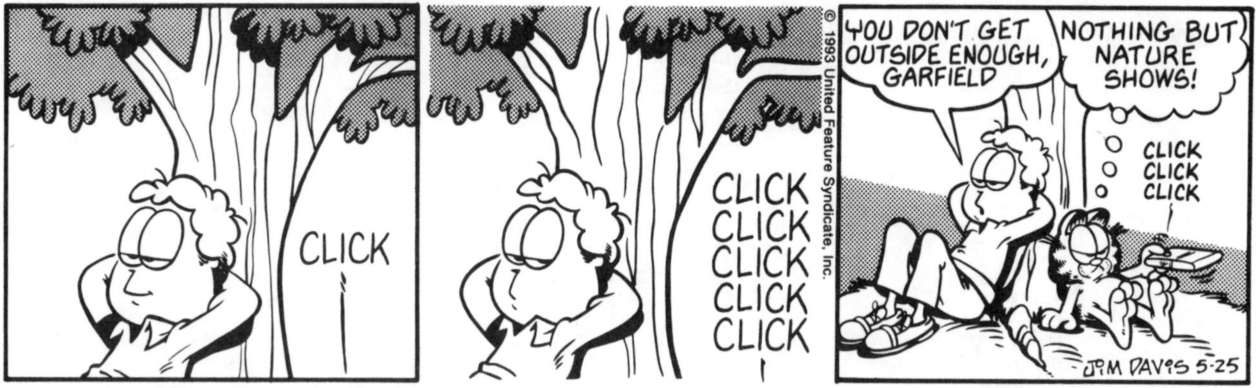
CLICK
CLICK CLICK CLICK CLICK CLICK
© 1993 United Feature Syndicate, Inc.
YOU DON'T GET OUTSIDE ENOUGH, GARFIELD
NOTHING BUT NATURE SHOWS!
CLICK CLICK CLICK
JIM DAVIS 5-25

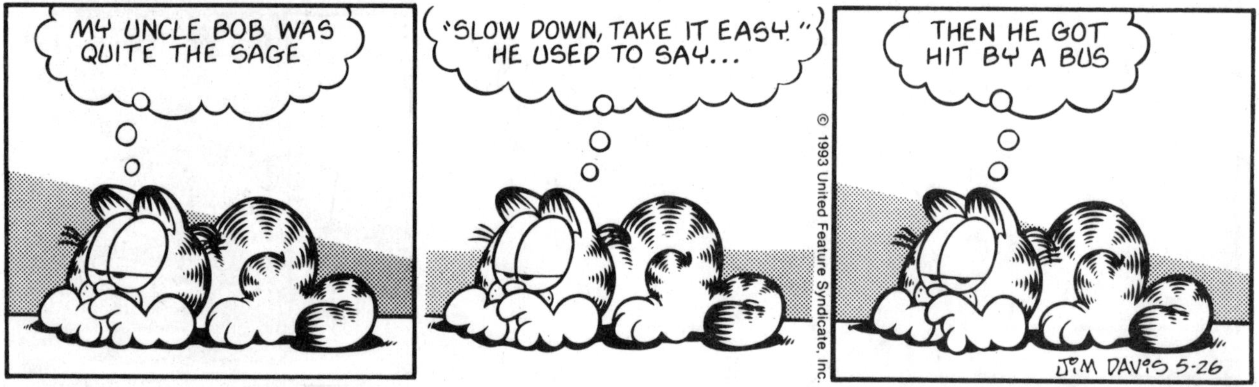
MY UNCLE BOB WAS QUITE THE SAGE
"SLOW DOWN, TAKE IT EASY." HE USED TO SAY...
THEN HE GOT HIT BY A BUS
JIM DAVIS 5-26

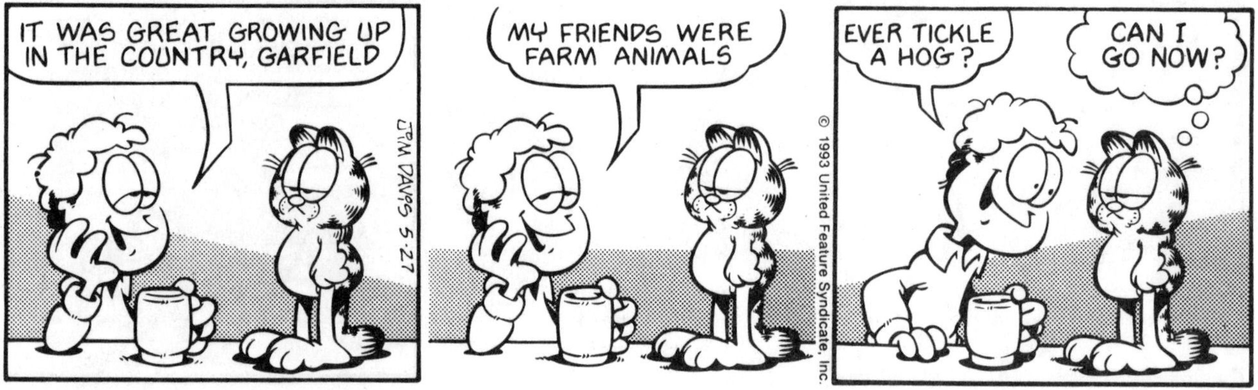
IT WAS GREAT GROWING UP IN THE COUNTRY, GARFIELD
JIM DAVIS 5-27
MY FRIENDS WERE FARM ANIMALS
EVER TICKLE A HOG?
CAN I GO NOW?

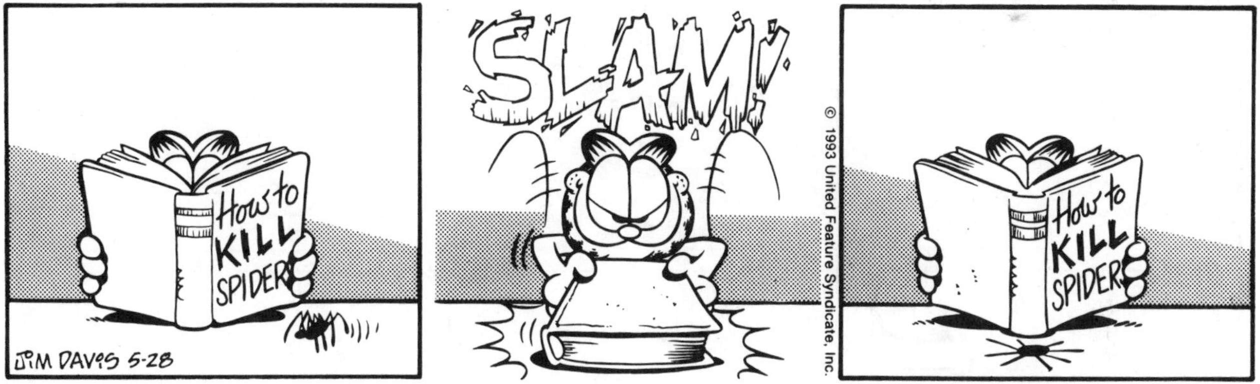
How to KILL SPIDER
JIM DAVIS 5-28
SLAM!
© 1993 United Feature Syndicate, Inc.
How to KILL SPIDER

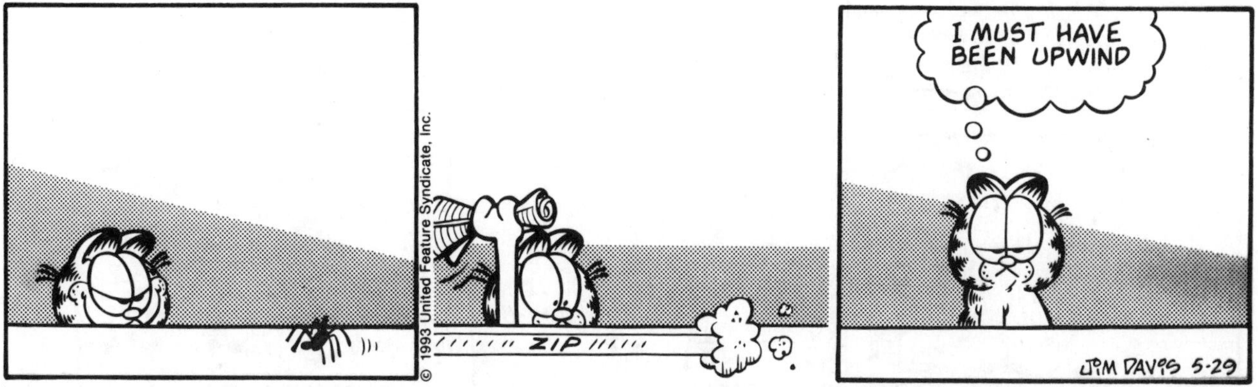
© 1993 United Feature Syndicate, Inc.
ZIP
I MUST HAVE BEEN UPWIND
JIM DAVIS 5-29

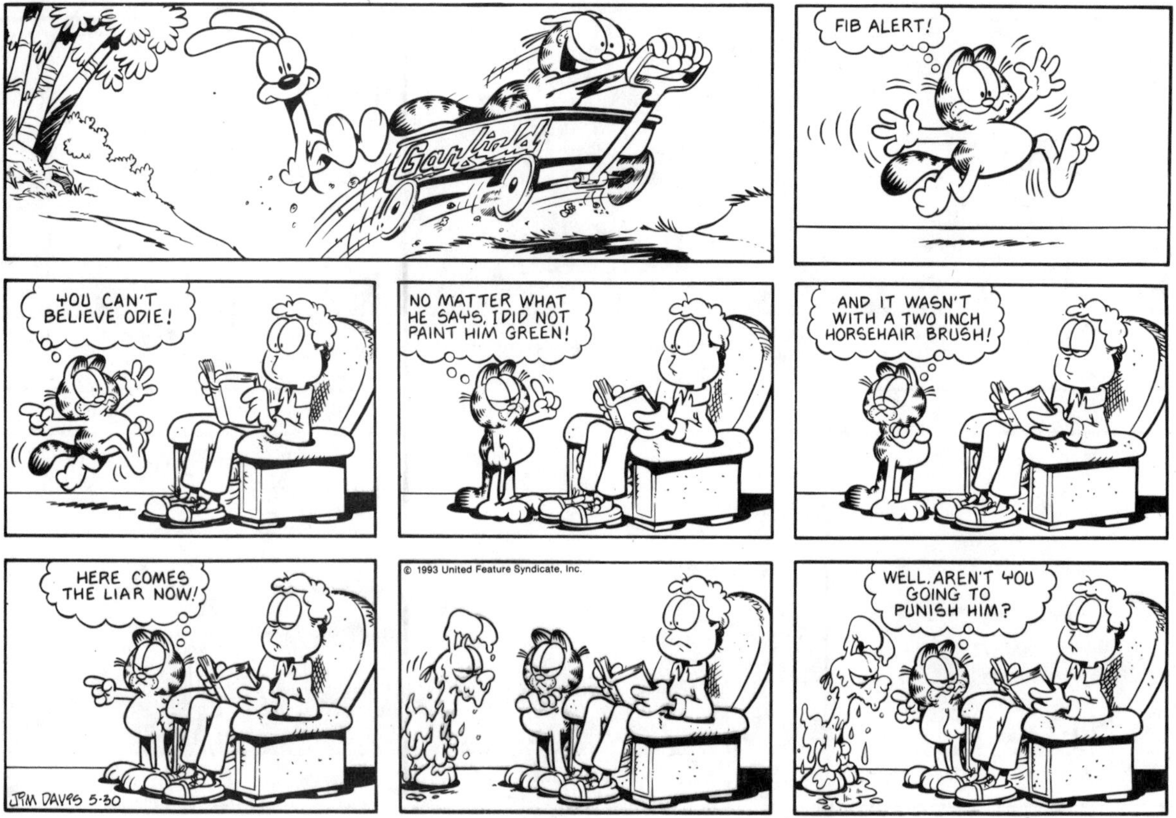
FIB ALERT!
YOU CAN'T BELIEVE ODIE!
NO MATTER WHAT HE SAYS, I DID NOT PAINT HIM GREEN!
AND IT WASN'T WITH A TWO INCH HORSEHAIR BRUSH!
HERE COMES THE LIAR NOW!
© 1993 United Feature Syndicate, Inc.
WELL, AREN'T YOU GOING TO PUNISH HIM?
JIM DAVIS 5-30

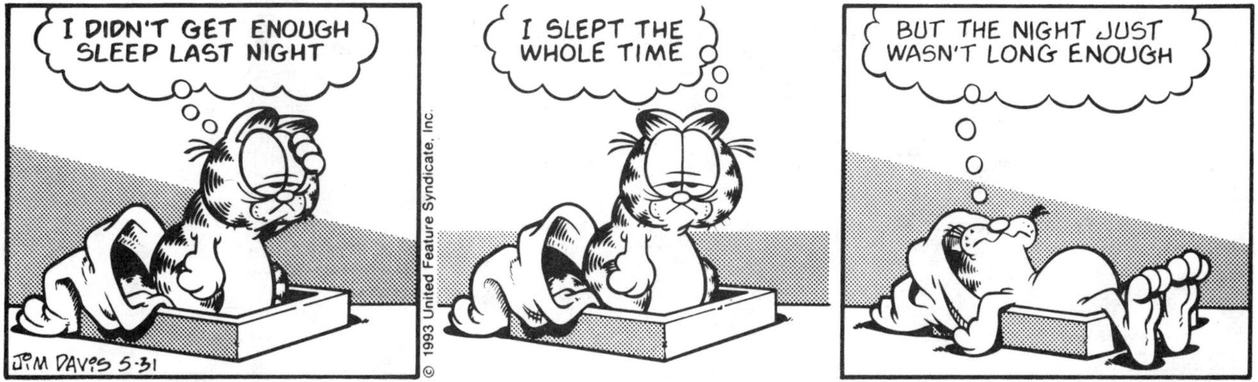
I DIDN'T GET ENOUGH SLEEP LAST NIGHT
JIM DAVIS 5-31
© 1993 United Feature Syndicate, Inc.
I SLEPT THE WHOLE TIME
BUT THE NIGHT JUST WASN'T LONG ENOUGH

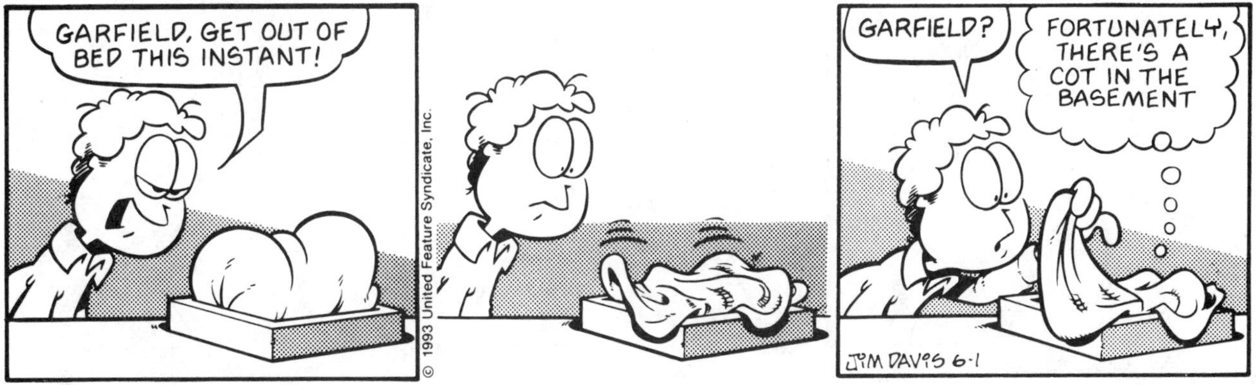
GARFIELD, GET OUT OF BED THIS INSTANT!
© 1993 United Feature Syndicate, Inc.
GARFIELD?
FORTUNATELY, THERE'S A COT IN THE BASEMENT
JIM DAVIS 6-1

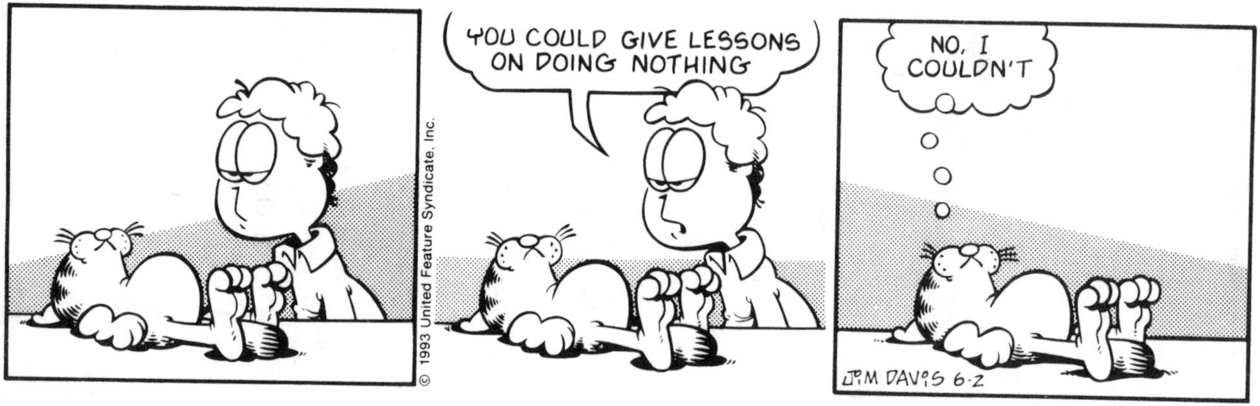
YOU COULD GIVE LESSONS ON DOING NOTHING
NO, I COULDN'T
JIM DAVIS 6-2
© 1993 United Feature Syndicate, Inc.

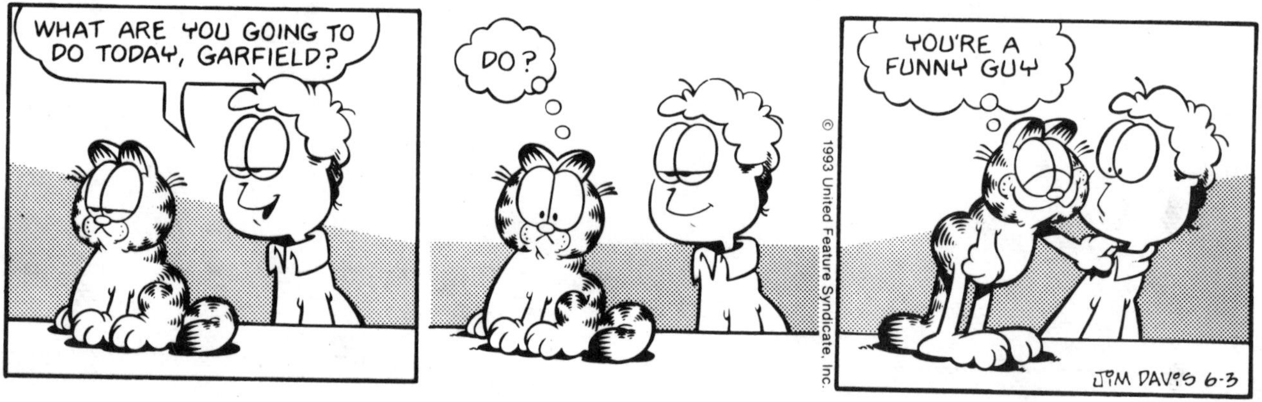
WHAT ARE YOU GOING TO DO TODAY, GARFIELD?
DO?
YOU'RE A FUNNY GUY
JIM DAVIS 6-3
© 1993 United Feature Syndicate, Inc.

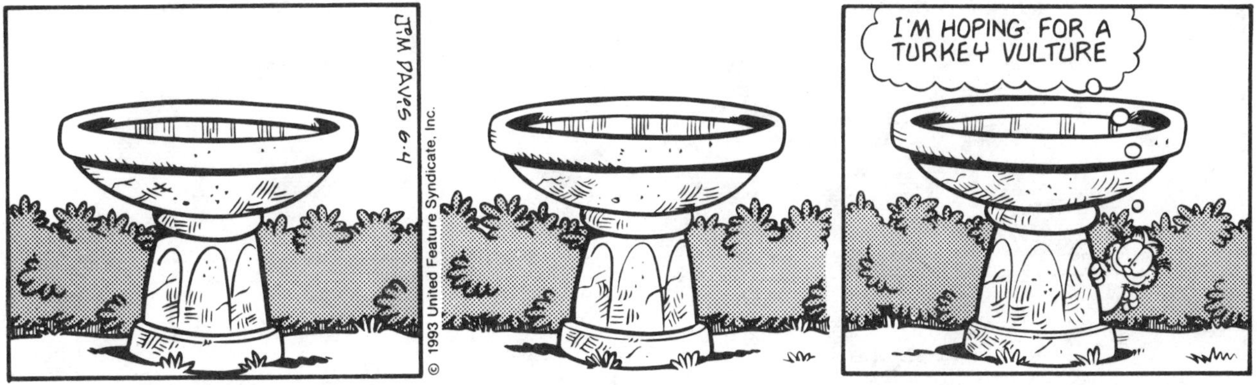
JIM DAVIS 6-4
© 1993 United Feature Syndicate, Inc.
I'M HOPING FOR A TURKEY VULTURE

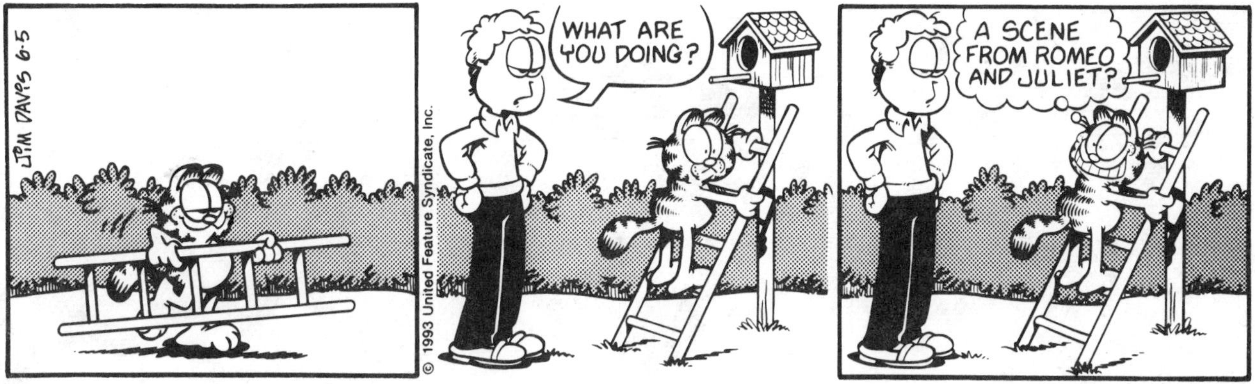
JIM DAVIS 6-5
© 1993 United Feature Syndicate, Inc.
WHAT ARE YOU DOING?
A SCENE FROM ROMEO AND JULIET?

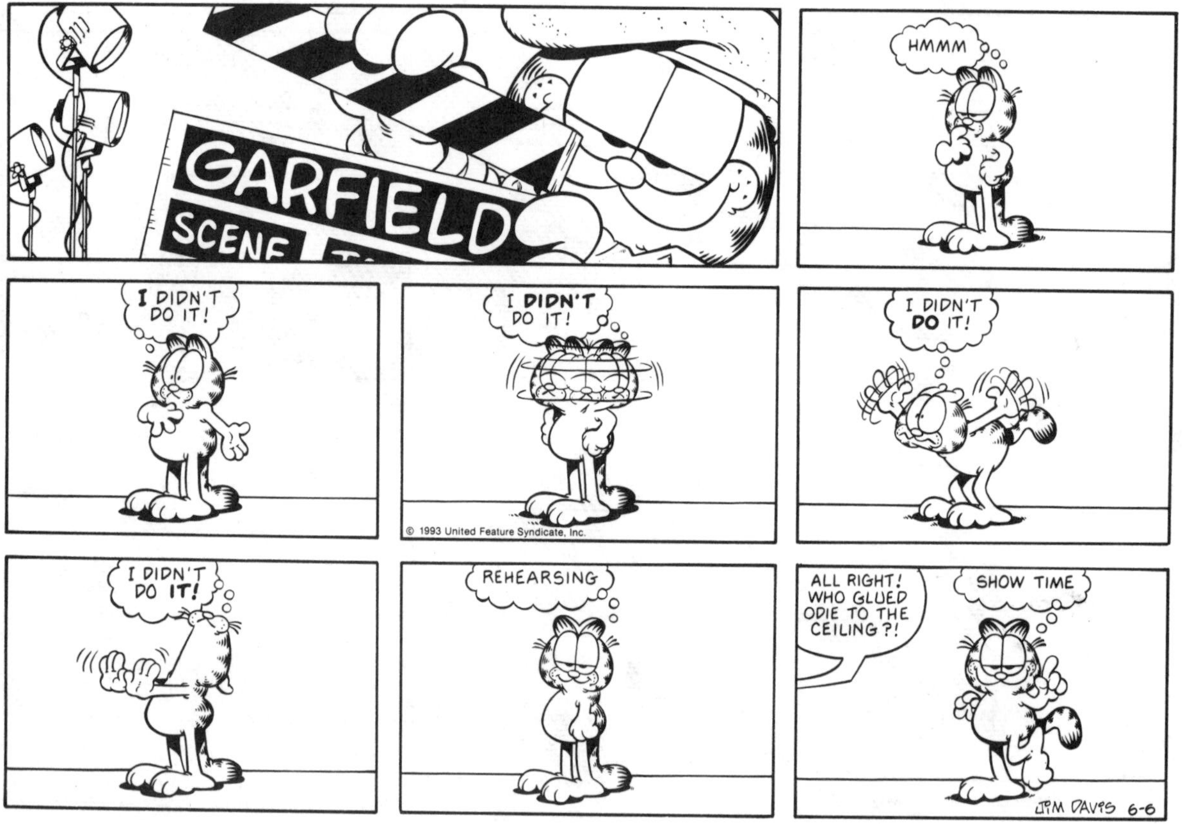
GARFIELD
SCENE
HMMM
I DIDN'T DO IT!
I DIDN'T DO IT!
I DIDN'T DO IT!
© 1993 United Feature Syndicate, Inc.
I DIDN'T DO IT!
REHEARSING
ALL RIGHT! WHO GLUED ODIE TO THE CEILING?!
SHOW TIME
JIM DAVIS 6-6

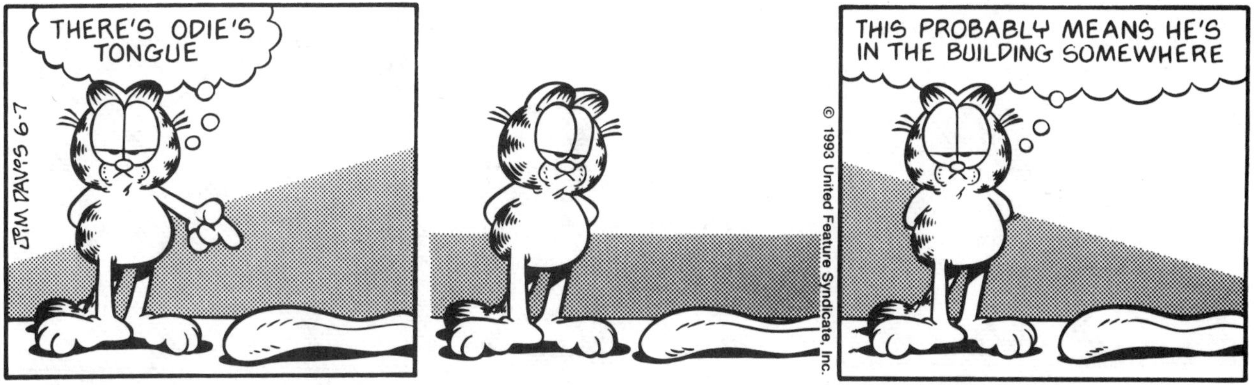
THERE'S ODIE'S TONGUE
JIM DAVIS 6-7
THIS PROBABLY MEANS HE'S IN THE BUILDING SOMEWHERE
© 1993 United Feature Syndicate, Inc.

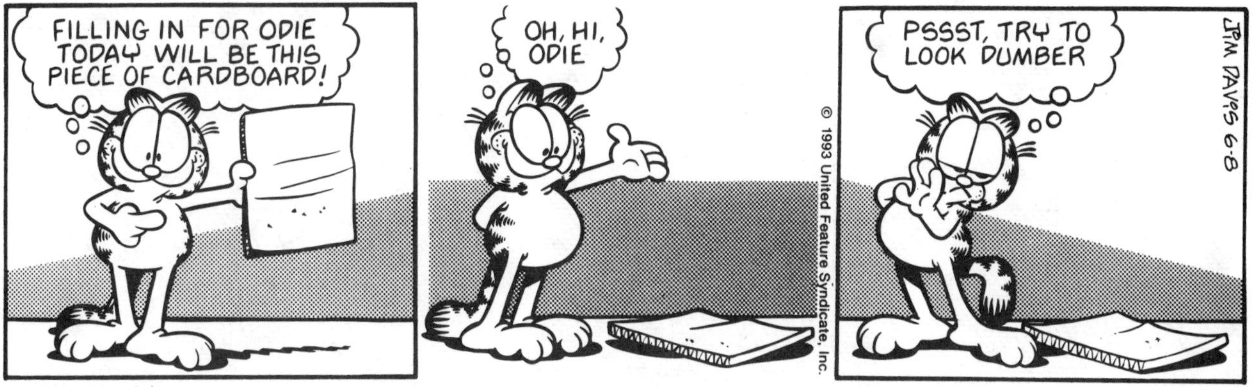
FILLING IN FOR ODIE TODAY WILL BE THIS PIECE OF CARDBOARD!
OH, HI, ODIE
PSSST, TRY TO LOOK DUMBER
JIM DAVIS 6-8
© 1993 United Feature Syndicate, Inc.

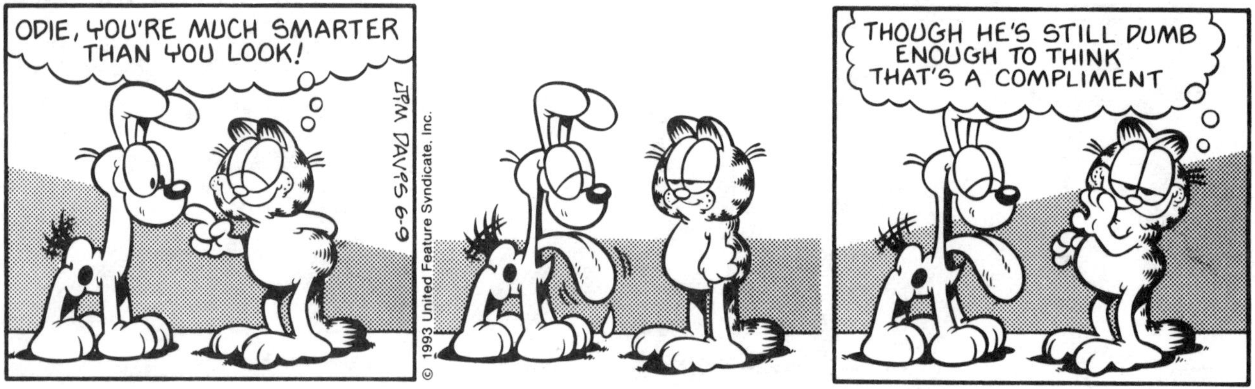
ODIE, YOU'RE MUCH SMARTER THAN YOU LOOK!
JIM DAVIS 6-9
© 1993 United Feature Syndicate, Inc.
THOUGH HE'S STILL DUMB ENOUGH TO THINK THAT'S A COMPLIMENT

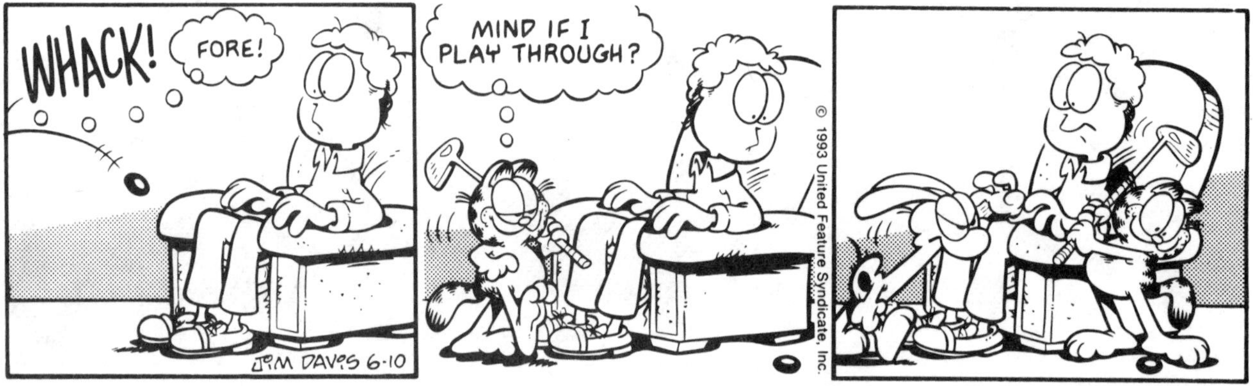
WHACK!
FORE!
JIM DAVIS 6-10
MIND IF I PLAY THROUGH?
© 1993 United Feature Syndicate, Inc.

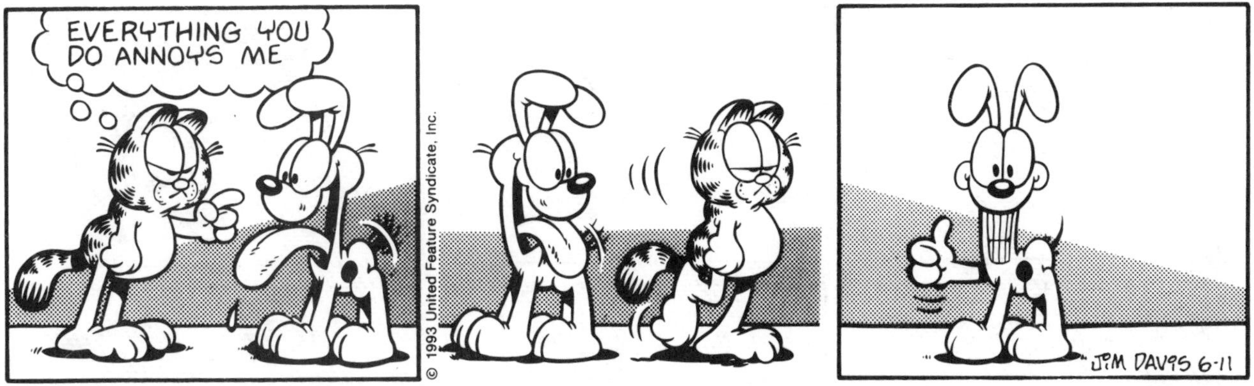
EVERYTHING YOU DO ANNOYS ME
© 1993 United Feature Syndicate, Inc.
JIM DAVIS 6-11

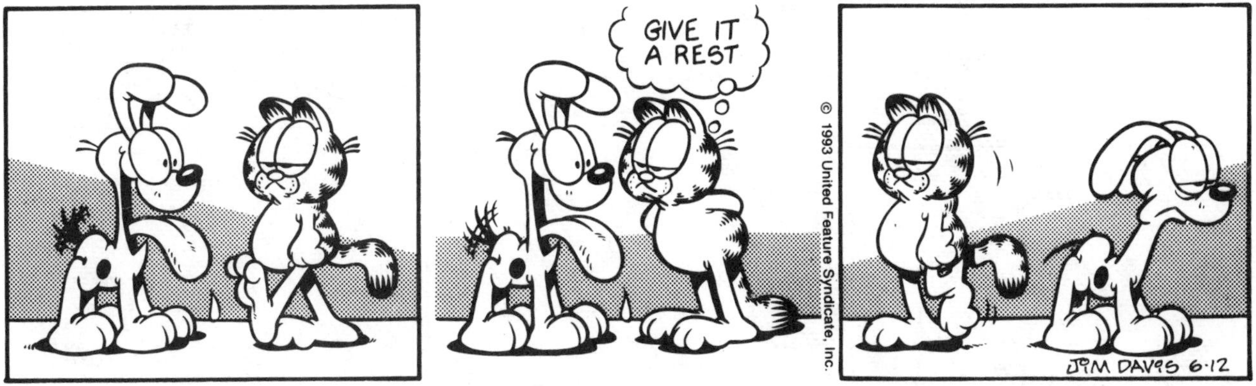
GIVE IT A REST
© 1993 United Feature Syndicate, Inc.
JIM DAVIS 6-12

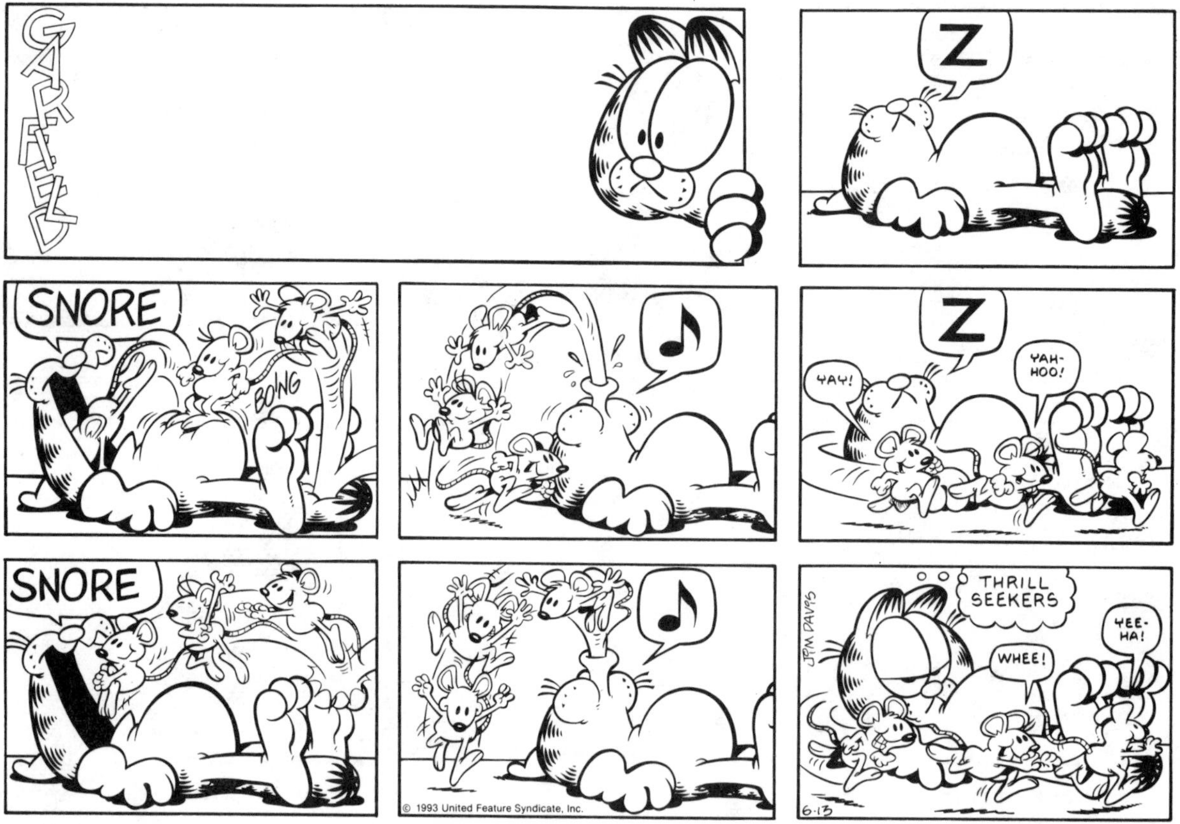
GARFIELD
Z
SNORE
BOING
♪
Z
YAY!
YAH-HOO!
SNORE
♪
JPM DAVPS
THRILL SEEKERS
WHEE!
YEE-HA!
6-13

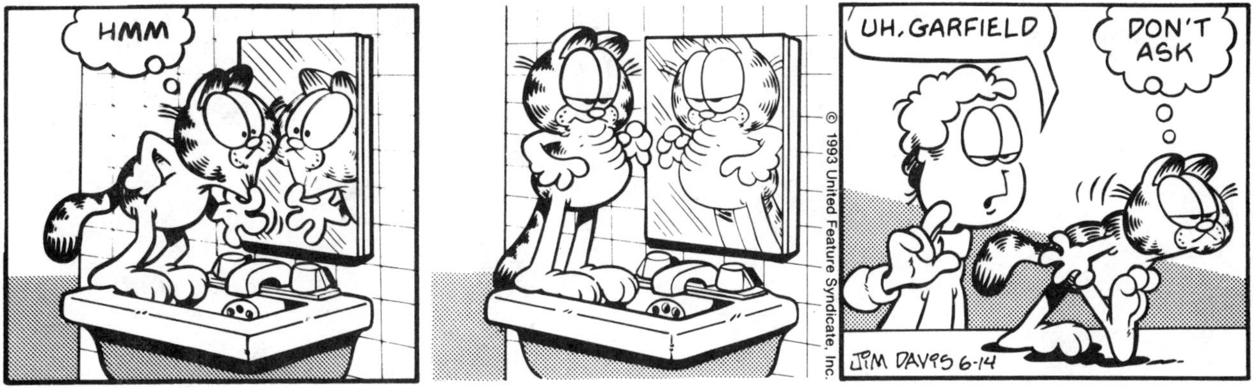
HMM
UH, GARFIELD
DON'T ASK
JIM DAVIS 6-14
© 1993 United Feature Syndicate, Inc.

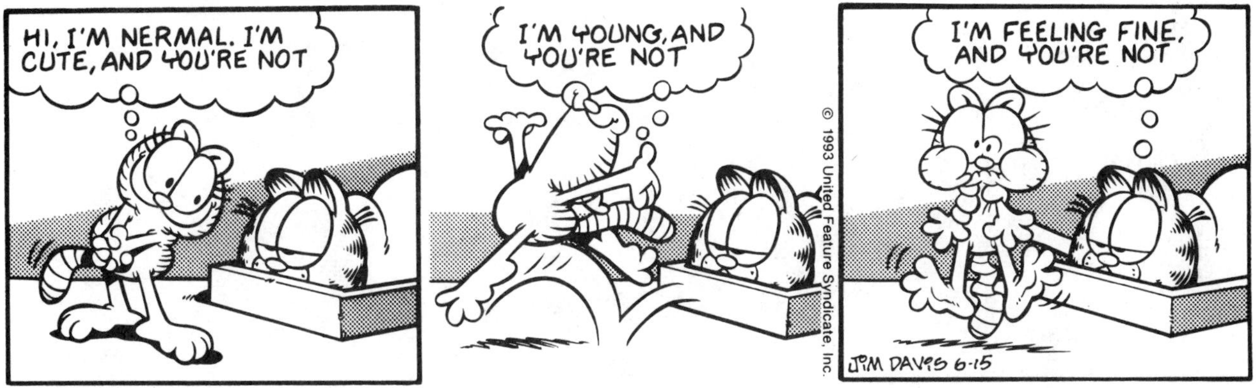
HI, I'M NERMAL. I'M CUTE, AND YOU'RE NOT
I'M YOUNG, AND YOU'RE NOT
I'M FEELING FINE, AND YOU'RE NOT
JIM DAVIS 6-15
© 1993 United Feature Syndicate, Inc.

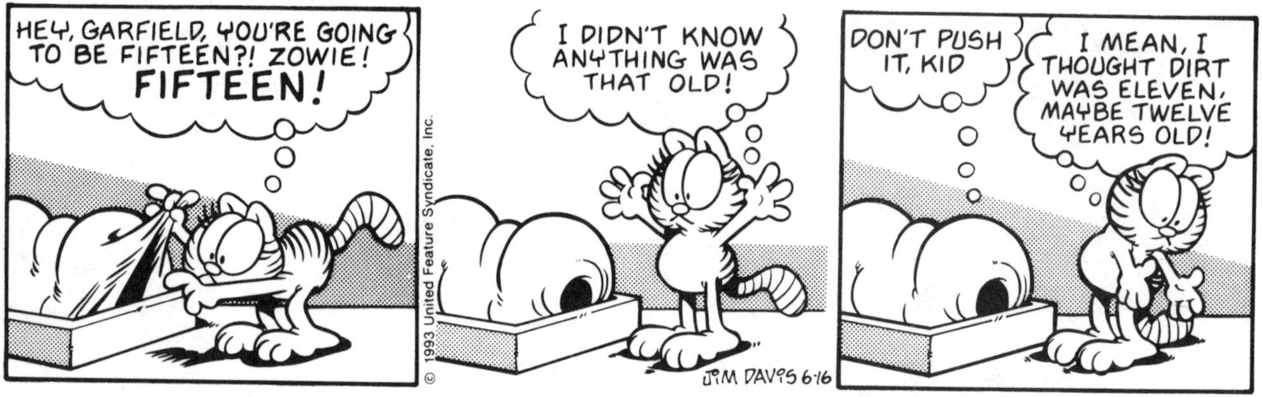
HEY, GARFIELD, YOU'RE GOING TO BE FIFTEEN?! ZOWIE! FIFTEEN!
I DIDN'T KNOW ANYTHING WAS THAT OLD!
DON'T PUSH IT, KID
I MEAN, I THOUGHT DIRT WAS ELEVEN, MAYBE TWELVE YEARS OLD!
JIM DAVIS 6·16
© 1993 United Feature Syndicate, Inc.

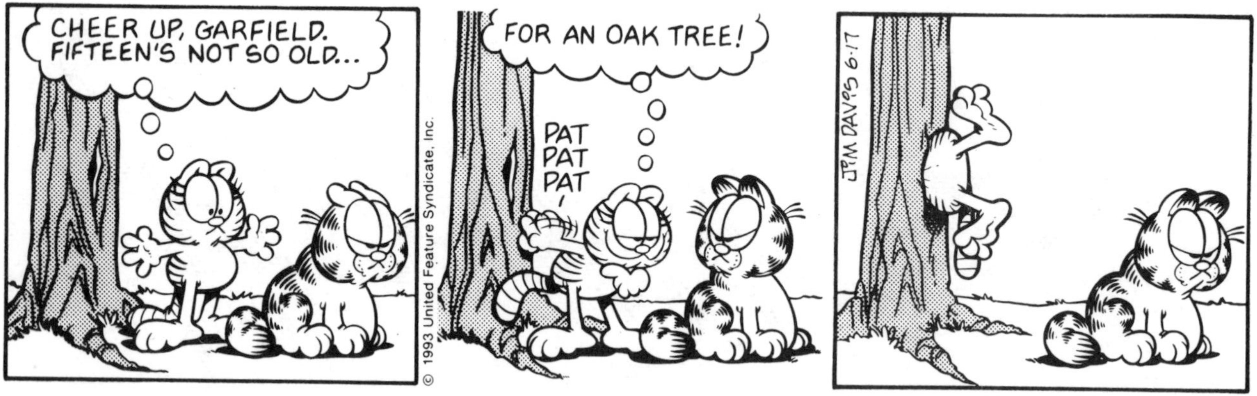
CHEER UP, GARFIELD. FIFTEEN'S NOT SO OLD...
FOR AN OAK TREE!
PAT PAT PAT
JIM DAVIS 6·17
© 1993 United Feature Syndicate, Inc.

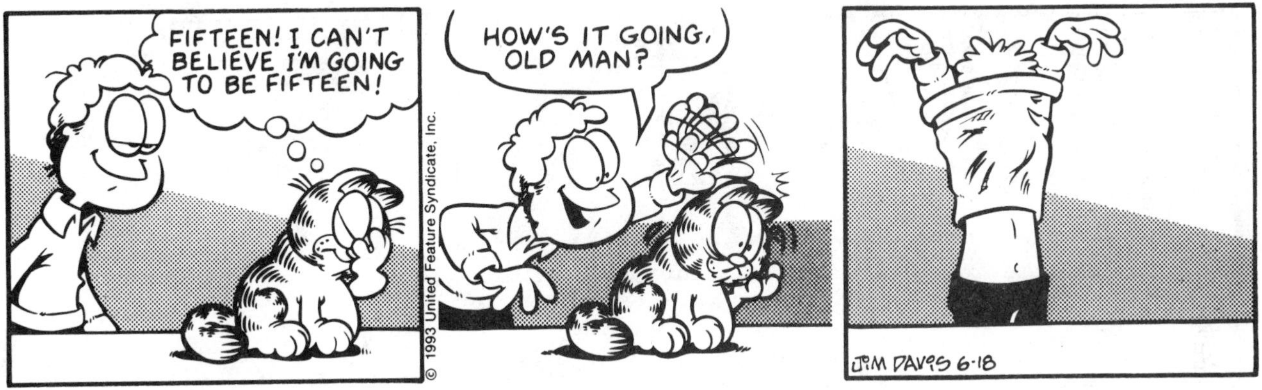
FIFTEEN! I CAN'T BELIEVE I'M GOING TO BE FIFTEEN!
HOW'S IT GOING, OLD MAN?
© 1993 United Feature Syndicate, Inc.
JIM DAVIS 6-18

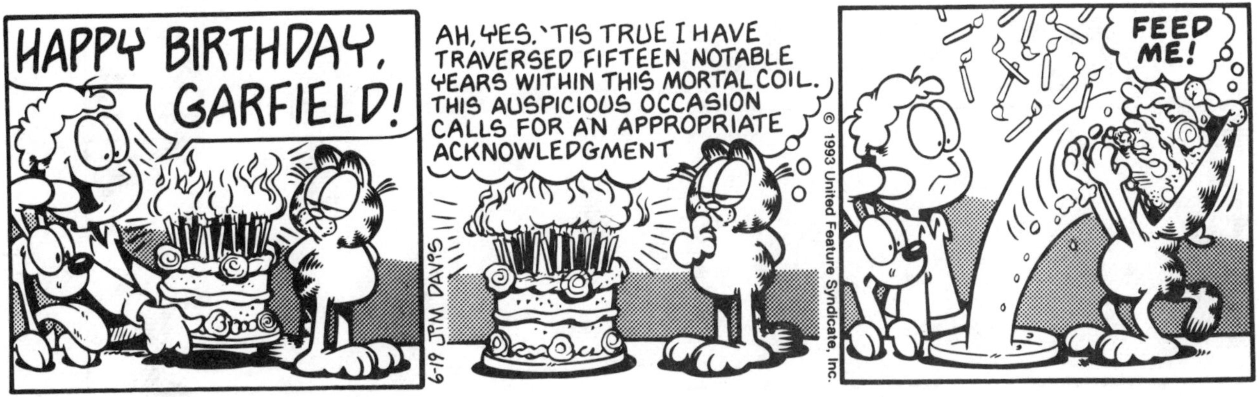
HAPPY BIRTHDAY, GARFIELD!
6-19 JIM DAVIS
AH, YES. 'TIS TRUE I HAVE TRAVERSED FIFTEEN NOTABLE YEARS WITHIN THIS MORTAL COIL. THIS AUSPICIOUS OCCASION CALLS FOR AN APPROPRIATE ACKNOWLEDGMENT
© 1993 United Feature Syndicate, Inc.
FEED ME!

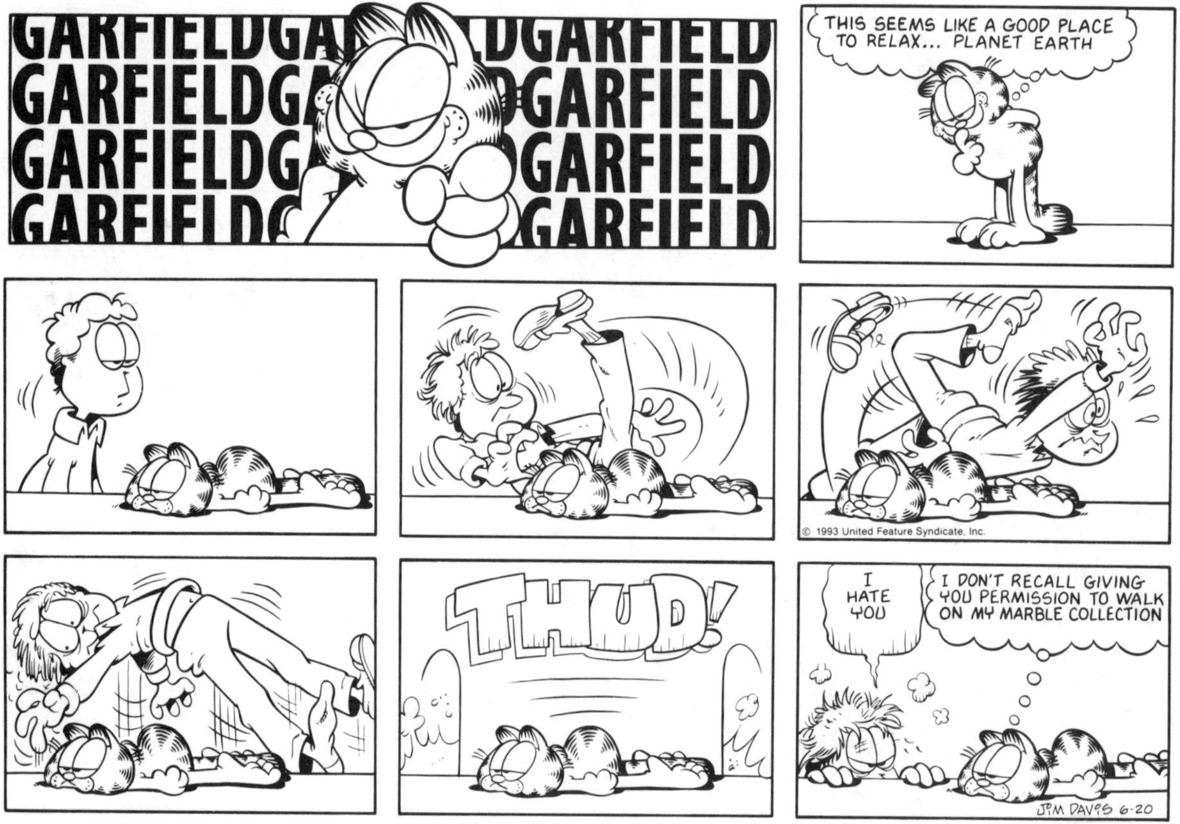

GARFIELD
THIS SEEMS LIKE A GOOD PLACE TO RELAX... PLANET EARTH
© 1993 United Feature Syndicate, Inc.
THUD!
I HATE YOU
I DON'T RECALL GIVING YOU PERMISSION TO WALK ON MY MARBLE COLLECTION
JIM DAVIS 6-20

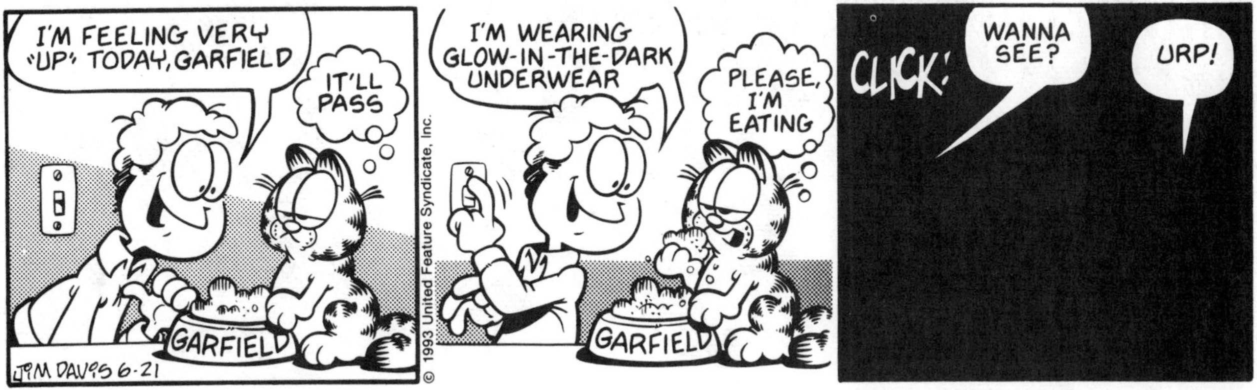
I'M FEELING VERY "UP" TODAY, GARFIELD
IT'LL PASS
GARFIELD
JIM DAVIS 6-21
© 1993 United Feature Syndicate, Inc.
I'M WEARING GLOW-IN-THE-DARK UNDERWEAR
PLEASE, I'M EATING
GARFIELD
CLICK!
WANNA SEE?
URP!

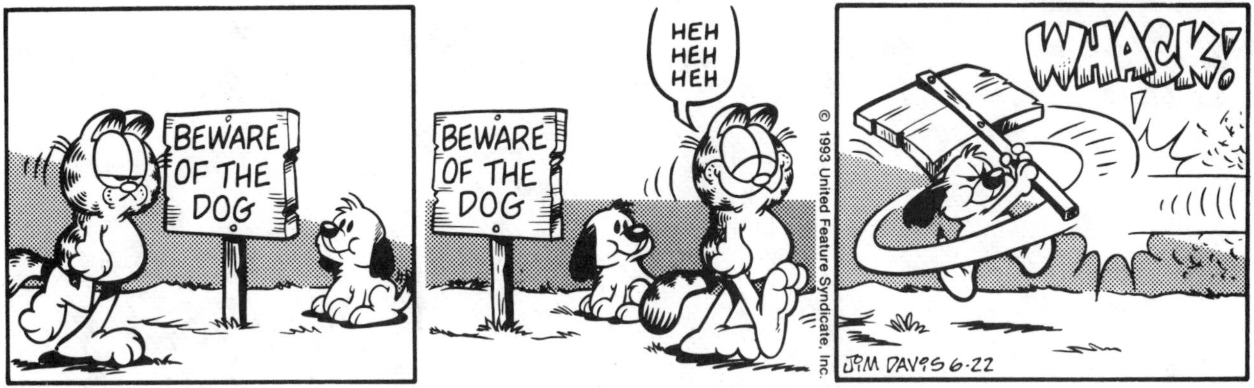
BEWARE OF THE DOG
BEWARE OF THE DOG
HEH HEH HEH
© 1993 United Feature Syndicate, Inc.
WHACK!
JIM DAVIS 6-22

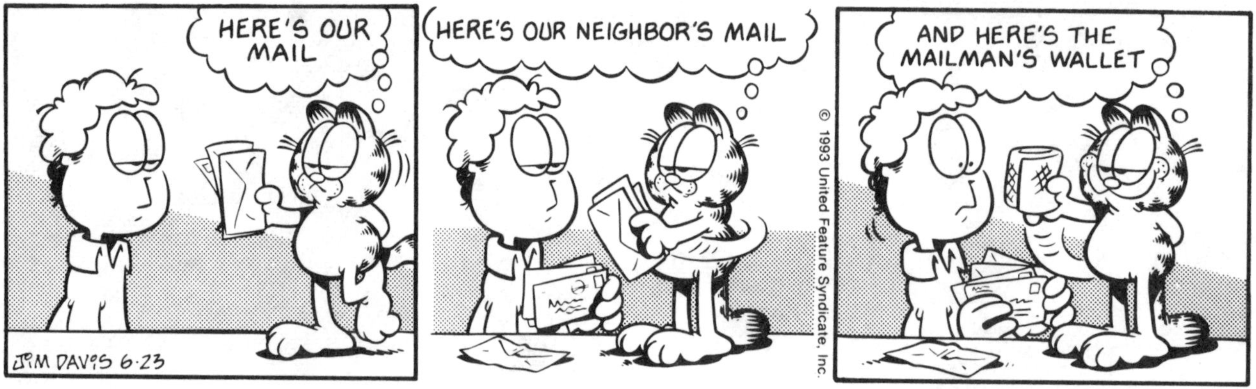
HERE'S OUR MAIL
JIM DAVIS 6-23
HERE'S OUR NEIGHBOR'S MAIL
© 1993 United Feature Syndicate, Inc.
AND HERE'S THE MAILMAN'S WALLET

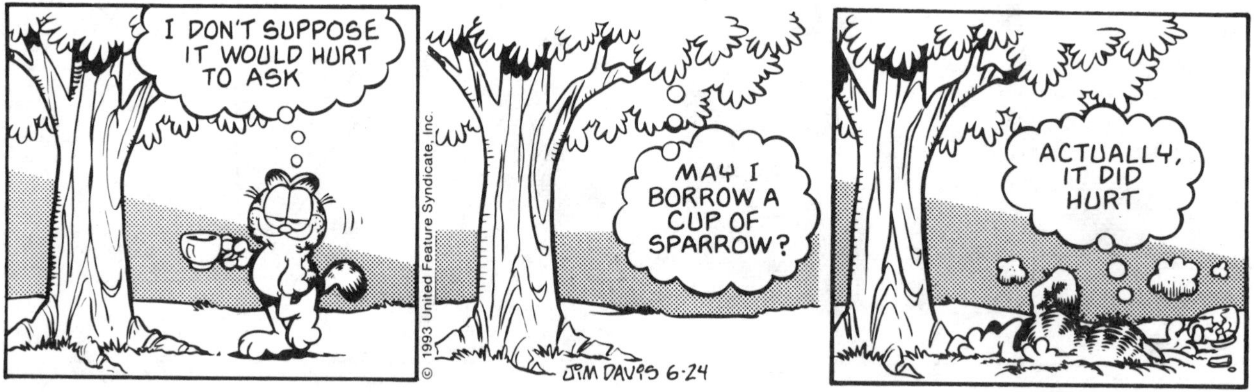
I DON'T SUPPOSE IT WOULD HURT TO ASK
© 1993 United Feature Syndicate, Inc.
MAY I BORROW A CUP OF SPARROW?
JIM DAVIS 6-24
ACTUALLY, IT DID HURT

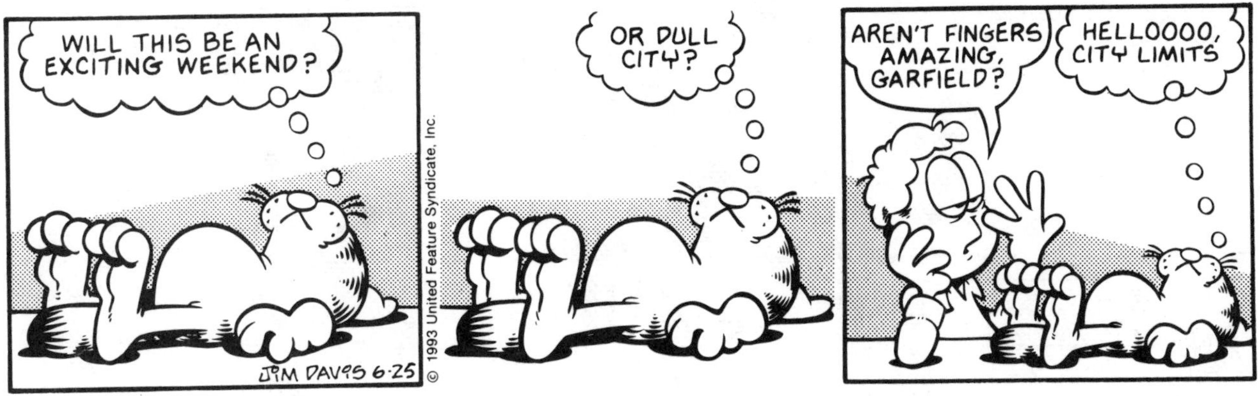
WILL THIS BE AN EXCITING WEEKEND?
JIM DAVIS 6-25
© 1993 United Feature Syndicate, Inc.
OR DULL CITY?
AREN'T FINGERS AMAZING, GARFIELD?
HELLOOOO, CITY LIMITS

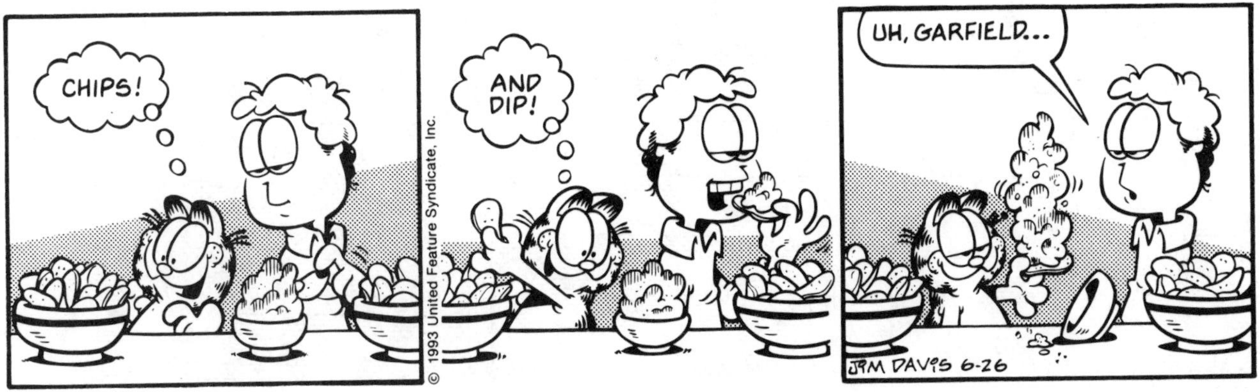
CHIPS!
© 1993 United Feature Syndicate, Inc.
AND DIP!
UH, GARFIELD...
JIM DAVIS 6-26

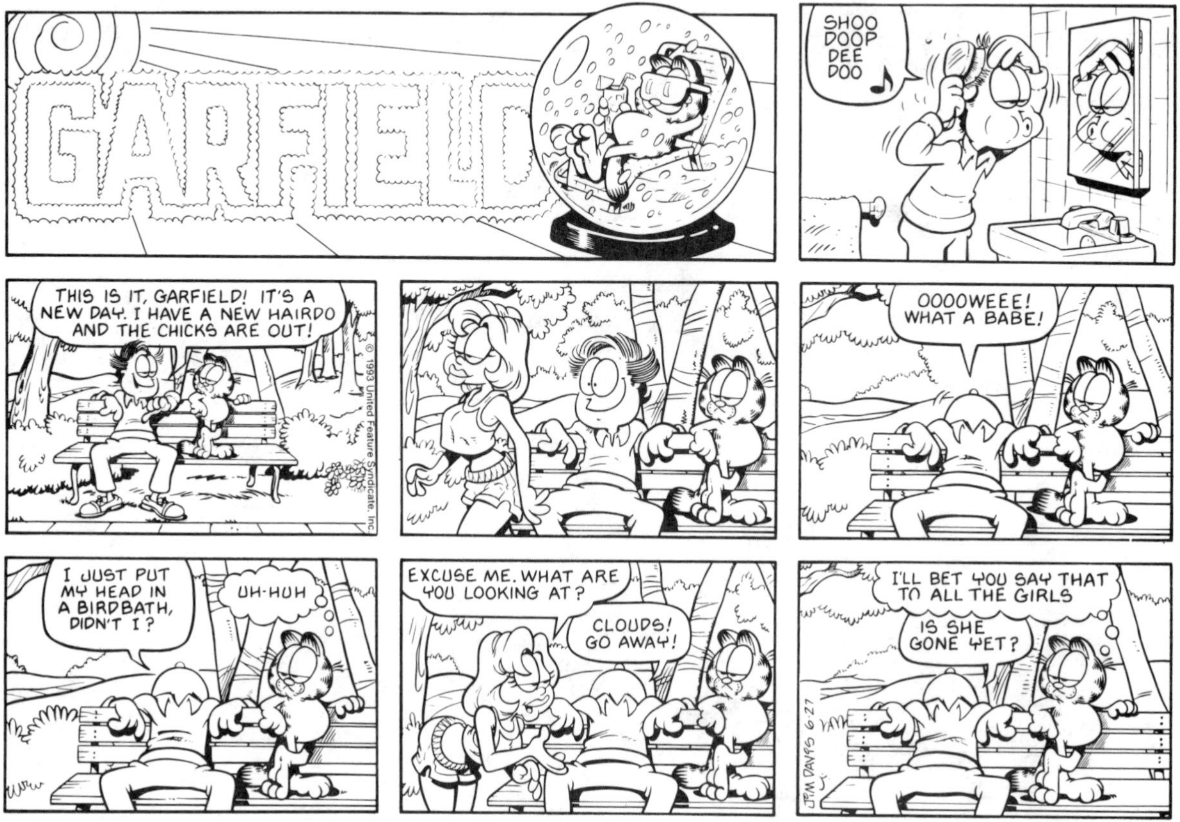
GARFIELD
SHOO DOOP DEE DOO
THIS IS IT, GARFIELD! IT'S A NEW DAY. I HAVE A NEW HAIRDO AND THE CHICKS ARE OUT!
© 1993 United Feature Syndicate, Inc.
OOOOWEEE! WHAT A BABE!
I JUST PUT MY HEAD IN A BIRDBATH, DIDN'T I?
UH-HUH
EXCUSE ME. WHAT ARE YOU LOOKING AT?
CLOUDS! GO AWAY!
I'LL BET YOU SAY THAT TO ALL THE GIRLS
IS SHE GONE YET?
JIM DAVIS 6-27

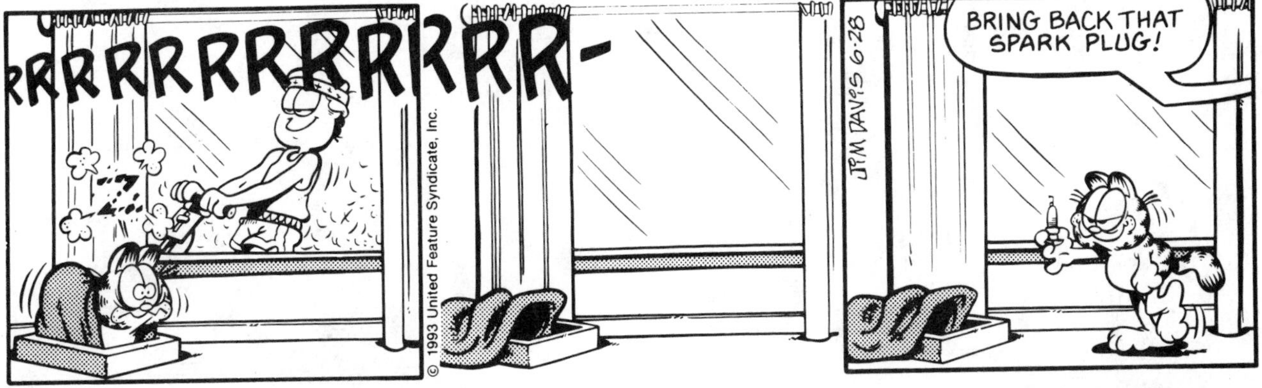
RRRRRRRRRRRR-
© 1993 United Feature Syndicate, Inc.
JIM DAVIS 6-28
BRING BACK THAT SPARK PLUG!

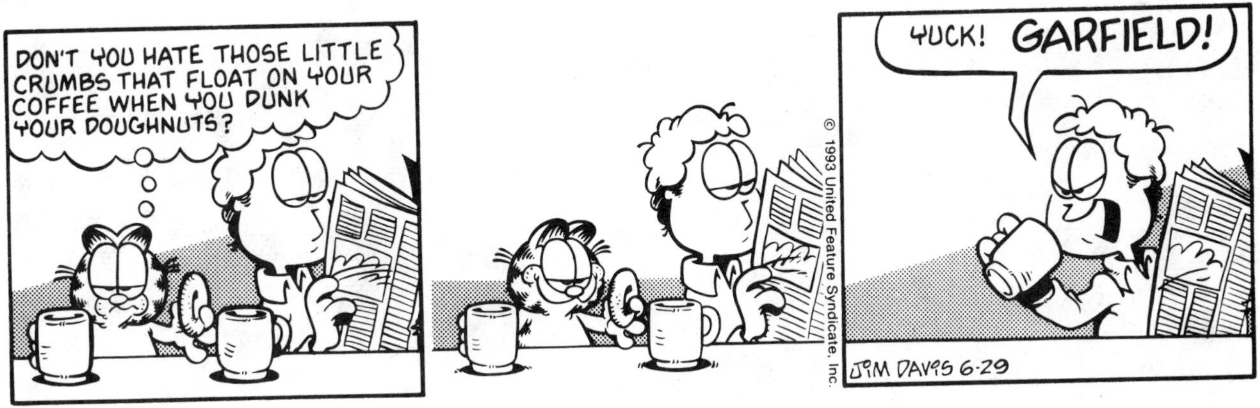
DON'T YOU HATE THOSE LITTLE CRUMBS THAT FLOAT ON YOUR COFFEE WHEN YOU DUNK YOUR DOUGHNUTS?
© 1993 United Feature Syndicate, Inc.
YUCK! GARFIELD!
JIM DAVIS 6-29

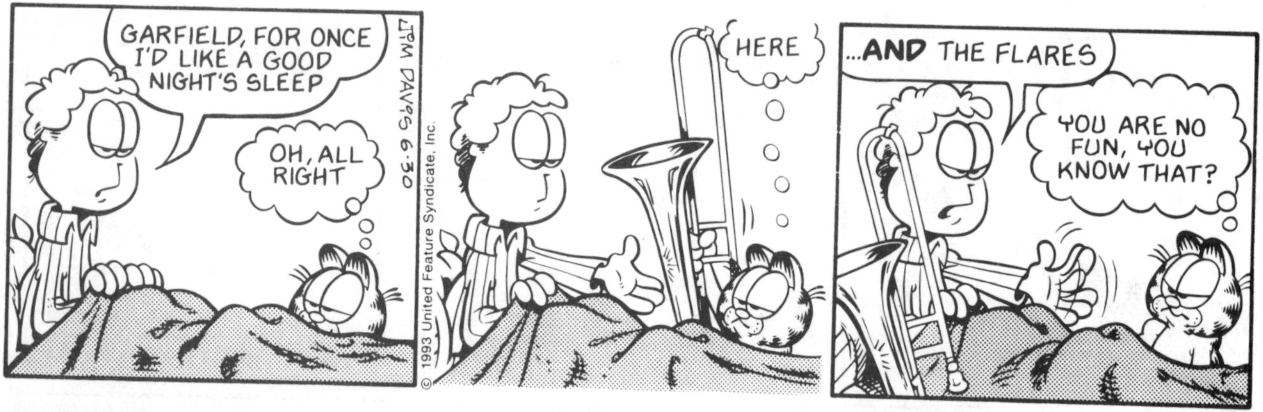
GARFIELD, FOR ONCE I'D LIKE A GOOD NIGHT'S SLEEP
OH, ALL RIGHT
JPM DAVPS 6-30
© 1993 United Feature Syndicate, Inc.
HERE
...**AND** THE FLARES
YOU ARE NO FUN, YOU KNOW THAT?

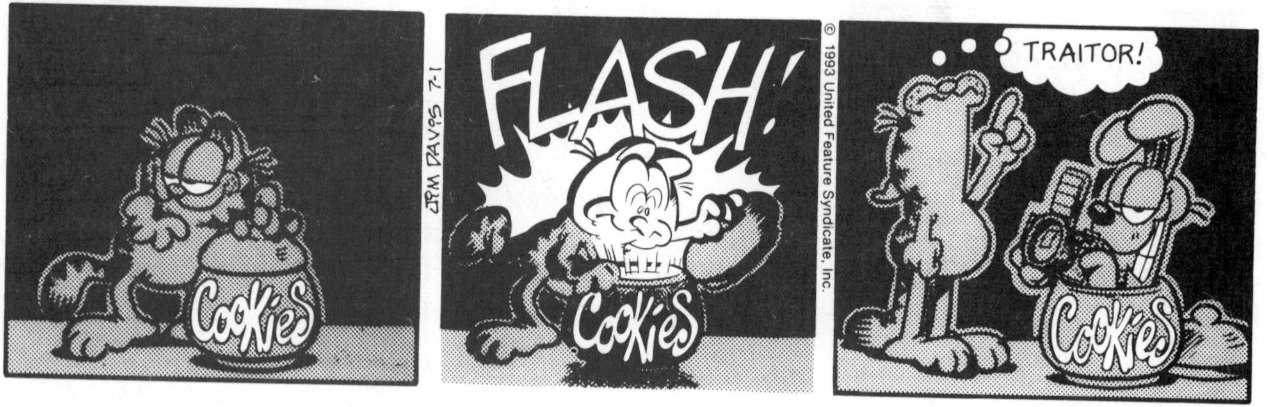
COOKIES
JPM DAVPS 7-1
FLASH!
COOKIES
© 1993 United Feature Syndicate, Inc.
TRAITOR!
COOKIES

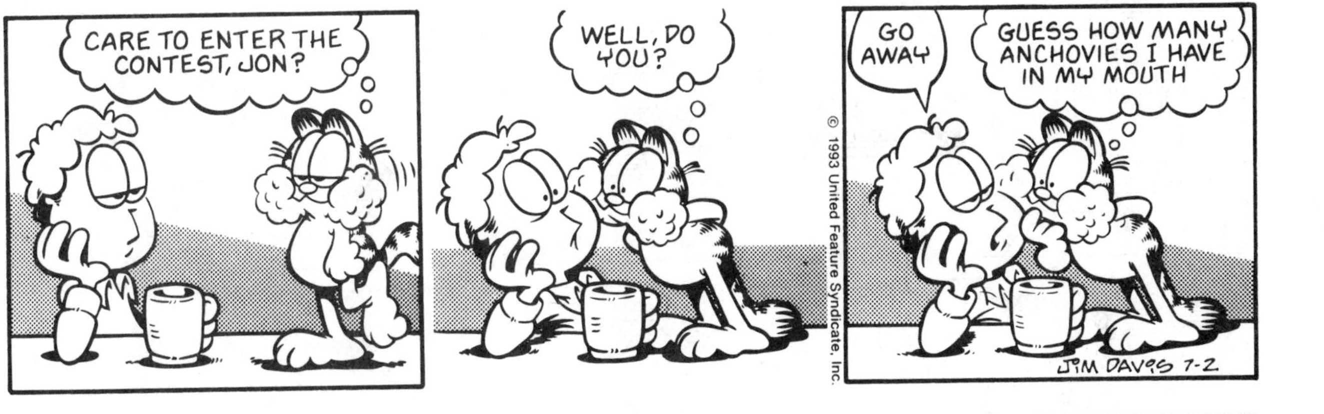
CARE TO ENTER THE CONTEST, JON?
WELL, DO YOU?
GO AWAY
GUESS HOW MANY ANCHOVIES I HAVE IN MY MOUTH
JIM DAVIS 7-2

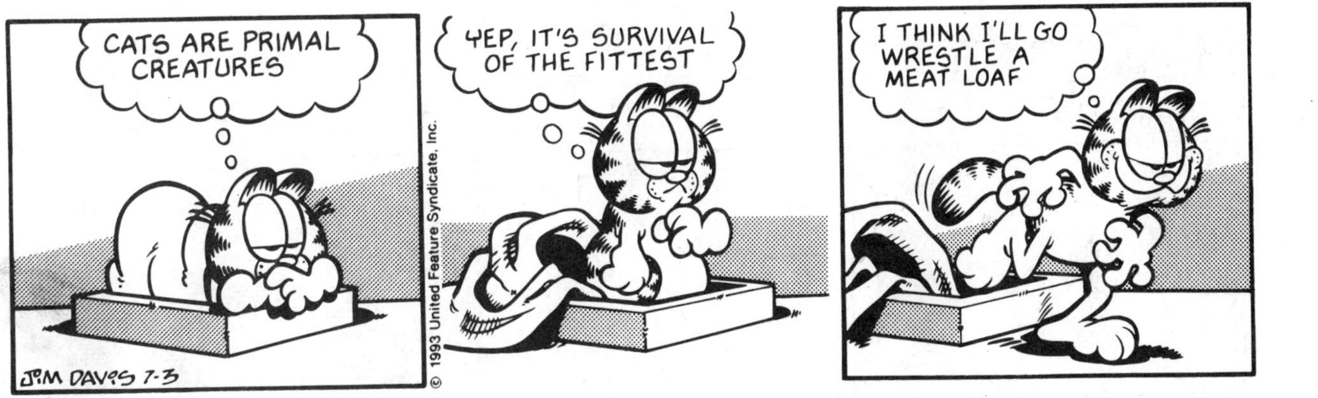
CATS ARE PRIMAL CREATURES
JIM DAVIS 7-3
YEP, IT'S SURVIVAL OF THE FITTEST
I THINK I'LL GO WRESTLE A MEAT LOAF

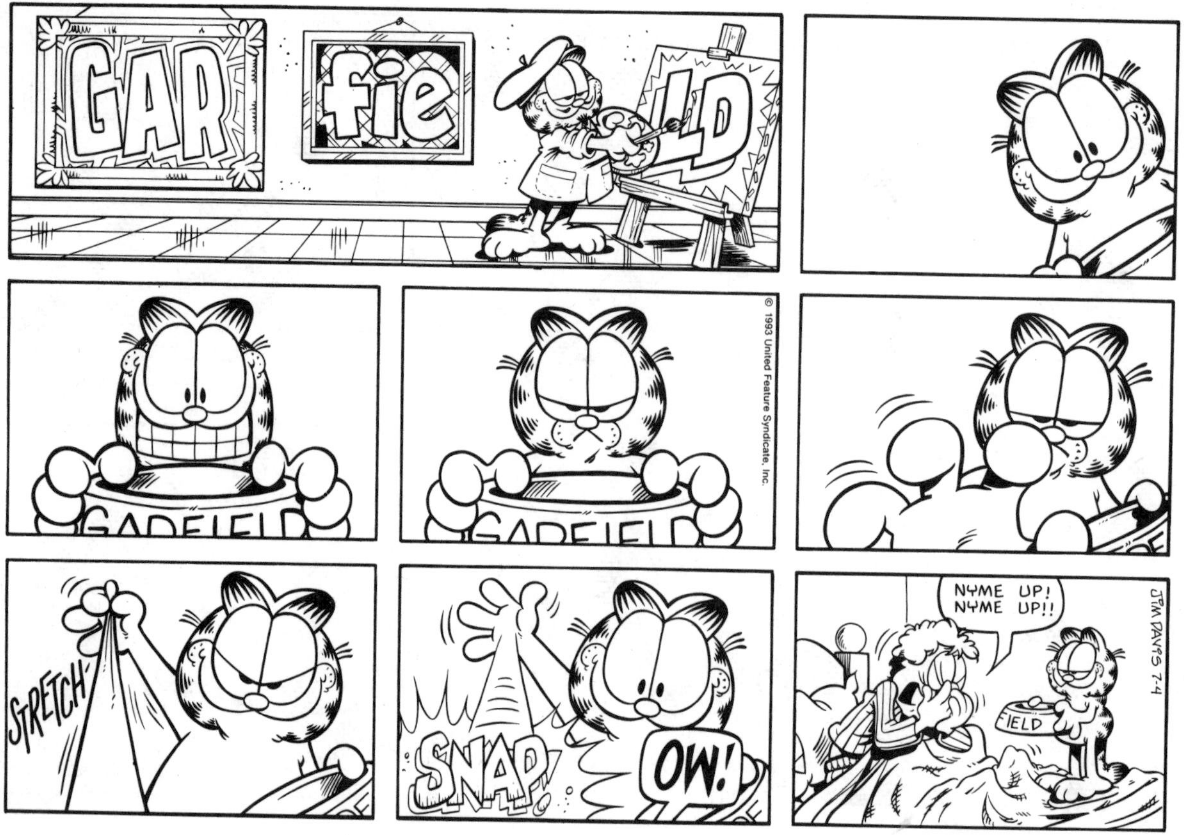
GAR
fie
LD
© 1993 United Feature Syndicate, Inc.
STRETCH
SNAP
OW!
NYME UP!
NYME UP!!
JIM DAVIS 7-4

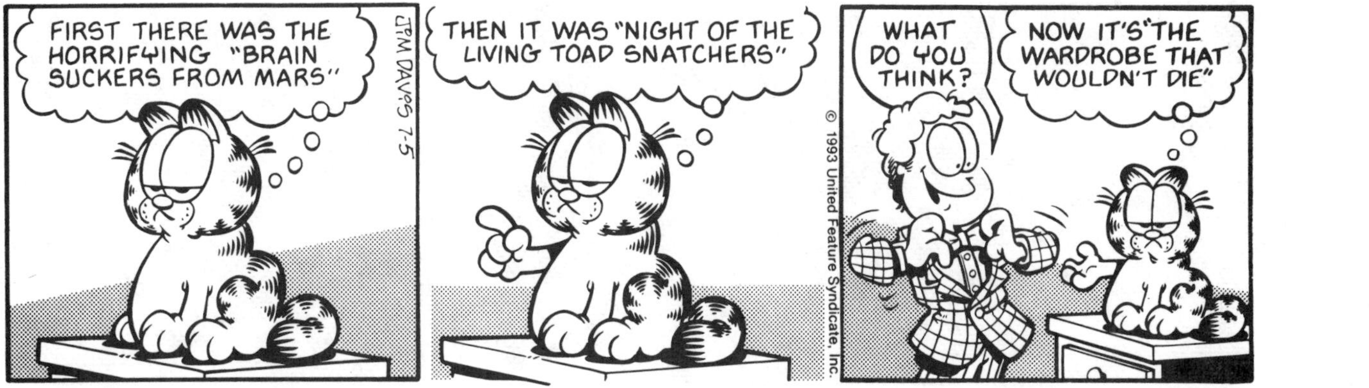
FIRST THERE WAS THE HORRIFYING "BRAIN SUCKERS FROM MARS"
JPM DAVIS 7-5
THEN IT WAS "NIGHT OF THE LIVING TOAD SNATCHERS"
WHAT DO YOU THINK?
NOW IT'S "THE WARDROBE THAT WOULDN'T DIE"
© 1993 United Feature Syndicate, Inc.

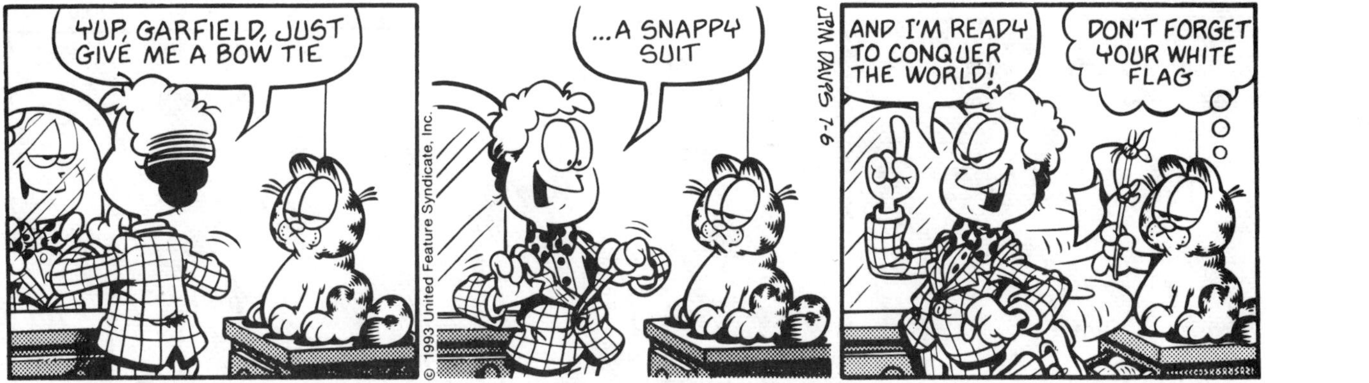
YUP, GARFIELD, JUST GIVE ME A BOW TIE
© 1993 United Feature Syndicate, Inc.
...A SNAPPY SUIT
JPM DAVIS 7-6
AND I'M READY TO CONQUER THE WORLD!
DON'T FORGET YOUR WHITE FLAG

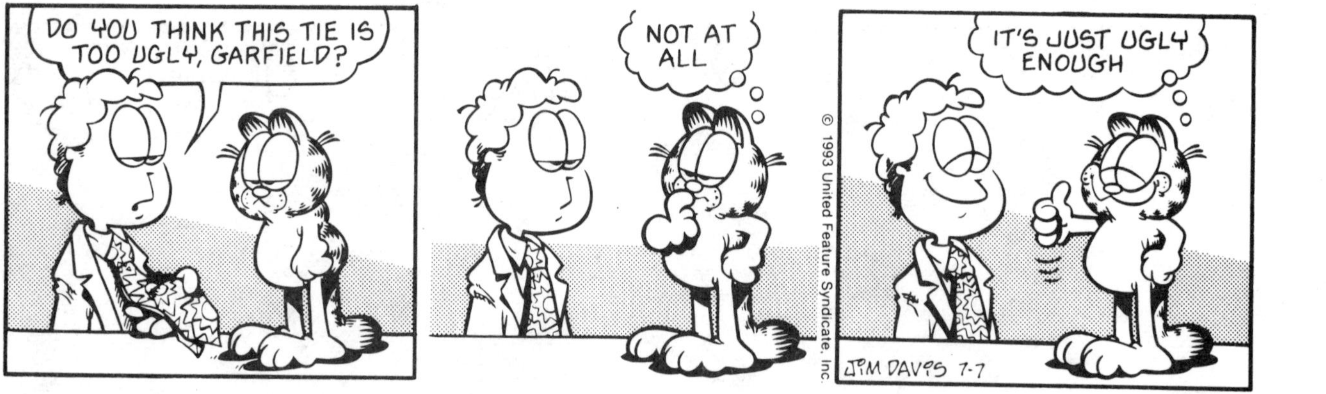
DO YOU THINK THIS TIE IS TOO UGLY, GARFIELD?
NOT AT ALL
IT'S JUST UGLY ENOUGH
JIM DAVIS 7-7

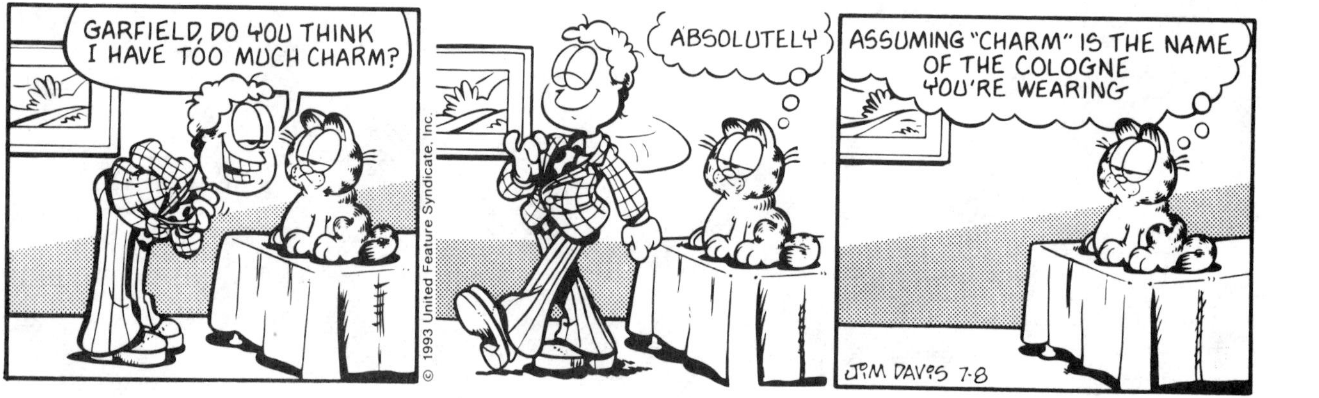
GARFIELD, DO YOU THINK I HAVE TOO MUCH CHARM?
ABSOLUTELY
ASSUMING "CHARM" IS THE NAME OF THE COLOGNE YOU'RE WEARING
JIM DAVIS 7-8

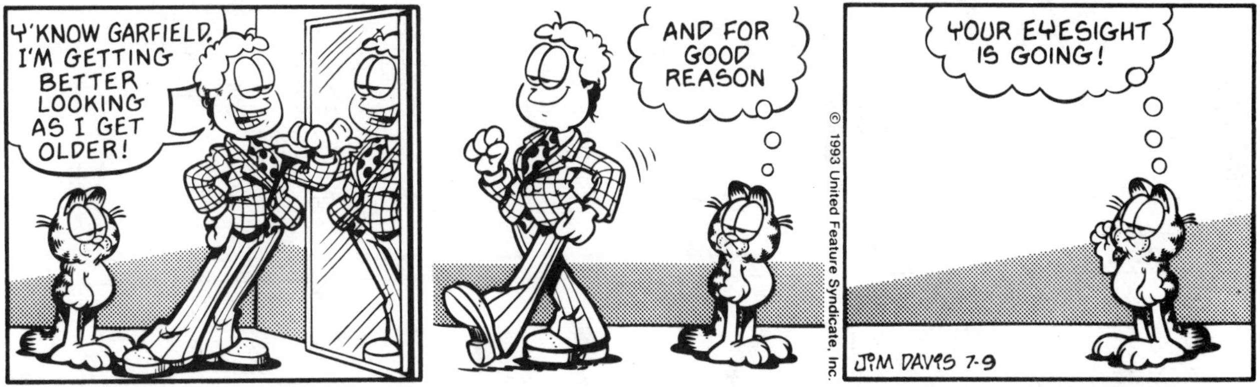
Y'KNOW GARFIELD, I'M GETTING BETTER LOOKING AS I GET OLDER!
AND FOR GOOD REASON
YOUR EYESIGHT IS GOING!
JIM DAVIS 7-9

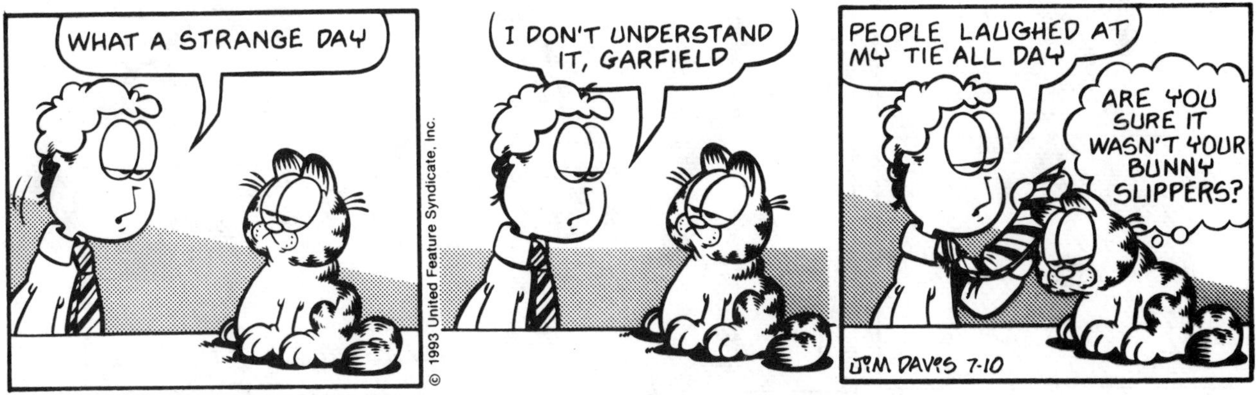
WHAT A STRANGE DAY
I DON'T UNDERSTAND IT, GARFIELD
PEOPLE LAUGHED AT MY TIE ALL DAY
ARE YOU SURE IT WASN'T YOUR BUNNY SLIPPERS?
JIM DAVIS 7-10

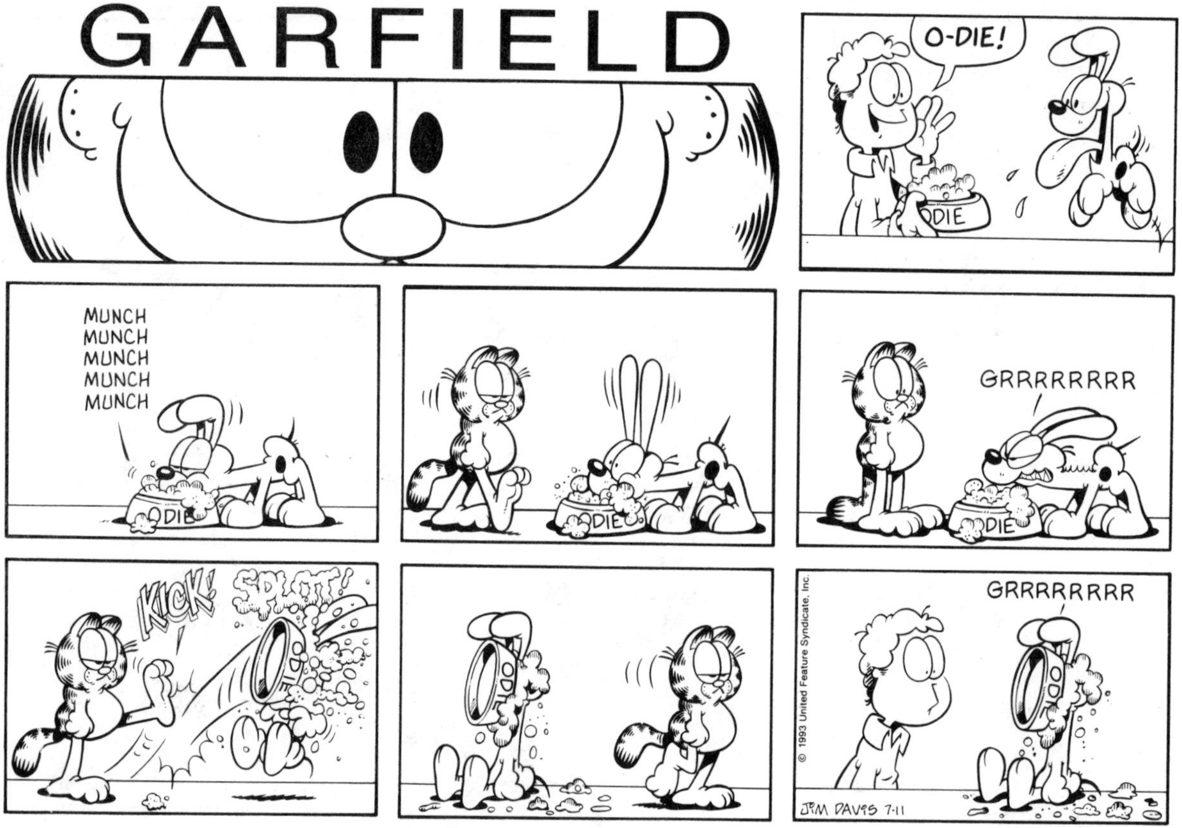
GARFIELD
O-DIE!
ODIE
MUNCH
MUNCH
MUNCH
MUNCH
MUNCH
ODIE
ODIE
GRRRRRRRR
ODIE
KICK!
SPLOT!
GRRRRRRRR
© 1993 United Feature Syndicate, Inc.
JIM DAVIS 7-11

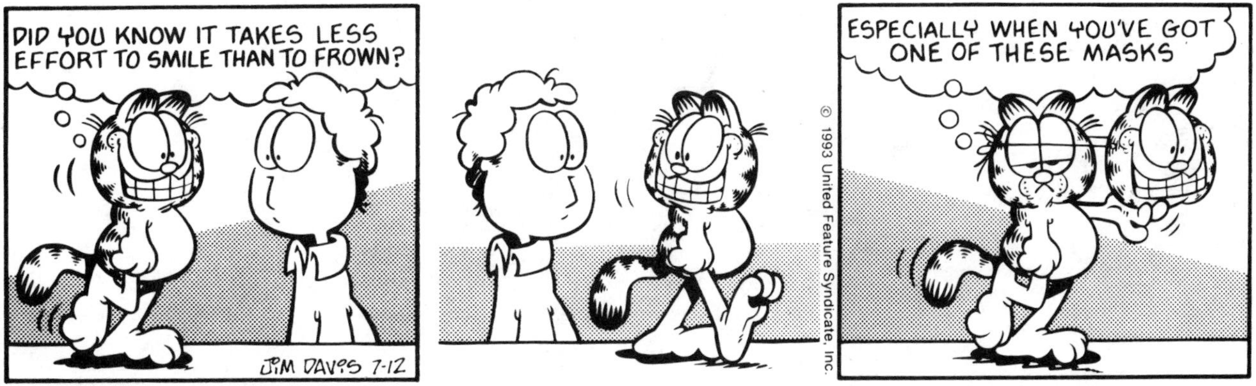

DID YOU KNOW IT TAKES LESS EFFORT TO SMILE THAN TO FROWN?
JIM DAVIS 7-12
© 1993 United Feature Syndicate, Inc.
ESPECIALLY WHEN YOU'VE GOT ONE OF THESE MASKS

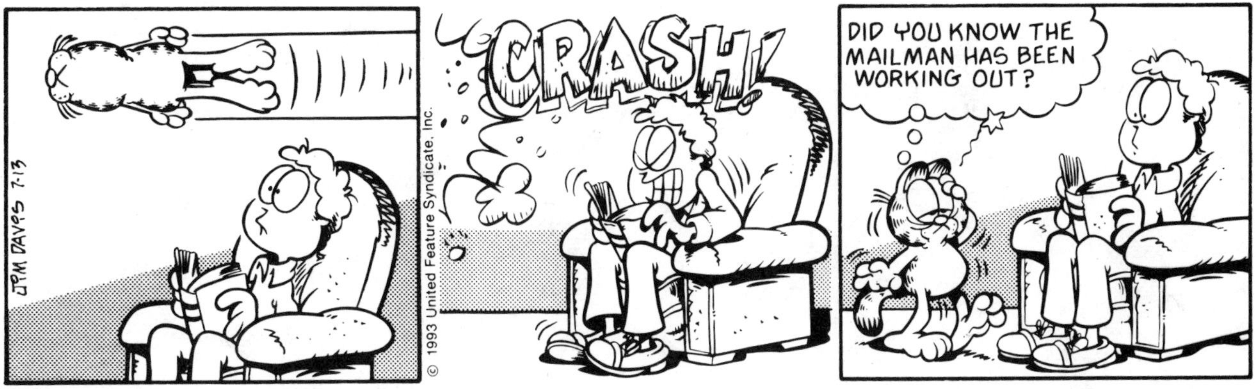

JIM DAVIS 7-13
© 1993 United Feature Syndicate, Inc.
CRASH!
DID YOU KNOW THE MAILMAN HAS BEEN WORKING OUT?

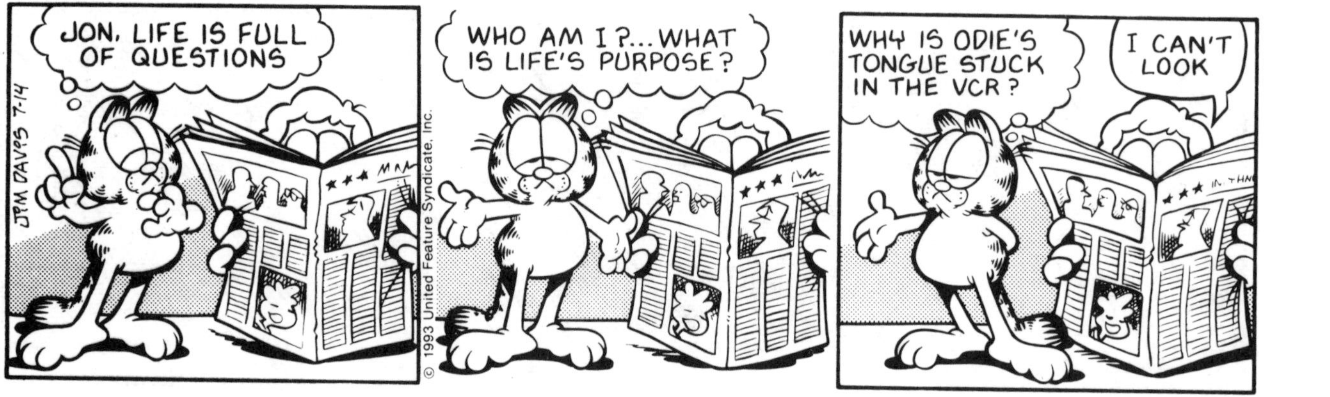
JON, LIFE IS FULL OF QUESTIONS
JIM DAVIS 7-14
WHO AM I?... WHAT IS LIFE'S PURPOSE?
© 1993 United Feature Syndicate, Inc.
WHY IS ODIE'S TONGUE STUCK IN THE VCR?
I CAN'T LOOK

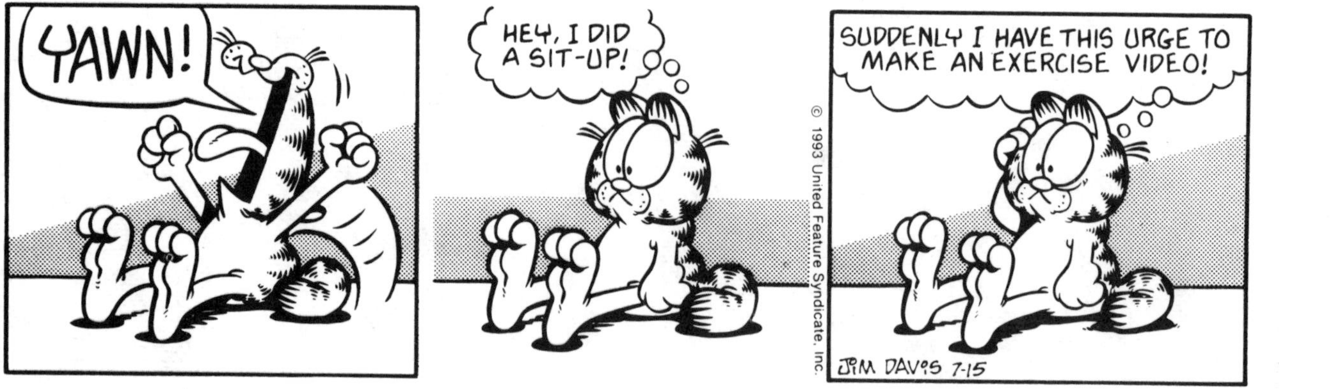
YAWN!
HEY, I DID A SIT-UP!
© 1993 United Feature Syndicate, Inc.
SUDDENLY I HAVE THIS URGE TO MAKE AN EXERCISE VIDEO!
JIM DAVIS 7-15

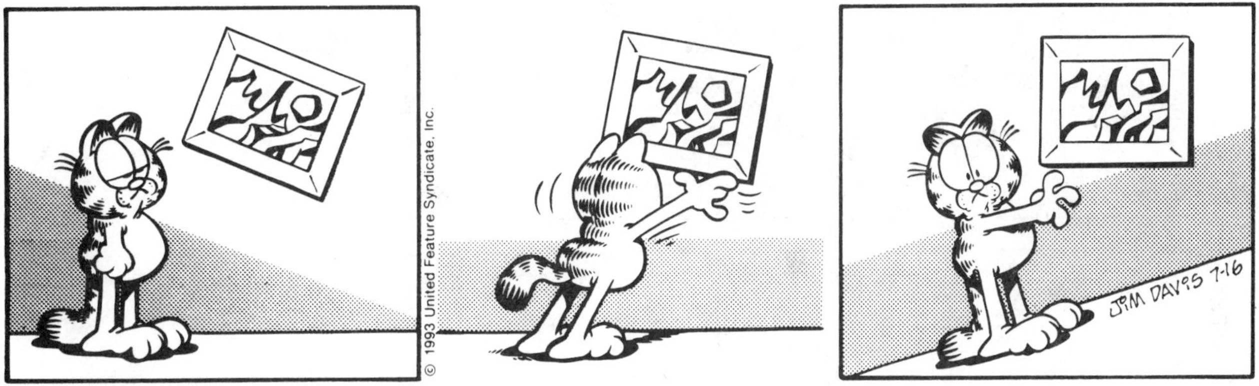

© 1993 United Feature Syndicate, Inc.
JIM DAVIS 7-16

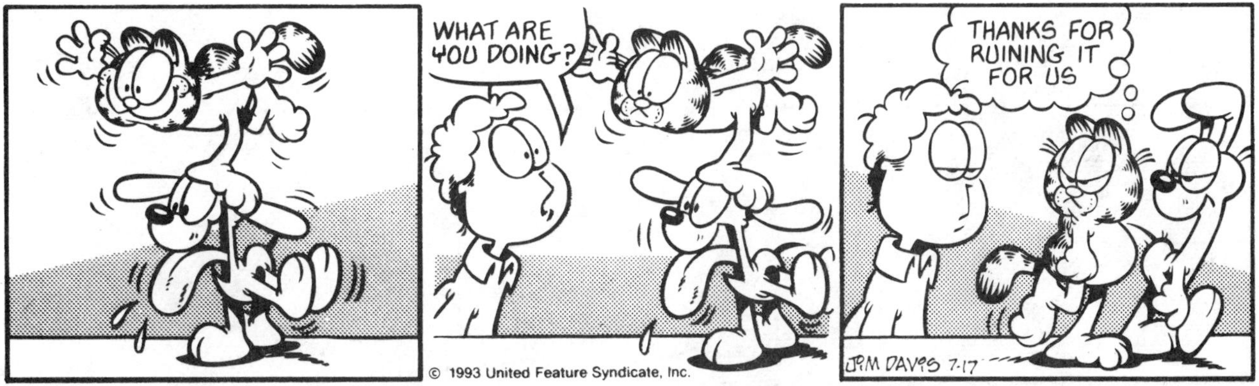

WHAT ARE YOU DOING?
THANKS FOR RUINING IT FOR US
© 1993 United Feature Syndicate, Inc.
JIM DAVIS 7-17

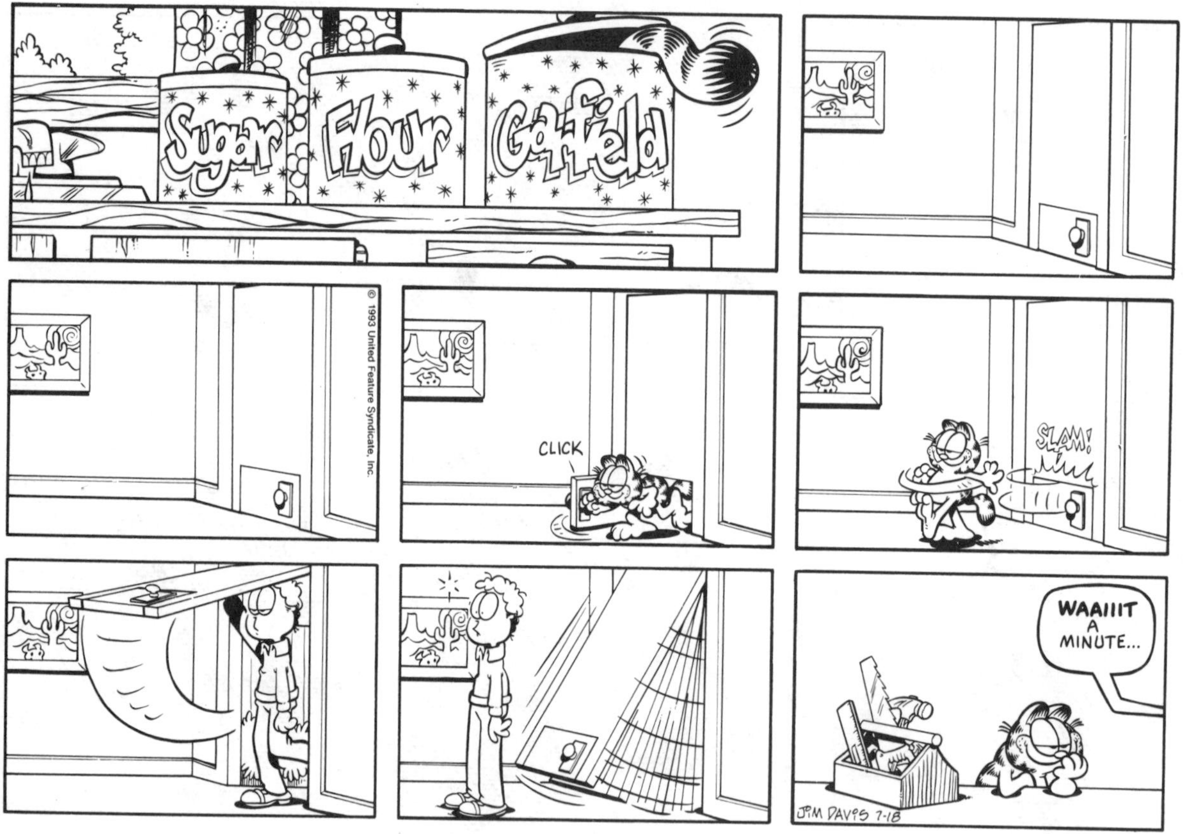
Sugar
Flour
Garfield
© 1993 United Feature Syndicate, Inc.
CLICK
SLAM!
WAAIIIT A MINUTE...
JIM DAVIS 7-18

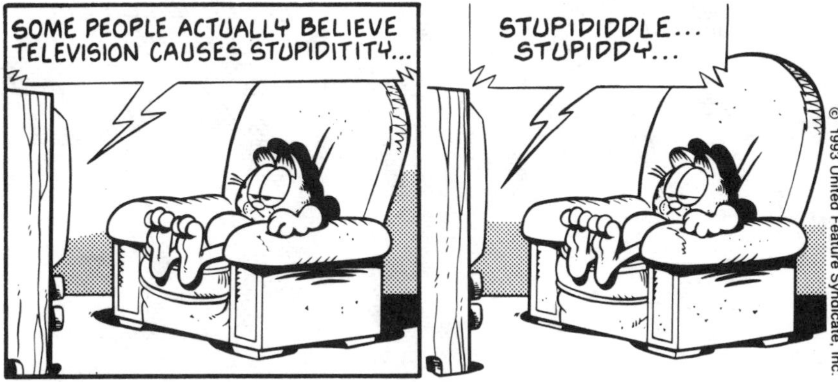
SOME PEOPLE ACTUALLY BELIEVE TELEVISION CAUSES STUPIDITITY...
STUPIDIDDLE... STUPIDDY...
NOT SMARTNESS!
NO KIDDING
© 1993 United Feature Syndicate, Inc.
JIM DAVIS 7-19

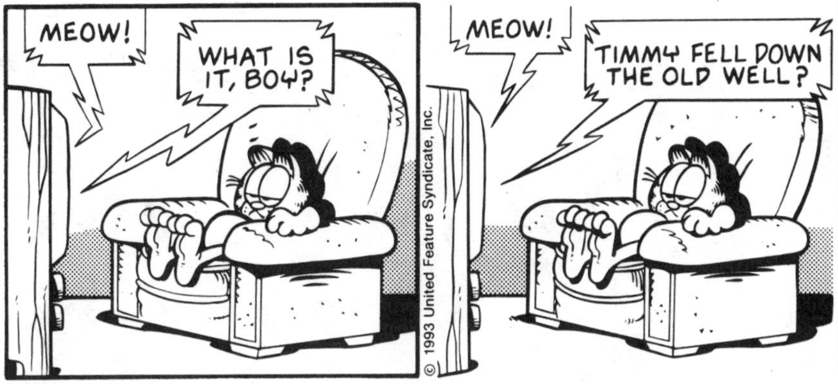
MEOW!
WHAT IS IT, BOY?
MEOW!
TIMMY FELL DOWN THE OLD WELL?
YOU PUSHED HIM, DIDN'T YOU?
MEOW!
YOU WANNA HERO?! GET A DOG!
© 1993 United Feature Syndicate, Inc.
JIM DAVIS 7-20

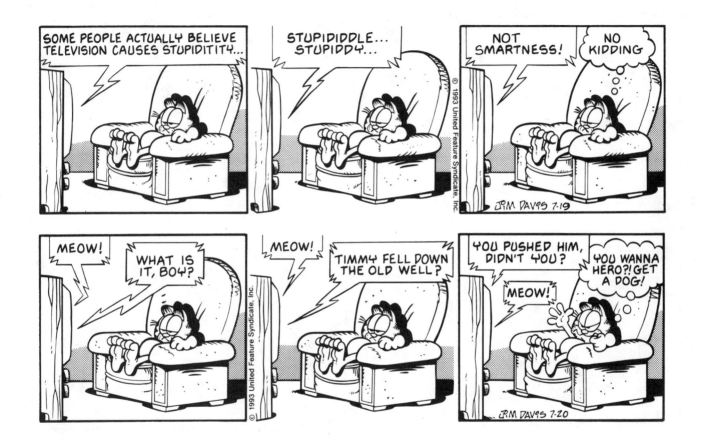

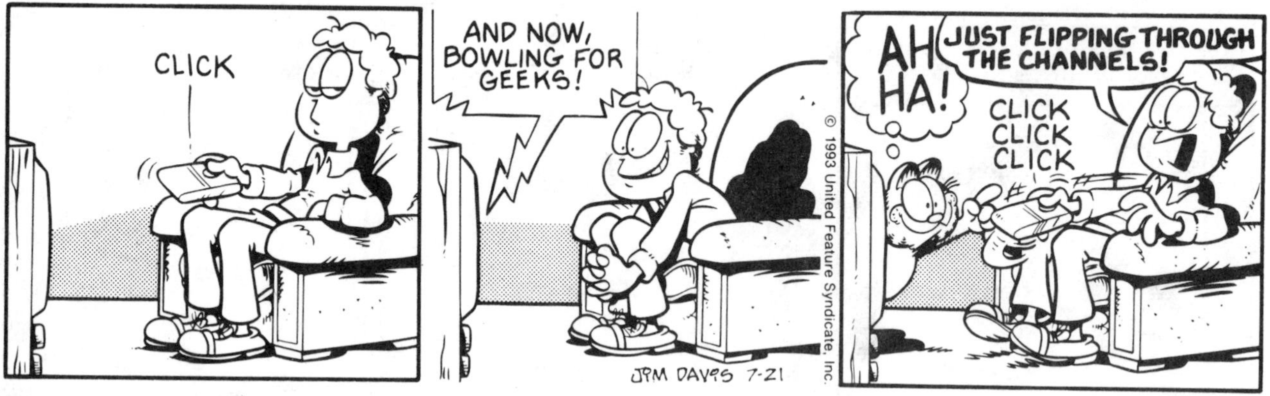
CLICK
AND NOW, BOWLING FOR GEEKS!
JIM DAVIS 7-21
© 1993 United Feature Syndicate, Inc.
AH HA!
JUST FLIPPING THROUGH THE CHANNELS!
CLICK CLICK CLICK

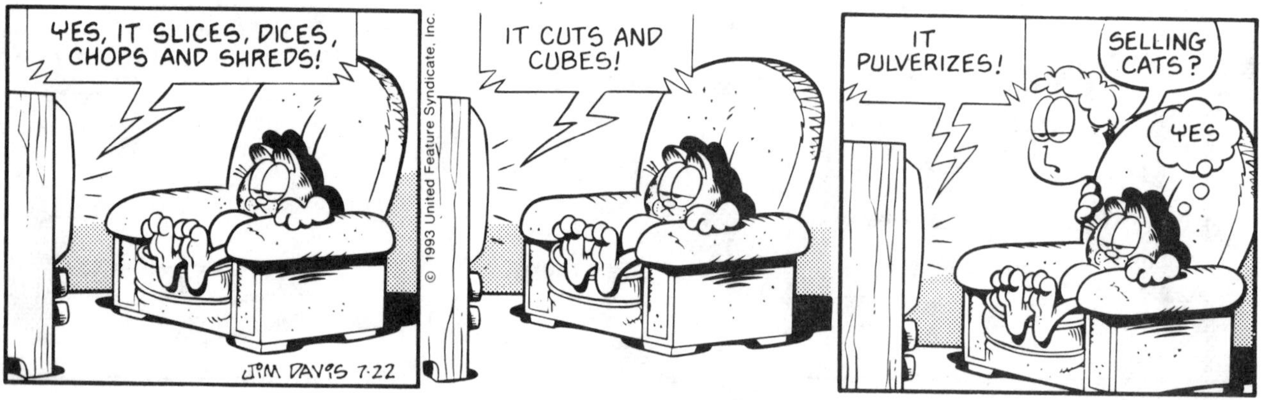
YES, IT SLICES, DICES, CHOPS AND SHREDS!
JIM DAVIS 7-22
© 1993 United Feature Syndicate, Inc.
IT CUTS AND CUBES!
IT PULVERIZES!
SELLING CATS?
YES

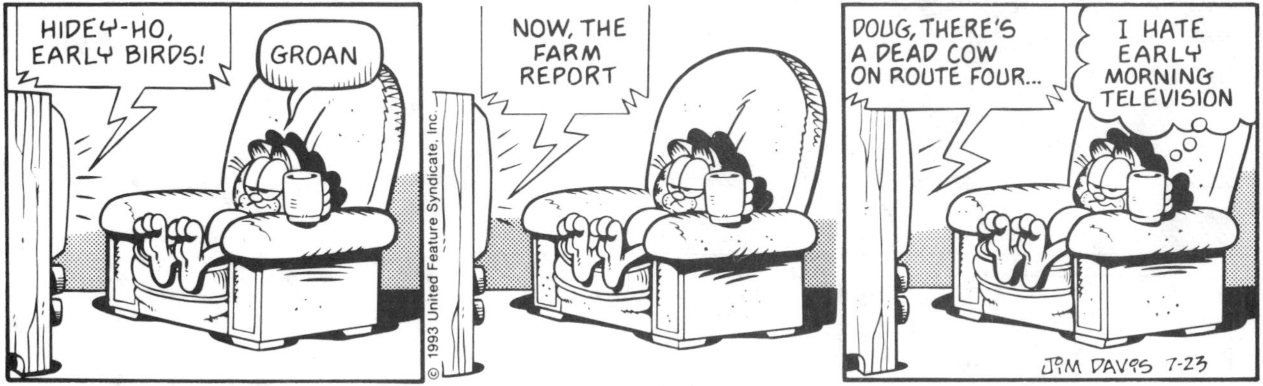
HIDEY-HO, EARLY BIRDS!
GROAN
NOW, THE FARM REPORT
DOUG, THERE'S A DEAD COW ON ROUTE FOUR...
I HATE EARLY MORNING TELEVISION
JIM DAVIS 7-23
© 1993 United Feature Syndicate, Inc.

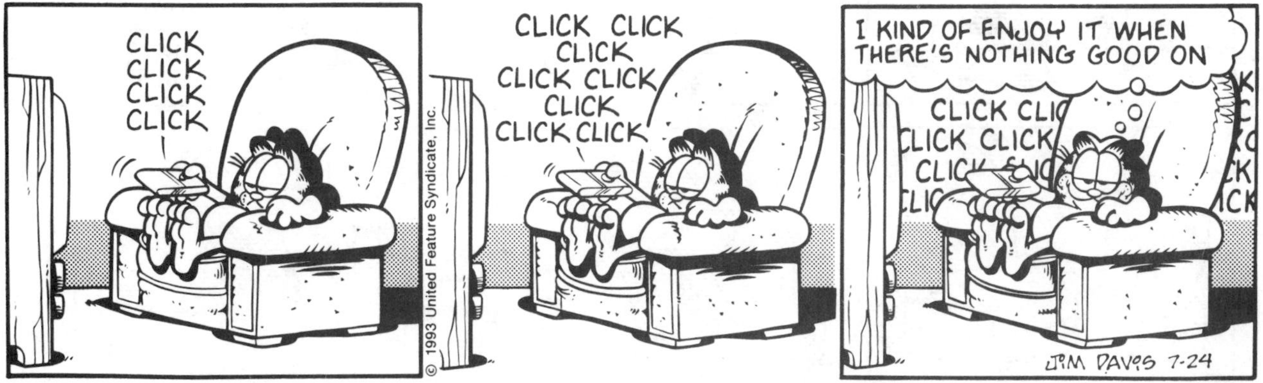
CLICK CLICK CLICK CLICK
CLICK CLICK CLICK CLICK CLICK CLICK CLICK CLICK
I KIND OF ENJOY IT WHEN THERE'S NOTHING GOOD ON
JIM DAVIS 7-24
© 1993 United Feature Syndicate, Inc.

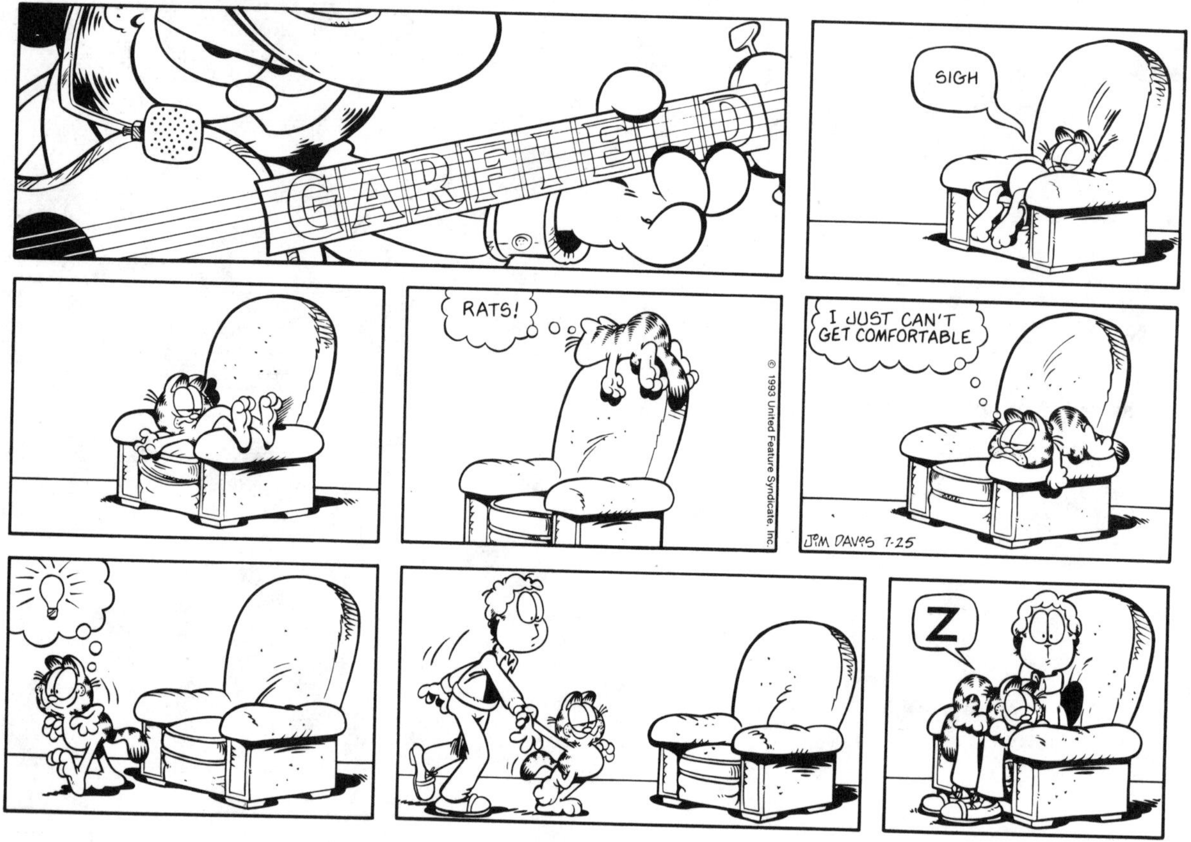
GARFIELD
SIGH
RATS!
I JUST CAN'T GET COMFORTABLE
© 1993 United Feature Syndicate, Inc.
JIM DAVIS 7-25
Z

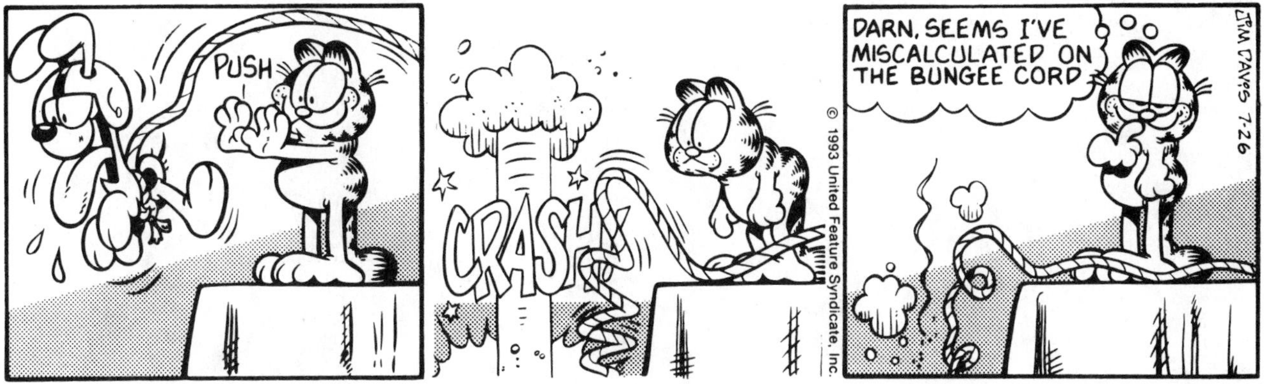

PUSH
CRASH
DARN, SEEMS I'VE MISCALCULATED ON THE BUNGEE CORD
JIM DAVIS 7-26
© 1993 United Feature Syndicate, Inc.

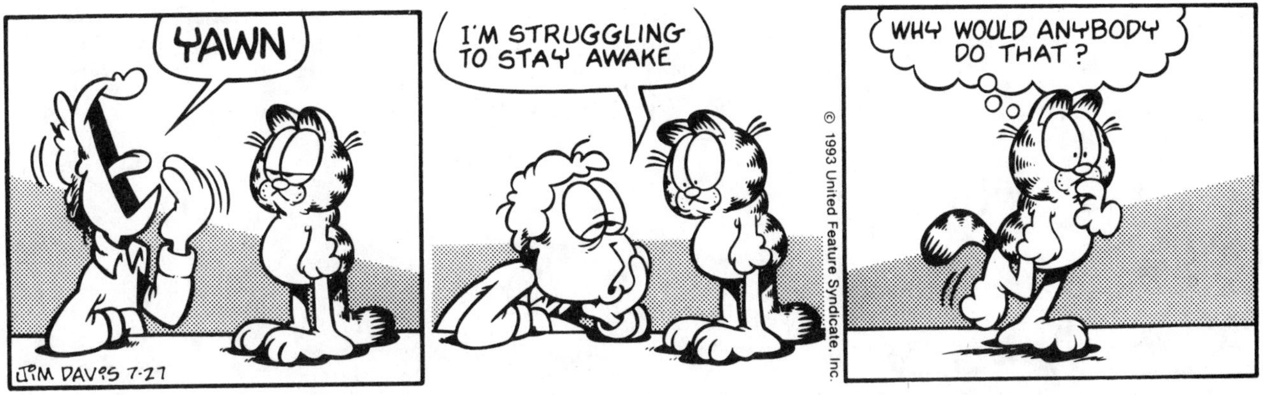

YAWN
JIM DAVIS 7-27
I'M STRUGGLING TO STAY AWAKE
WHY WOULD ANYBODY DO THAT?
© 1993 United Feature Syndicate, Inc.

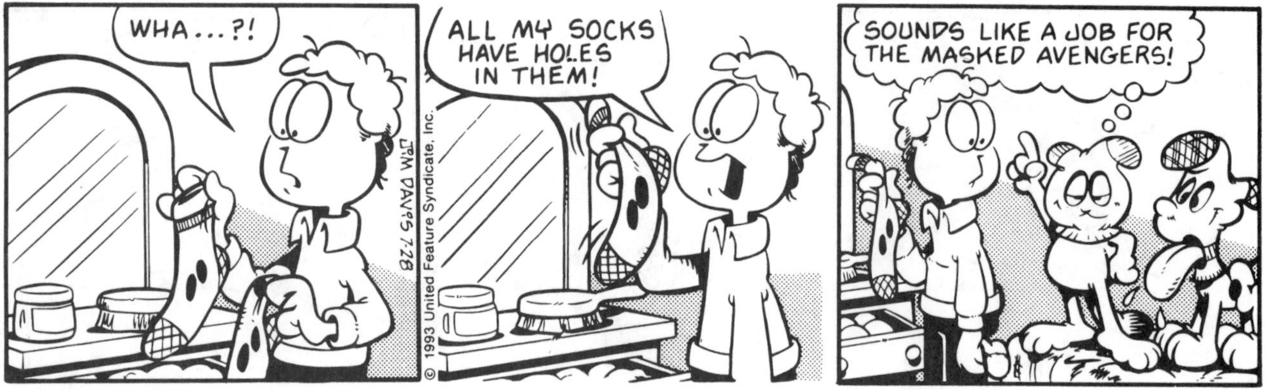
WHA...?!
JIM DAVIS 7-28
© 1993 United Feature Syndicate, Inc.
ALL MY SOCKS HAVE HOLES IN THEM!
SOUNDS LIKE A JOB FOR THE MASKED AVENGERS!

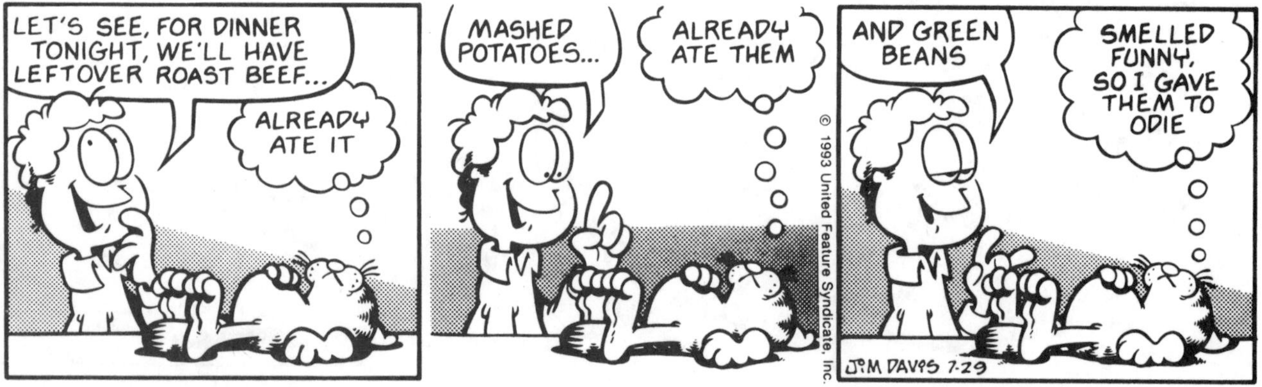
LET'S SEE, FOR DINNER TONIGHT, WE'LL HAVE LEFTOVER ROAST BEEF...
ALREADY ATE IT
MASHED POTATOES...
ALREADY ATE THEM
© 1993 United Feature Syndicate, Inc.
AND GREEN BEANS
SMELLED FUNNY, SO I GAVE THEM TO ODIE
JIM DAVIS 7-29

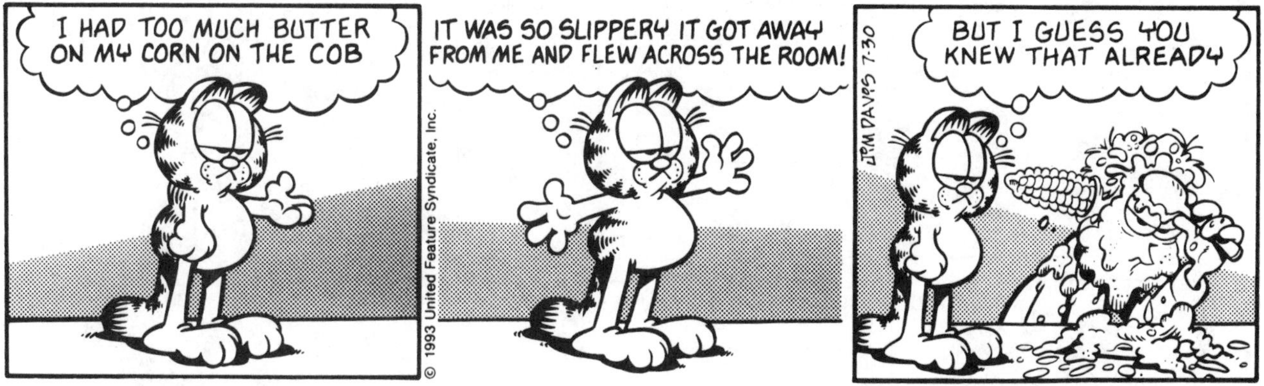
I HAD TOO MUCH BUTTER ON MY CORN ON THE COB
IT WAS SO SLIPPERY IT GOT AWAY FROM ME AND FLEW ACROSS THE ROOM!
BUT I GUESS YOU KNEW THAT ALREADY
JIM DAVIS 7-30
© 1993 United Feature Syndicate, Inc.

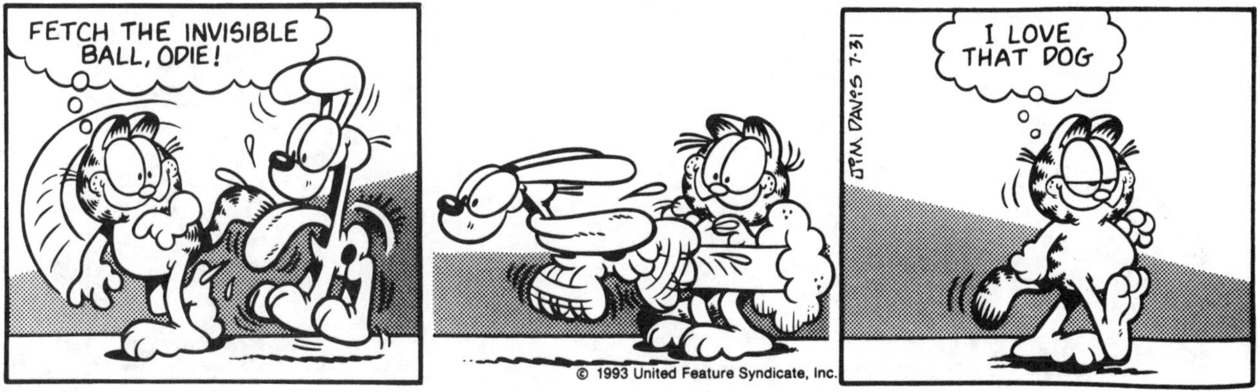
FETCH THE INVISIBLE BALL, ODIE!
I LOVE THAT DOG
JIM DAVIS 7-31
© 1993 United Feature Syndicate, Inc.

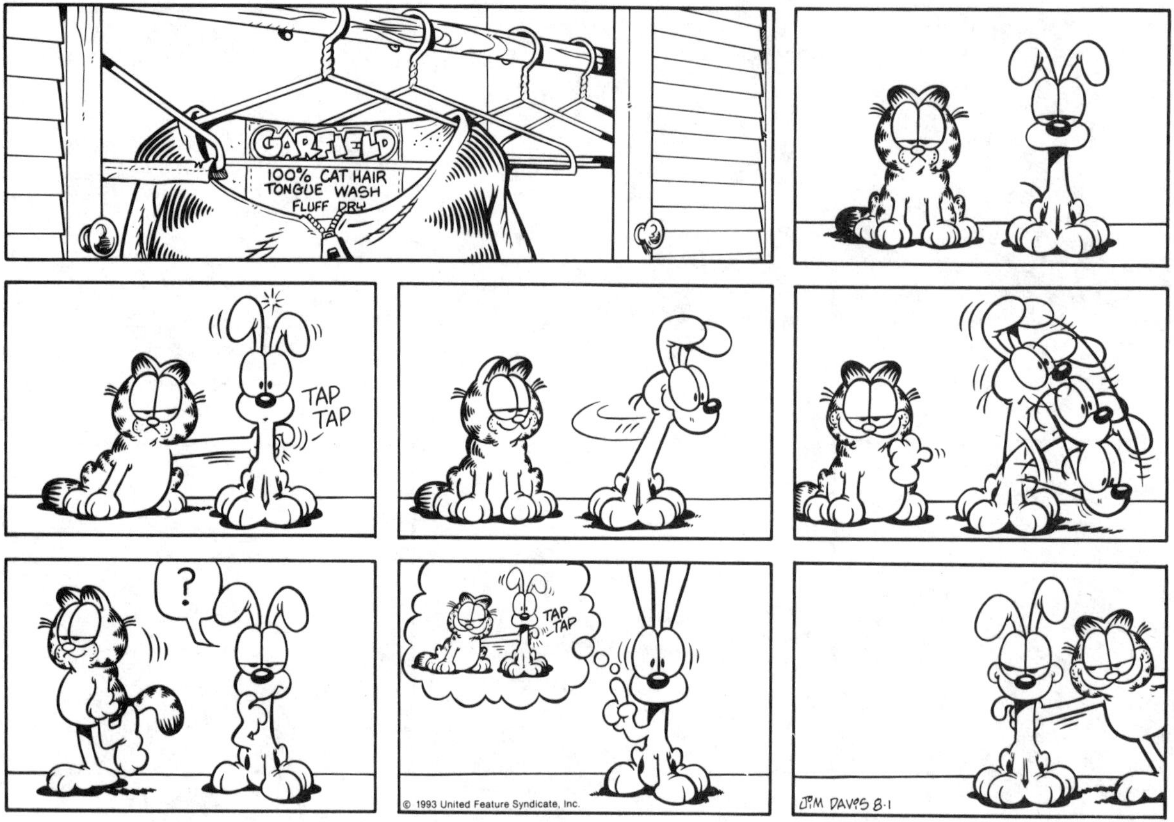
GARFIELD
100% CAT HAIR
TONGUE WASH
FLUFF DRY
TAP
TAP
?
TAP
TAP
© 1993 United Feature Syndicate, Inc.
JIM DAVIS 8-1

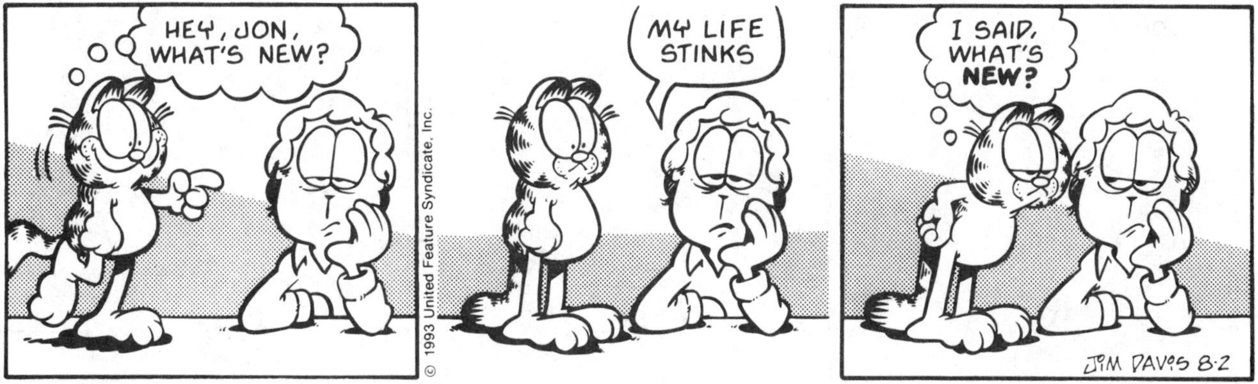
HEY, JON, WHAT'S NEW?
MY LIFE STINKS
I SAID, WHAT'S **NEW?**
JIM DAVIS 8-2

© 1993 United Feature Syndicate, Inc.

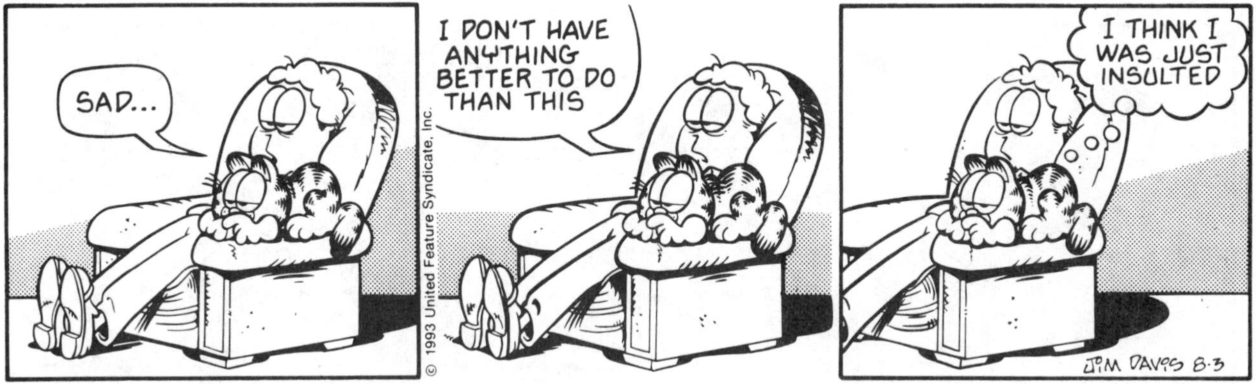
SAD...
I DON'T HAVE ANYTHING BETTER TO DO THAN THIS
I THINK I WAS JUST INSULTED
JIM DAVIS 8-3

© 1993 United Feature Syndicate, Inc.

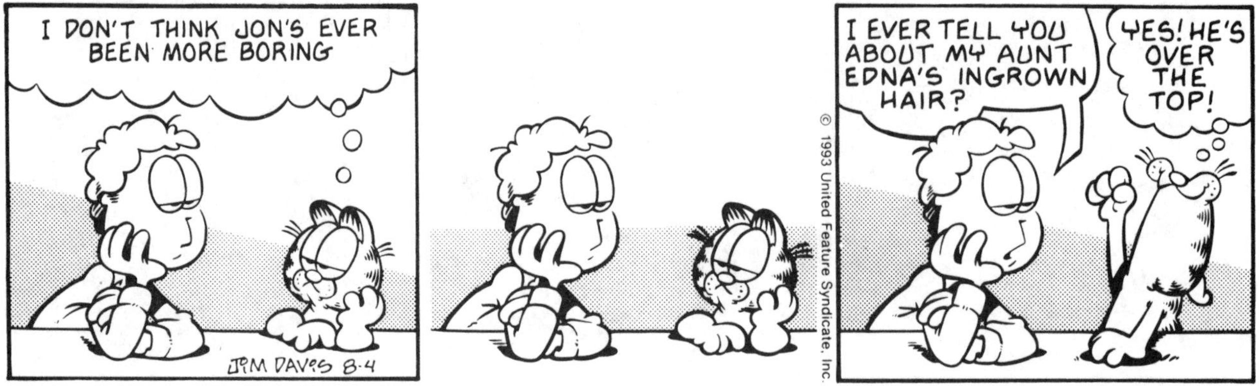
I DON'T THINK JON'S EVER BEEN MORE BORING
JIM DAVIS 8-4
© 1993 United Feature Syndicate, Inc.
I EVER TELL YOU ABOUT MY AUNT EDNA'S INGROWN HAIR?
YES! HE'S OVER THE TOP!

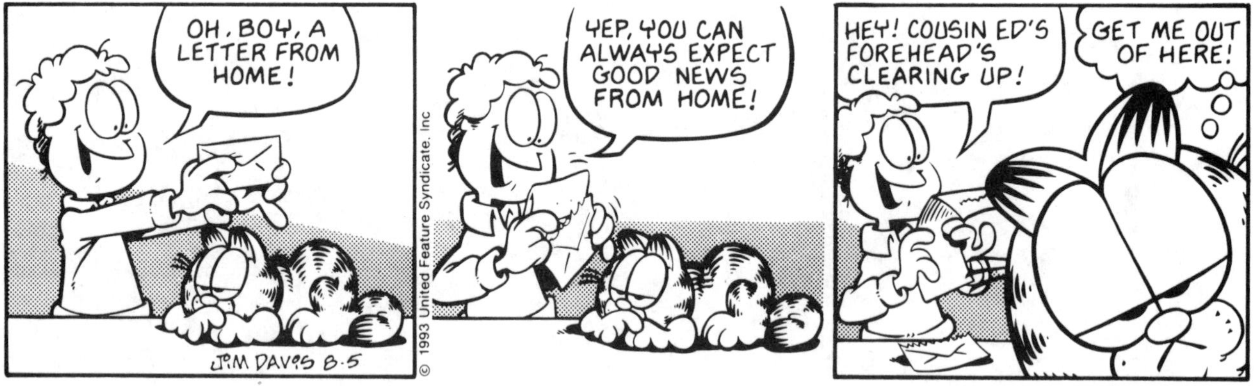
OH, BOY, A LETTER FROM HOME!
JIM DAVIS 8-5
© 1993 United Feature Syndicate, Inc
YEP, YOU CAN ALWAYS EXPECT GOOD NEWS FROM HOME!
HEY! COUSIN ED'S FOREHEAD'S CLEARING UP!
GET ME OUT OF HERE!

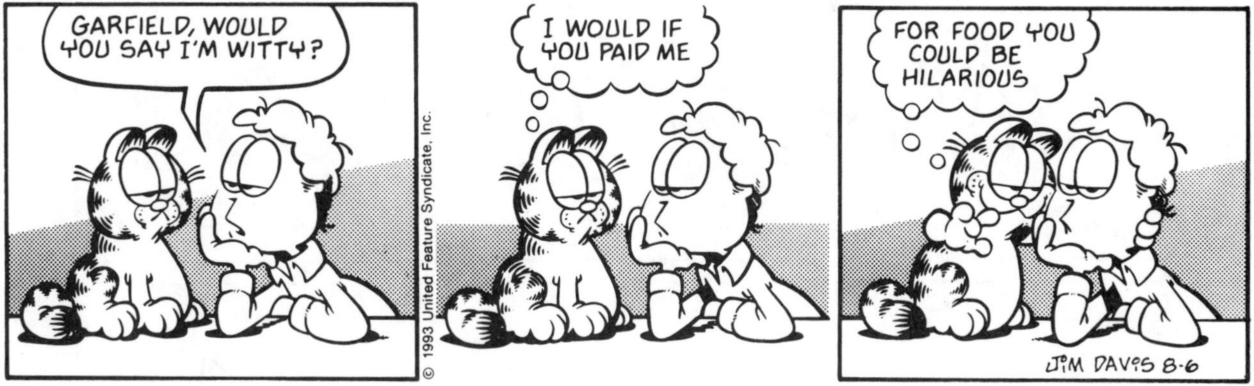
GARFIELD, WOULD YOU SAY I'M WITTY?
I WOULD IF YOU PAID ME
FOR FOOD YOU COULD BE HILARIOUS
© 1993 United Feature Syndicate, Inc.
JIM DAVIS 8-6

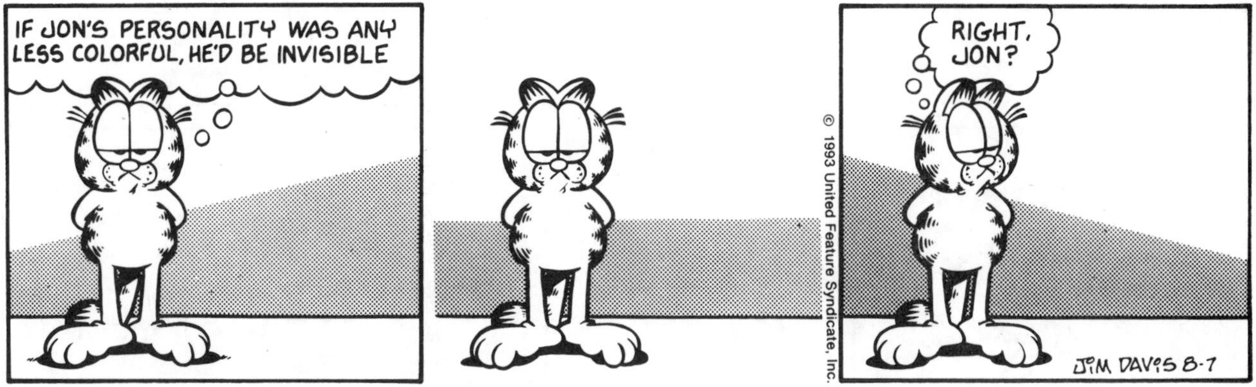
IF JON'S PERSONALITY WAS ANY LESS COLORFUL, HE'D BE INVISIBLE
RIGHT, JON?
© 1993 United Feature Syndicate, Inc.
JIM DAVIS 8-7

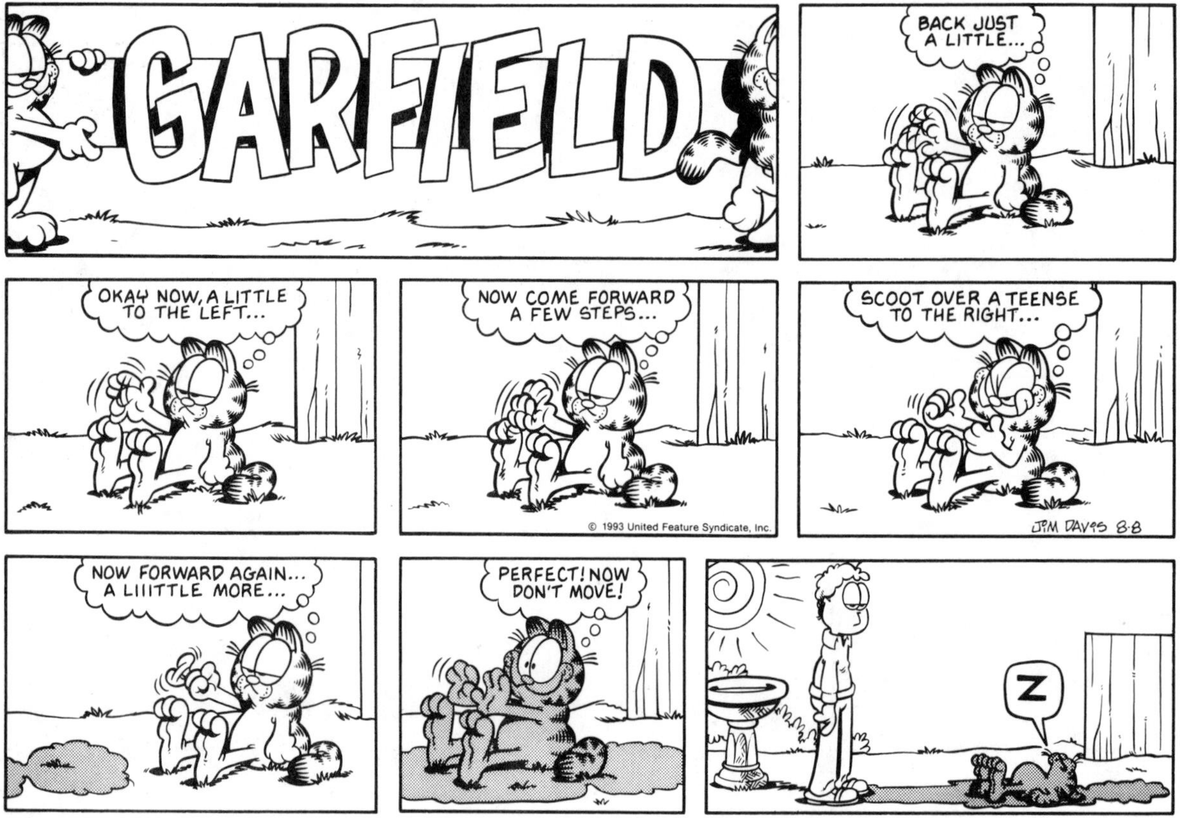

GARFIELD
BACK JUST A LITTLE...
OKAY NOW, A LITTLE TO THE LEFT...
NOW COME FORWARD A FEW STEPS...
SCOOT OVER A TEENSE TO THE RIGHT...
© 1993 United Feature Syndicate, Inc.
JIM DAVIS 8-8
NOW FORWARD AGAIN... A LIIITTLE MORE...
PERFECT! NOW DON'T MOVE!
Z

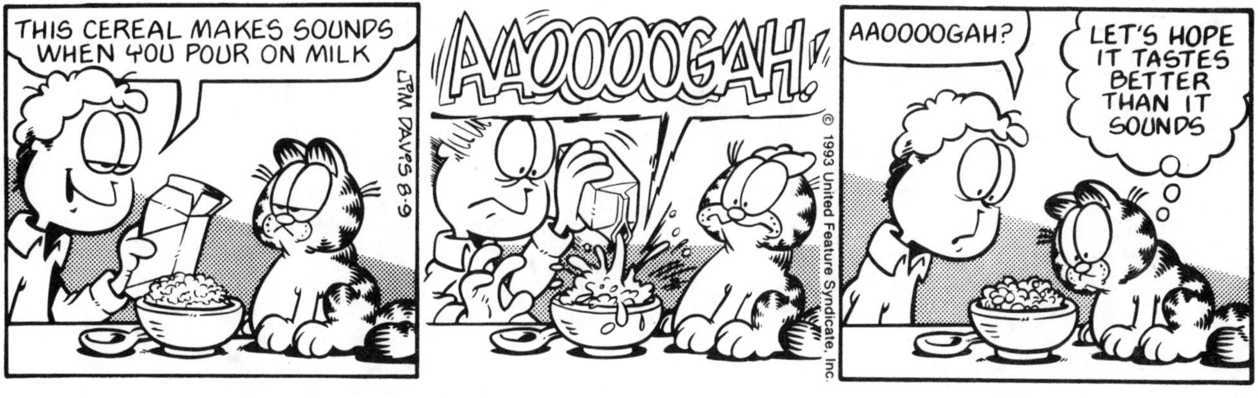
THIS CEREAL MAKES SOUNDS WHEN YOU POUR ON MILK
JIM DAVIS 8-9
AAOOOOGAH!
© 1993 United Feature Syndicate, Inc.
AAOOOOGAH?
LET'S HOPE IT TASTES BETTER THAN IT SOUNDS

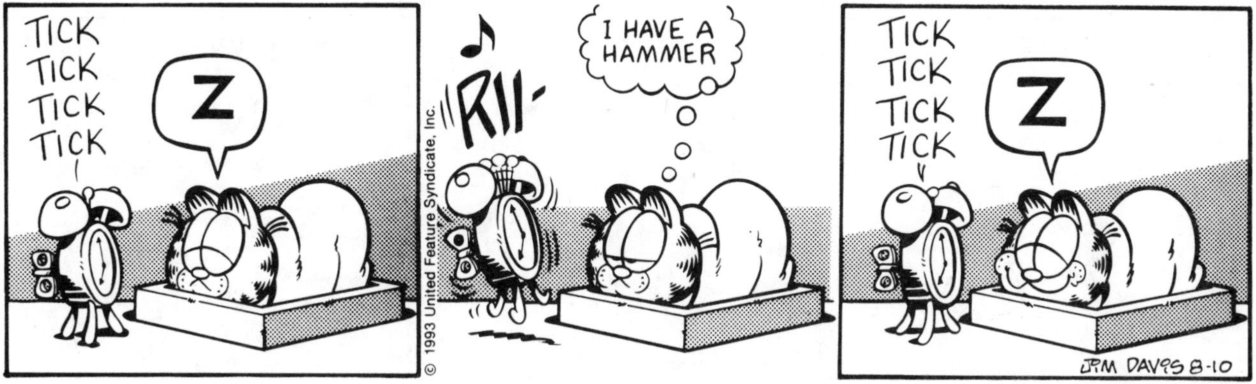
TICK TICK TICK TICK
Z
© 1993 United Feature Syndicate, Inc.
RII-
I HAVE A HAMMER
TICK TICK TICK TICK
Z
JIM DAVIS 8-10

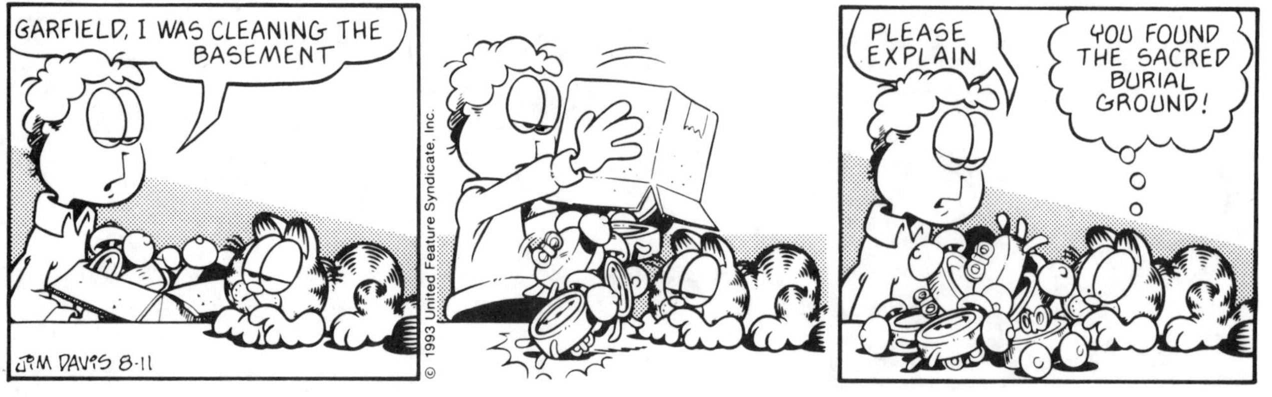
GARFIELD, I WAS CLEANING THE BASEMENT
PLEASE EXPLAIN
YOU FOUND THE SACRED BURIAL GROUND!
JIM DAVIS 8-11
© 1993 United Feature Syndicate, Inc.

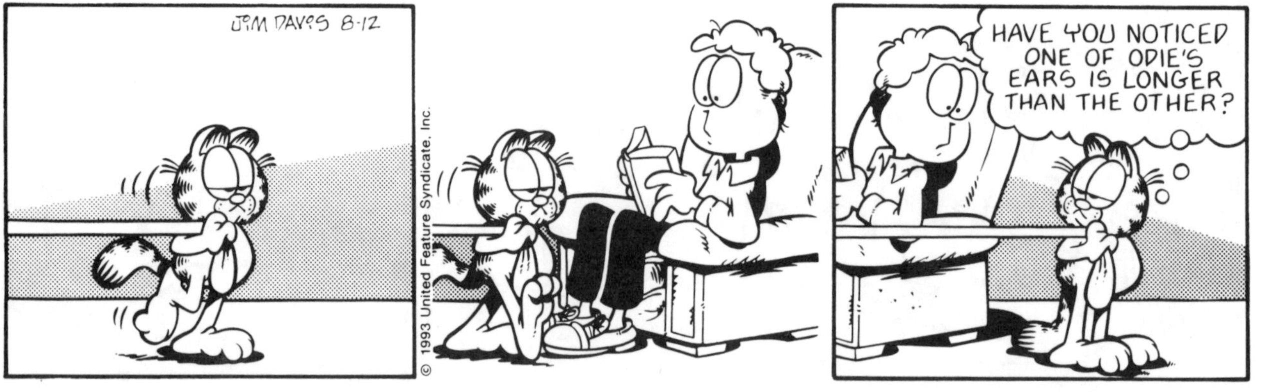
JIM DAVIS 8-12
© 1993 United Feature Syndicate, Inc.
HAVE YOU NOTICED ONE OF ODIE'S EARS IS LONGER THAN THE OTHER?

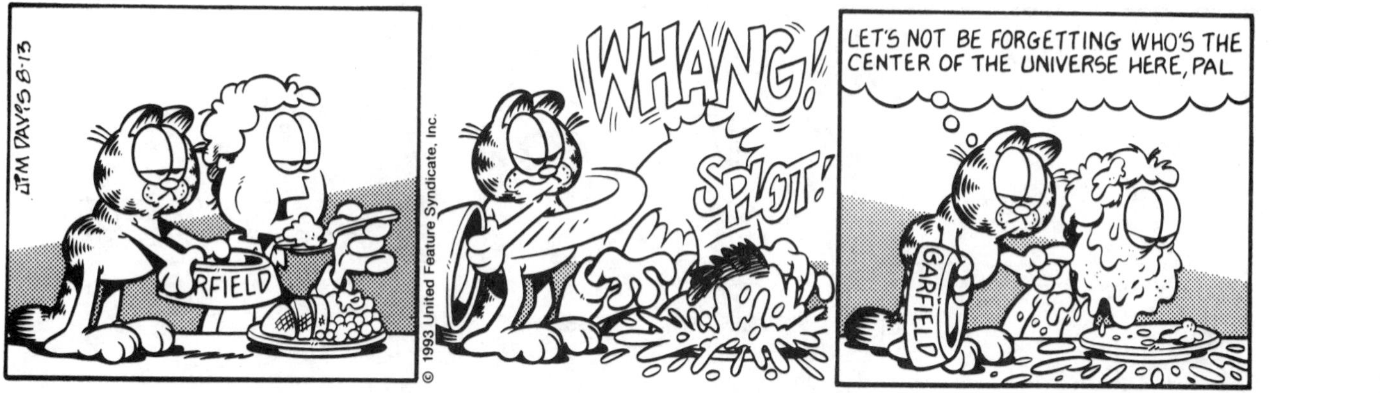
JIM DAVIS 8-13
RFIELD
© 1993 United Feature Syndicate, Inc.
WHANG!
SPLOT!
LET'S NOT BE FORGETTING WHO'S THE CENTER OF THE UNIVERSE HERE, PAL
GARFIELD

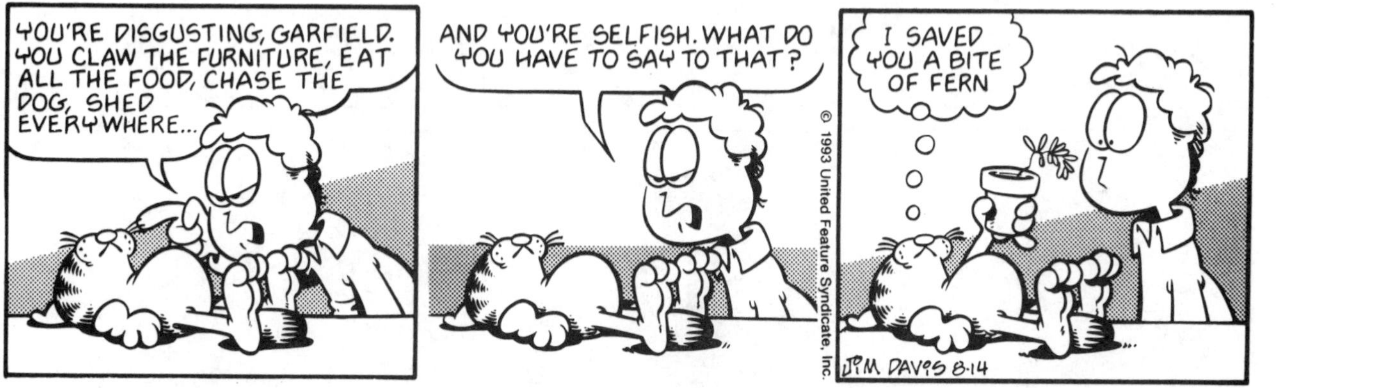
YOU'RE DISGUSTING, GARFIELD. YOU CLAW THE FURNITURE, EAT ALL THE FOOD, CHASE THE DOG, SHED EVERYWHERE...
AND YOU'RE SELFISH. WHAT DO YOU HAVE TO SAY TO THAT?
© 1993 United Feature Syndicate, Inc.
I SAVED YOU A BITE OF FERN
JIM DAVIS 8-14

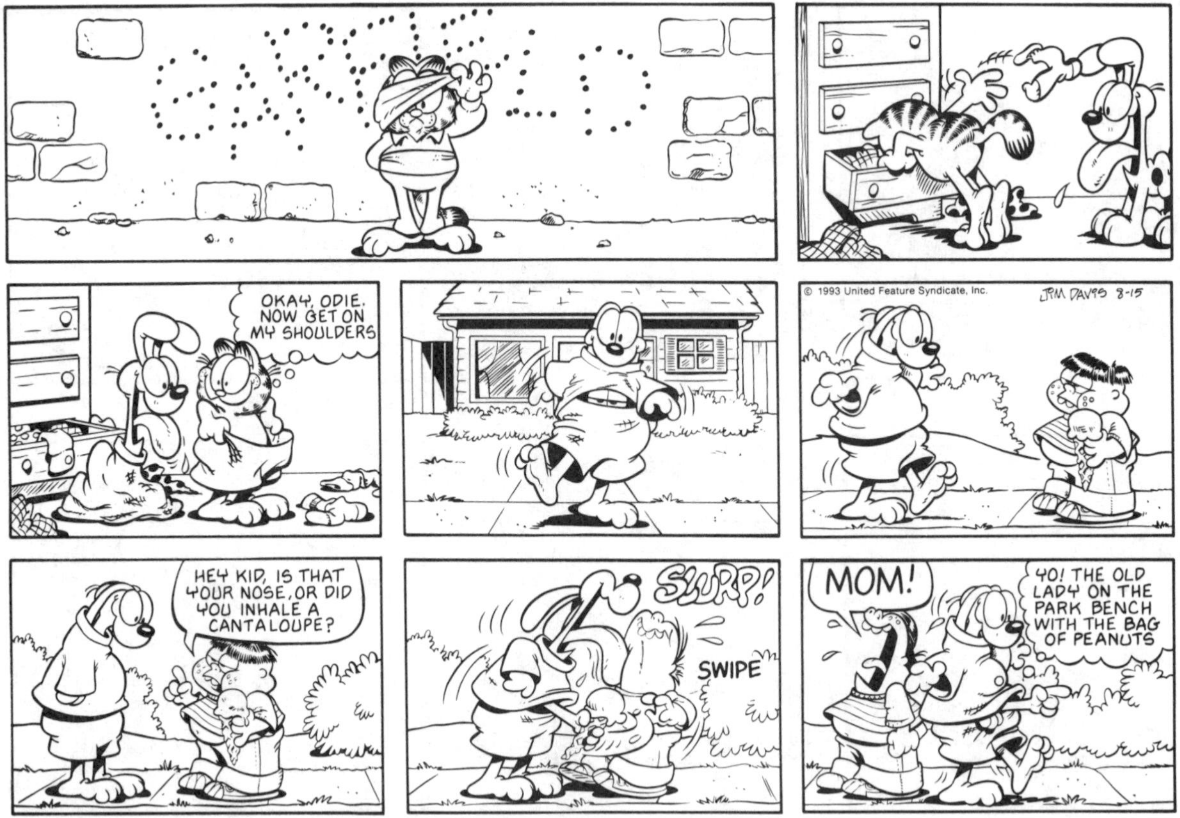
GARFIELD
OKAY, ODIE. NOW GET ON MY SHOULDERS
© 1993 United Feature Syndicate, Inc.
JIM DAVIS 8-15
HEY KID, IS THAT YOUR NOSE, OR DID YOU INHALE A CANTALOUPE?
SLURP!
SWIPE
MOM!
YO! THE OLD LADY ON THE PARK BENCH WITH THE BAG OF PEANUTS

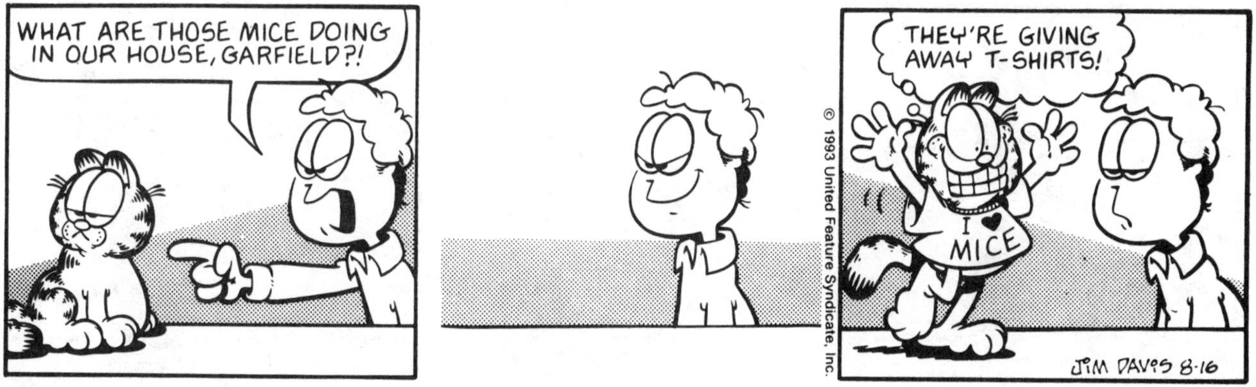
WHAT ARE THOSE MICE DOING IN OUR HOUSE, GARFIELD?!
THEY'RE GIVING AWAY T-SHIRTS!
I ♥ MICE
© 1993 United Feature Syndicate, Inc.
JIM DAVIS 8-16

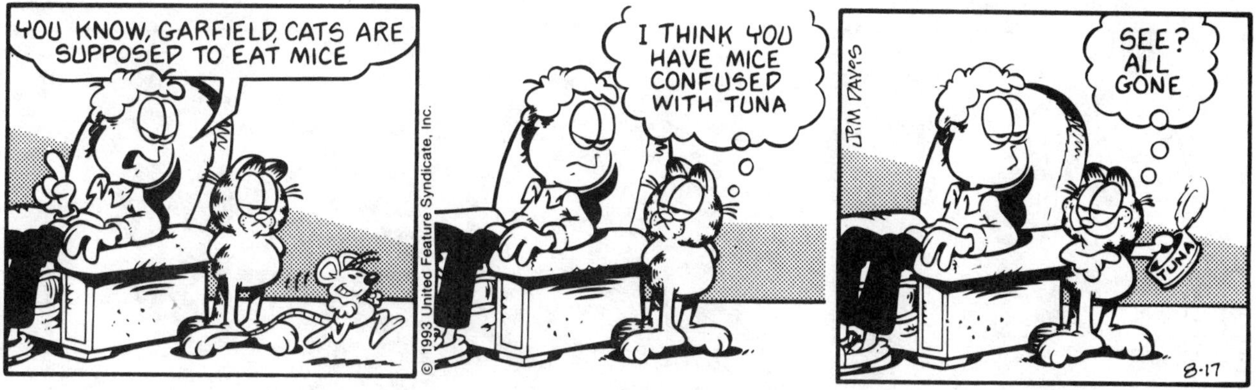
YOU KNOW, GARFIELD, CATS ARE SUPPOSED TO EAT MICE
I THINK YOU HAVE MICE CONFUSED WITH TUNA
SEE? ALL GONE
TUNA
© 1993 United Feature Syndicate, Inc.
JIM DAVIS
8-17

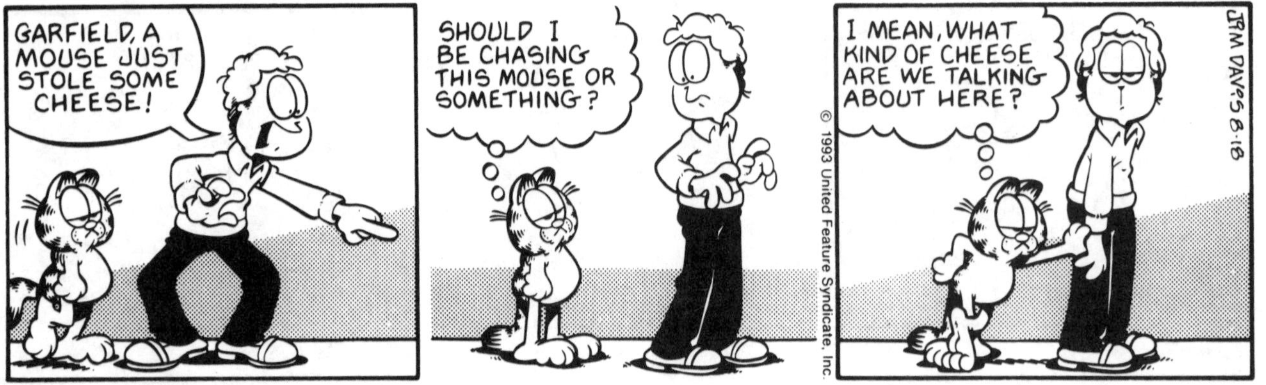
GARFIELD, A MOUSE JUST STOLE SOME CHEESE!
SHOULD I BE CHASING THIS MOUSE OR SOMETHING?
I MEAN, WHAT KIND OF CHEESE ARE WE TALKING ABOUT HERE?
JIM DAVIS 8-18
© 1993 United Feature Syndicate, Inc.

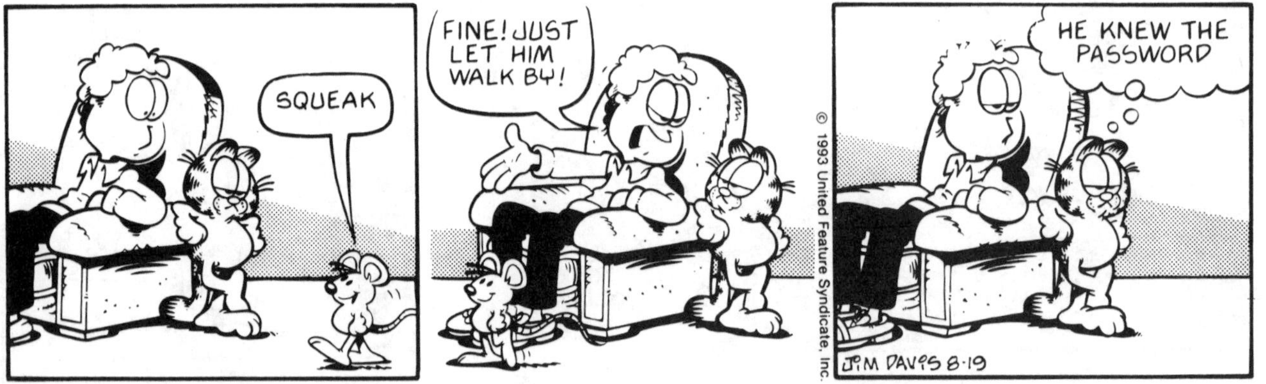
SQUEAK
FINE! JUST LET HIM WALK BY!
HE KNEW THE PASSWORD
JIM DAVIS 8-19
© 1993 United Feature Syndicate, Inc.

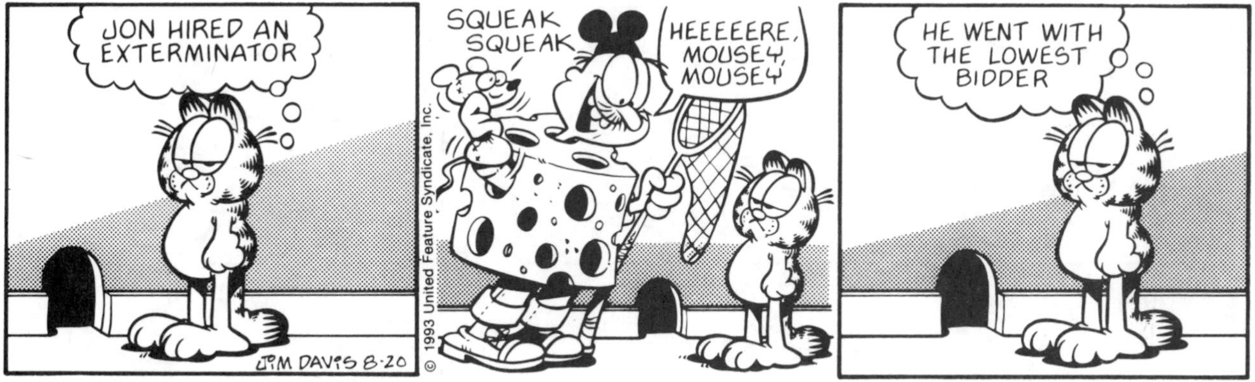
JON HIRED AN EXTERMINATOR
JIM DAVIS 8-20
SQUEAK SQUEAK
HEEEEEERE, MOUSEY, MOUSEY
© 1993 United Feature Syndicate, Inc.
HE WENT WITH THE LOWEST BIDDER

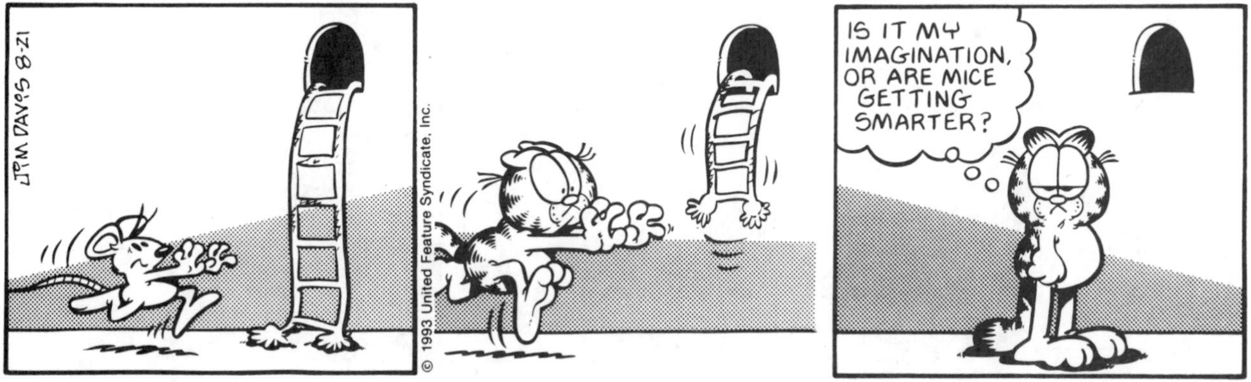
JIM DAVIS 8-21
© 1993 United Feature Syndicate, Inc.
IS IT MY IMAGINATION, OR ARE MICE GETTING SMARTER?

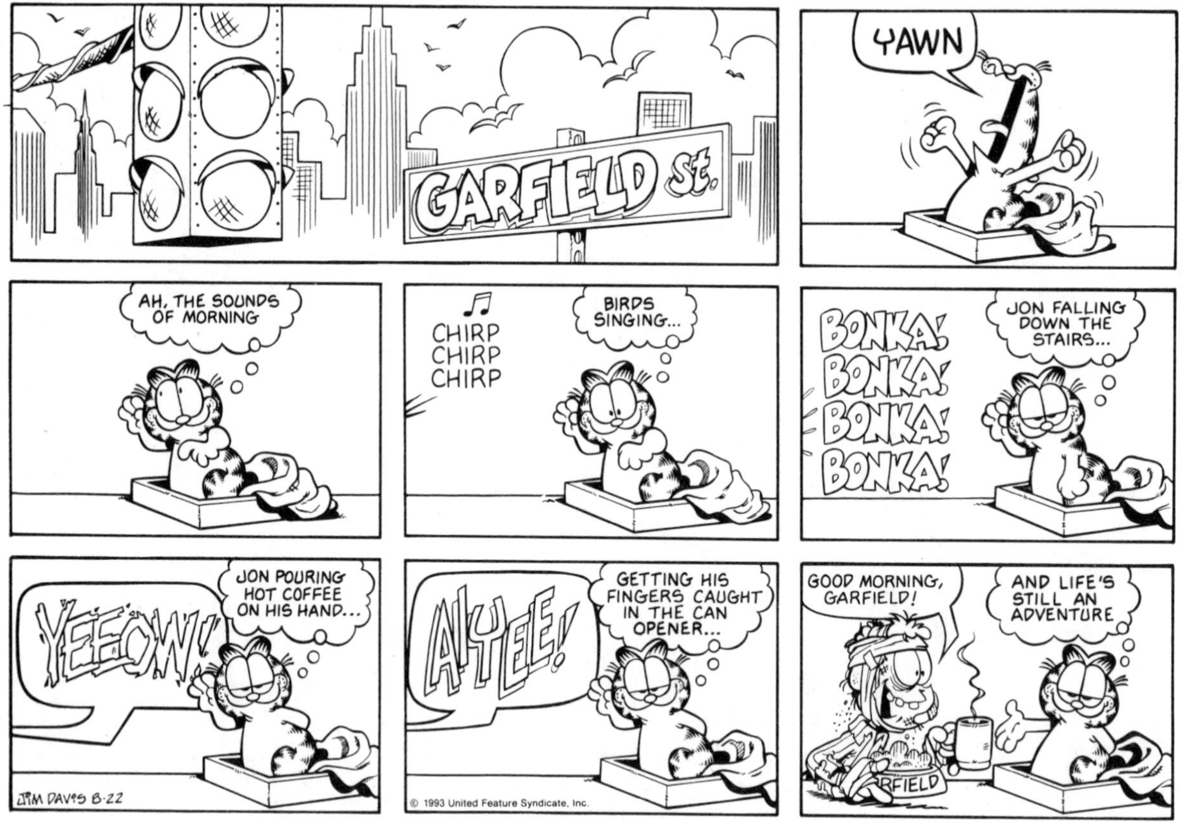
GARFIELD St.
YAWN
AH, THE SOUNDS OF MORNING
CHIRP
CHIRP
CHIRP
BIRDS SINGING...
BONKA!
BONKA!
BONKA!
BONKA!
JON FALLING DOWN THE STAIRS...
YEEOW!
JON POURING HOT COFFEE ON HIS HAND...
AIYEE!
GETTING HIS FINGERS CAUGHT IN THE CAN OPENER...
GOOD MORNING, GARFIELD!
AND LIFE'S STILL AN ADVENTURE
JIM DAVIS 8-22
© 1993 United Feature Syndicate, Inc.

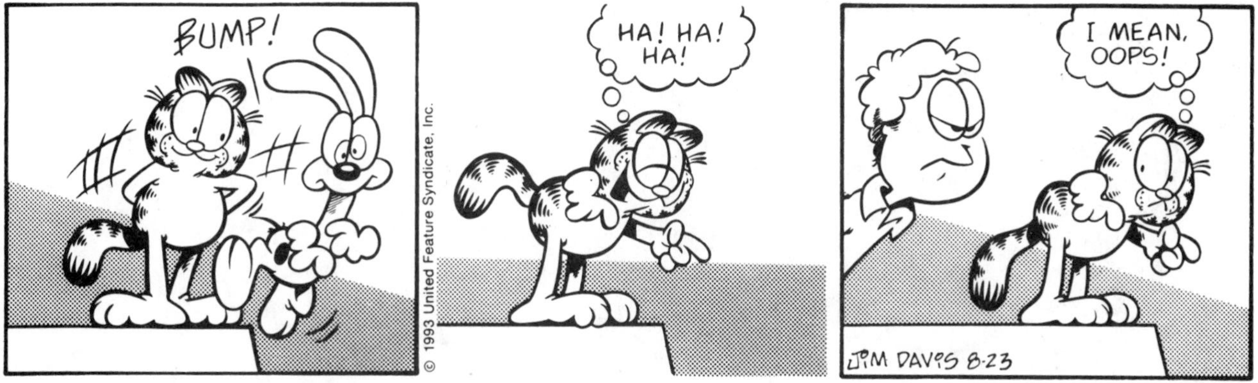
BUMP!
HA! HA! HA!
I MEAN, OOPS!
© 1993 United Feature Syndicate, Inc.
JIM DAVIS 8-23

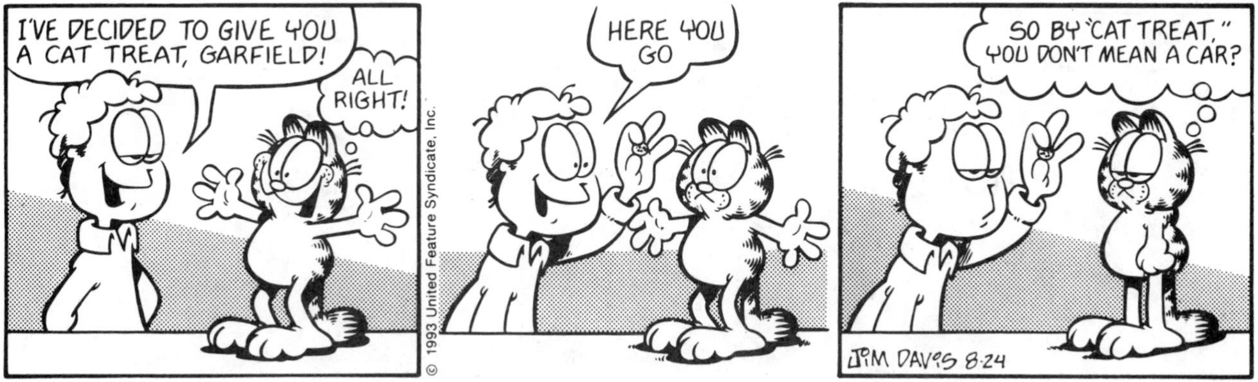
I'VE DECIDED TO GIVE YOU A CAT TREAT, GARFIELD!
ALL RIGHT!
HERE YOU GO
SO BY "CAT TREAT," YOU DON'T MEAN A CAR?
© 1993 United Feature Syndicate, Inc.
JIM DAVIS 8-24

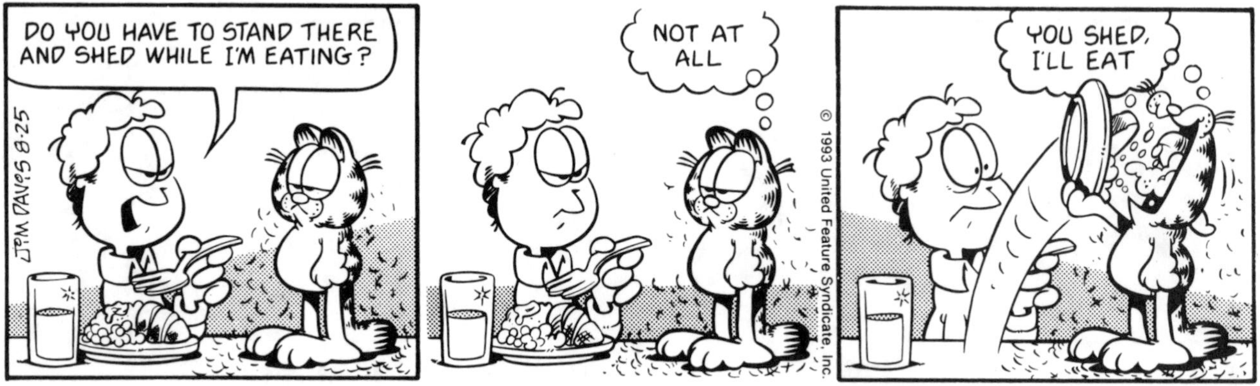
DO YOU HAVE TO STAND THERE AND SHED WHILE I'M EATING?
JIM DAVIS 8·25
NOT AT ALL
YOU SHED, I'LL EAT
© 1993 United Feature Syndicate, Inc.

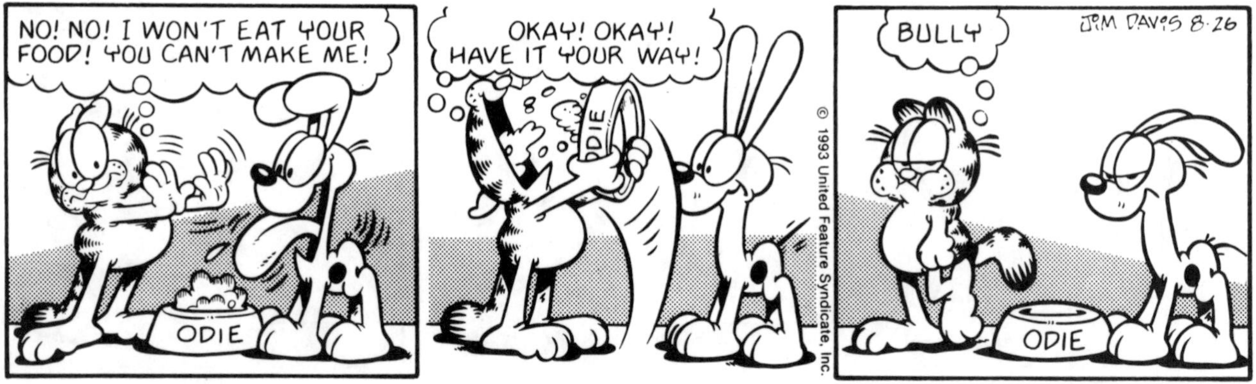
NO! NO! I WON'T EAT YOUR FOOD! YOU CAN'T MAKE ME!
ODIE
OKAY! OKAY! HAVE IT YOUR WAY!
ODIE
BULLY
JIM DAVIS 8·26
ODIE
© 1993 United Feature Syndicate, Inc.

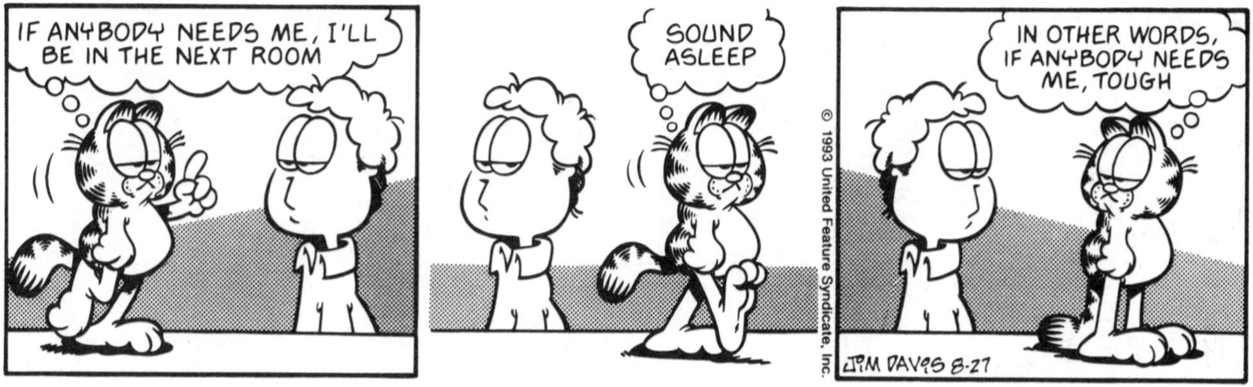
IF ANYBODY NEEDS ME, I'LL BE IN THE NEXT ROOM
SOUND ASLEEP
IN OTHER WORDS, IF ANYBODY NEEDS ME, TOUGH
© 1993 United Feature Syndicate, Inc.
JIM DAVIS 8-27

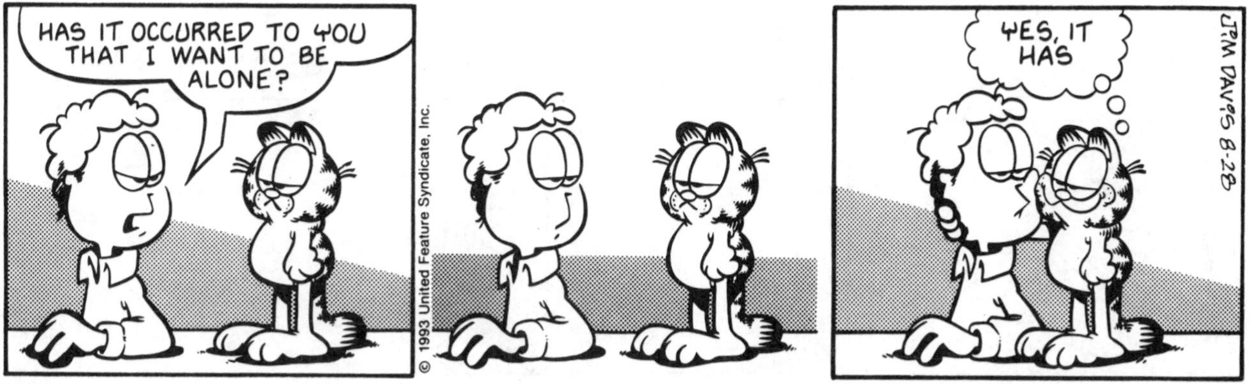
HAS IT OCCURRED TO YOU THAT I WANT TO BE ALONE?
YES, IT HAS
© 1993 United Feature Syndicate, Inc.
JIM DAVIS 8-28

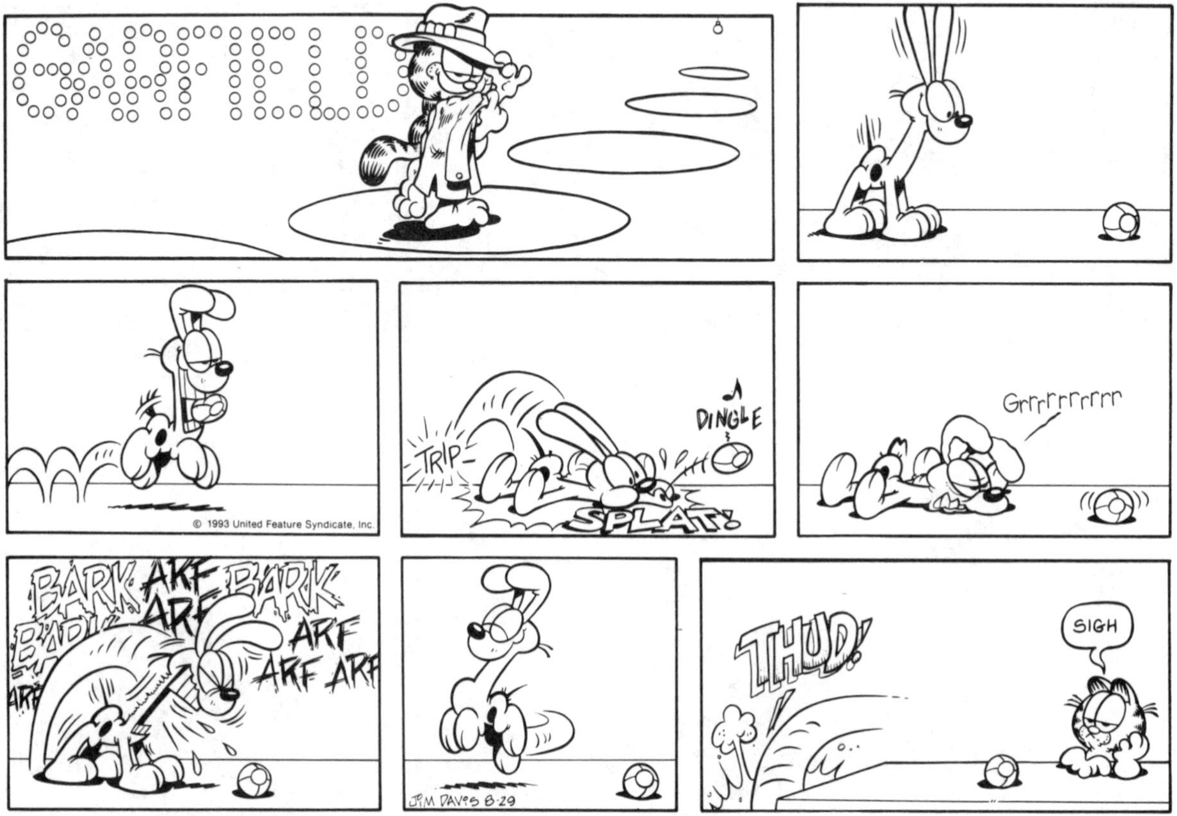

© 1993 United Feature Syndicate, Inc.
TRIP-
DINGLE
SPLAT!
Grrrrrrrrr
BARK ARF BARK
BARK ARF
ARF
ARF
ARF ARF
JIM DAVIS 8-29
THUD!
SIGH

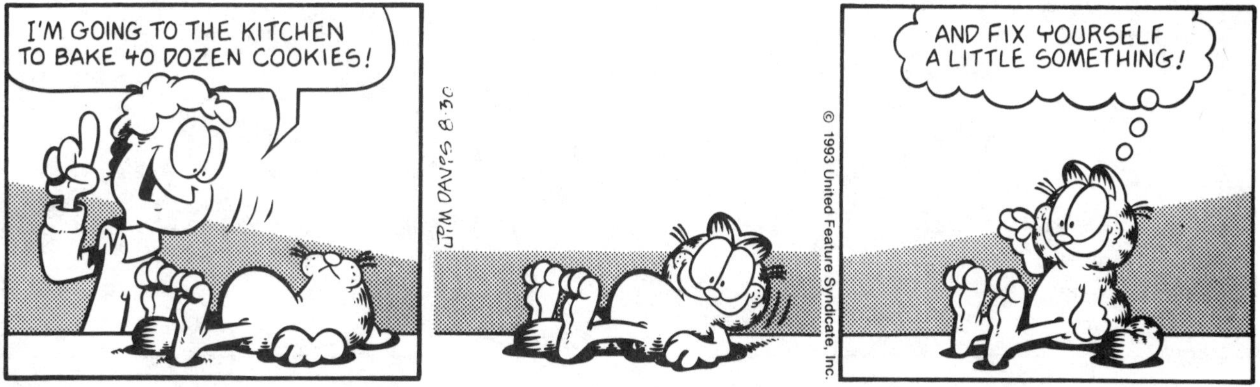
I'M GOING TO THE KITCHEN TO BAKE 40 DOZEN COOKIES!
JIM DAVIS 8-30
AND FIX YOURSELF A LITTLE SOMETHING!

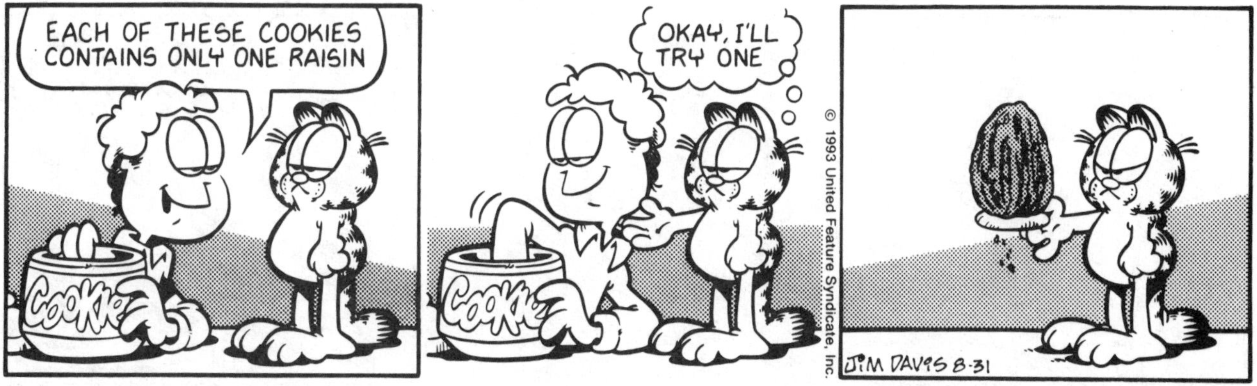
EACH OF THESE COOKIES CONTAINS ONLY ONE RAISIN
COOKIES
OKAY, I'LL TRY ONE
JIM DAVIS 8-31

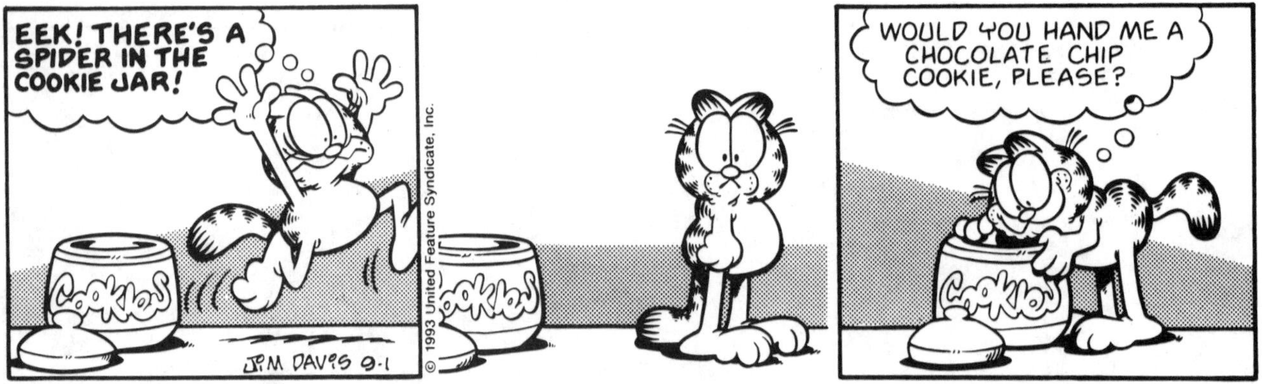
EEK! THERE'S A SPIDER IN THE COOKIE JAR!
COOKIES
JIM DAVIS 9-1
© 1993 United Feature Syndicate, Inc.
WOULD YOU HAND ME A CHOCOLATE CHIP COOKIE, PLEASE?

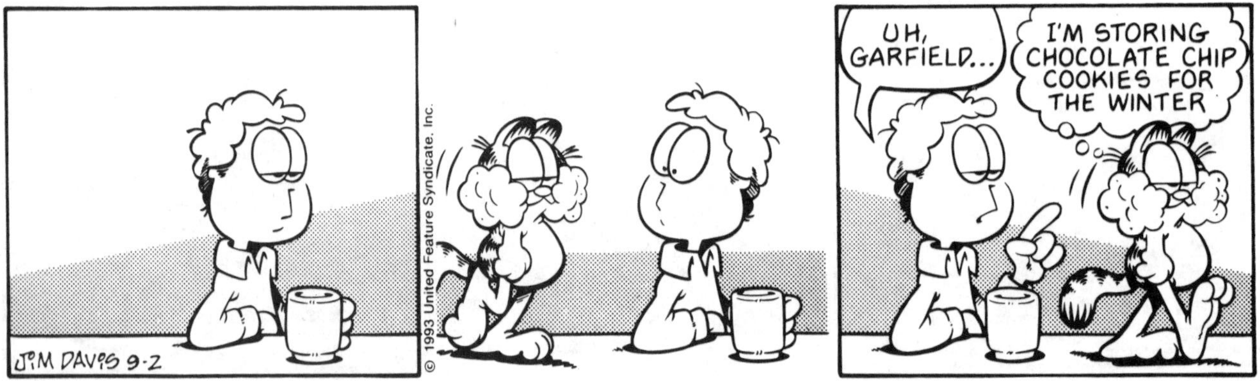
JIM DAVIS 9-2
© 1993 United Feature Syndicate, Inc.
UH, GARFIELD...
I'M STORING CHOCOLATE CHIP COOKIES FOR THE WINTER

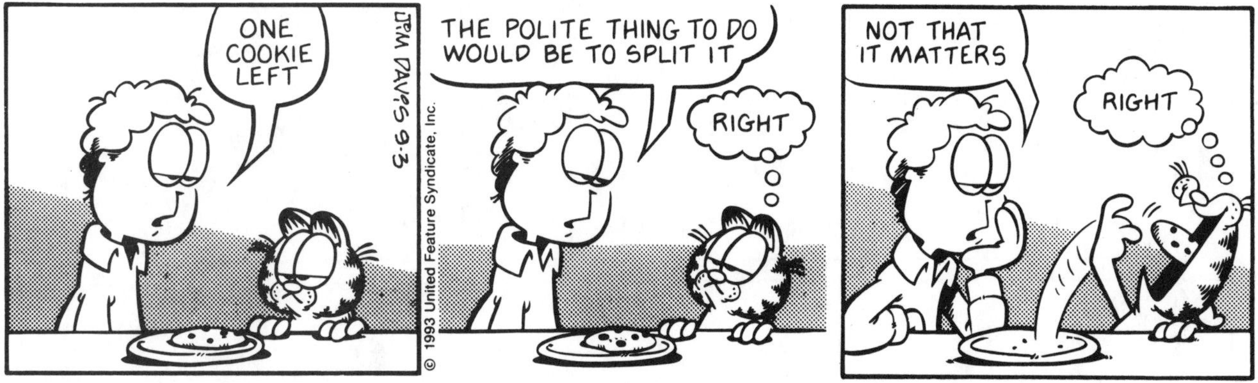
ONE COOKIE LEFT
JIM DAVIS 9-3
© 1993 United Feature Syndicate, Inc.
THE POLITE THING TO DO WOULD BE TO SPLIT IT
RIGHT
NOT THAT IT MATTERS
RIGHT

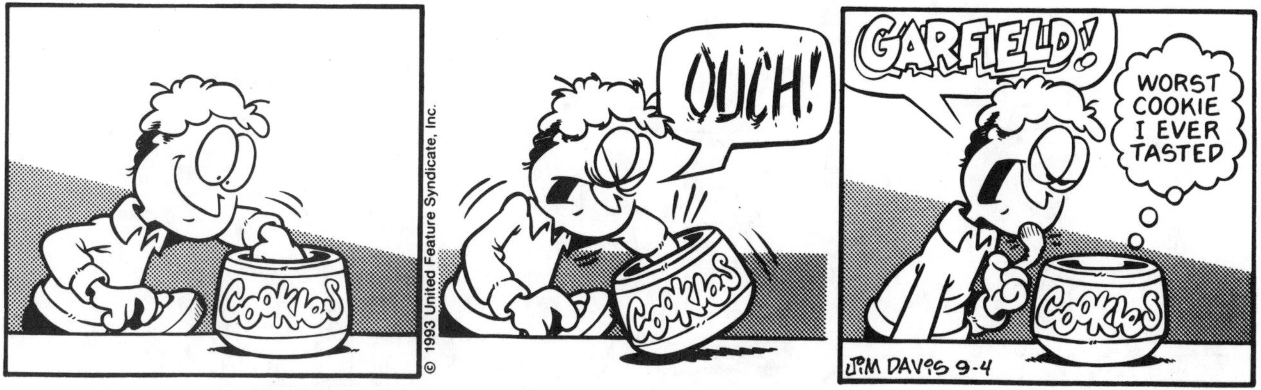
© 1993 United Feature Syndicate, Inc.
COOKIES
OUCH!
COOKIES
GARFIELD!
WORST COOKIE I EVER TASTED
COOKIES
JIM DAVIS 9-4

SNIP
SNIP

I'VE REALLY DONE IT THIS TIME, GARFIELD!

HO BOY...

I'VE MADE A SUIT OUT OF THE SUNDAY FUNNIES!

NOW, WHEN WOMEN COME UP TO ME TO READ THE COMICS, I'LL SAY SOMETHING FUNNY, IF YOU KNOW WHAT I MEAN

CITY PARK

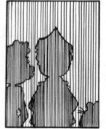

YOUR PUNCH LINE IS SHOWING

NOW THAT'S FUNNY

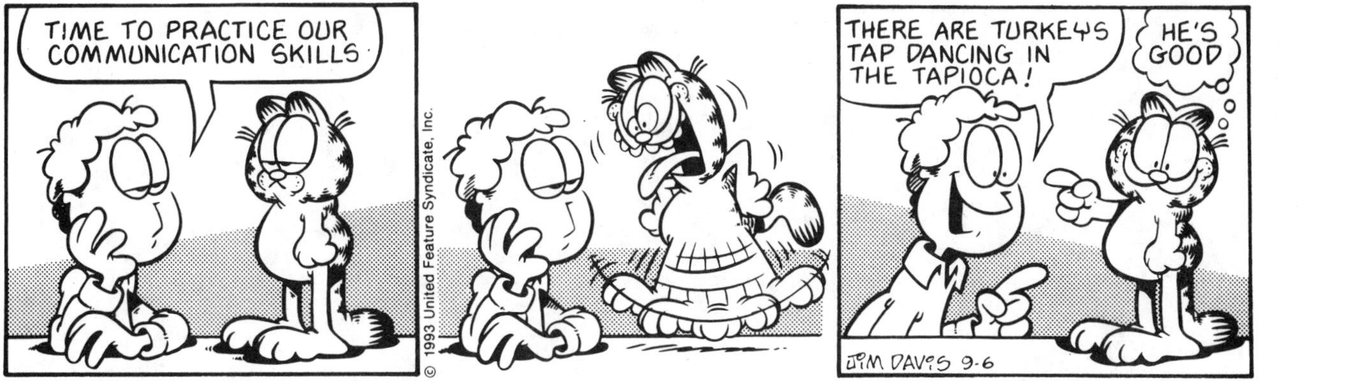
TIME TO PRACTICE OUR COMMUNICATION SKILLS
© 1993 United Feature Syndicate, Inc.
THERE ARE TURKEYS TAP DANCING IN THE TAPIOCA!
HE'S GOOD
JIM DAVIS 9-6

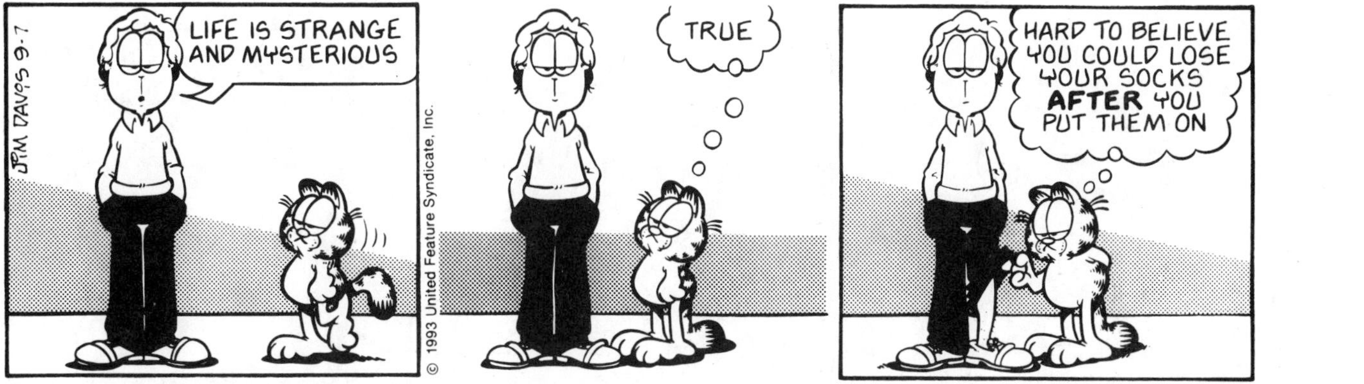
JIM DAVIS 9-7
LIFE IS STRANGE AND MYSTERIOUS
© 1993 United Feature Syndicate, Inc.
TRUE
HARD TO BELIEVE YOU COULD LOSE YOUR SOCKS **AFTER** YOU PUT THEM ON

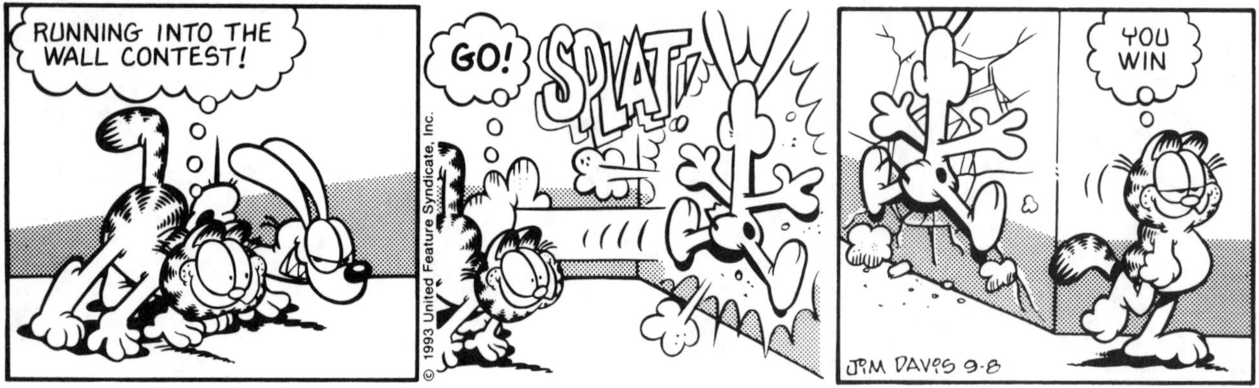
RUNNING INTO THE WALL CONTEST!
GO!
SPLAT!
YOU WIN
© 1993 United Feature Syndicate, Inc.
JIM DAVIS 9-8

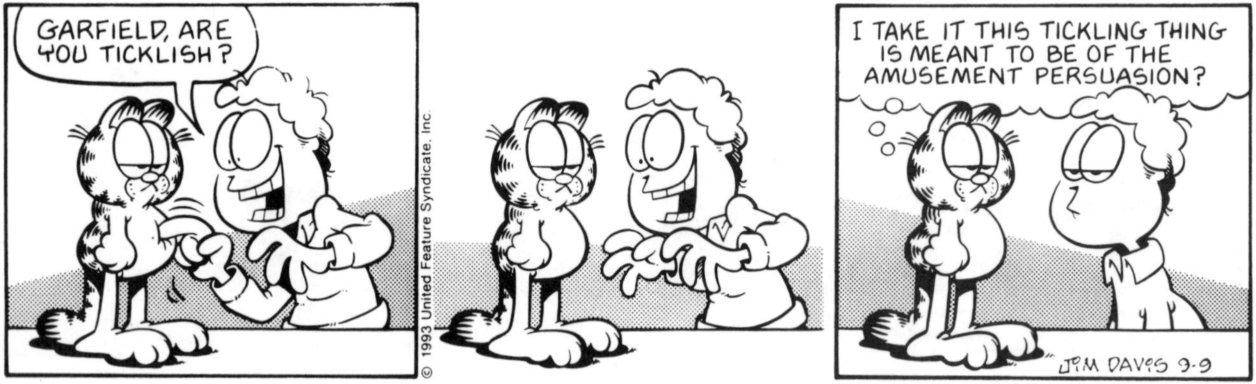
GARFIELD, ARE YOU TICKLISH?
I TAKE IT THIS TICKLING THING IS MEANT TO BE OF THE AMUSEMENT PERSUASION?
© 1993 United Feature Syndicate, Inc.
JIM DAVIS 9-9

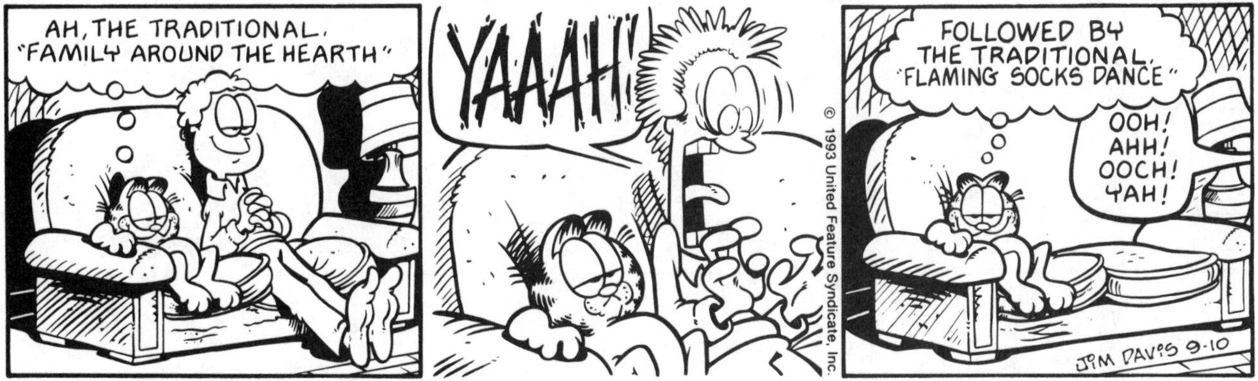
AH, THE TRADITIONAL "FAMILY AROUND THE HEARTH"
YAAAH!
FOLLOWED BY THE TRADITIONAL "FLAMING SOCKS DANCE"
OOH! AHH! OOCH! YAH!
© 1993 United Feature Syndicate, Inc.
JIM DAVIS 9-10

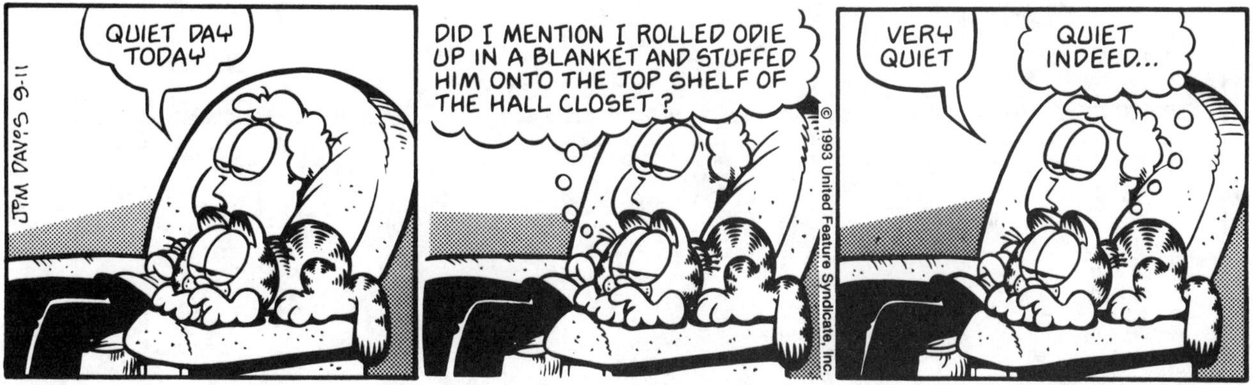
JIM DAVIS 9-11
QUIET DAY TODAY
DID I MENTION I ROLLED ODIE UP IN A BLANKET AND STUFFED HIM ONTO THE TOP SHELF OF THE HALL CLOSET ?
VERY QUIET
QUIET INDEED...
© 1993 United Feature Syndicate, Inc.

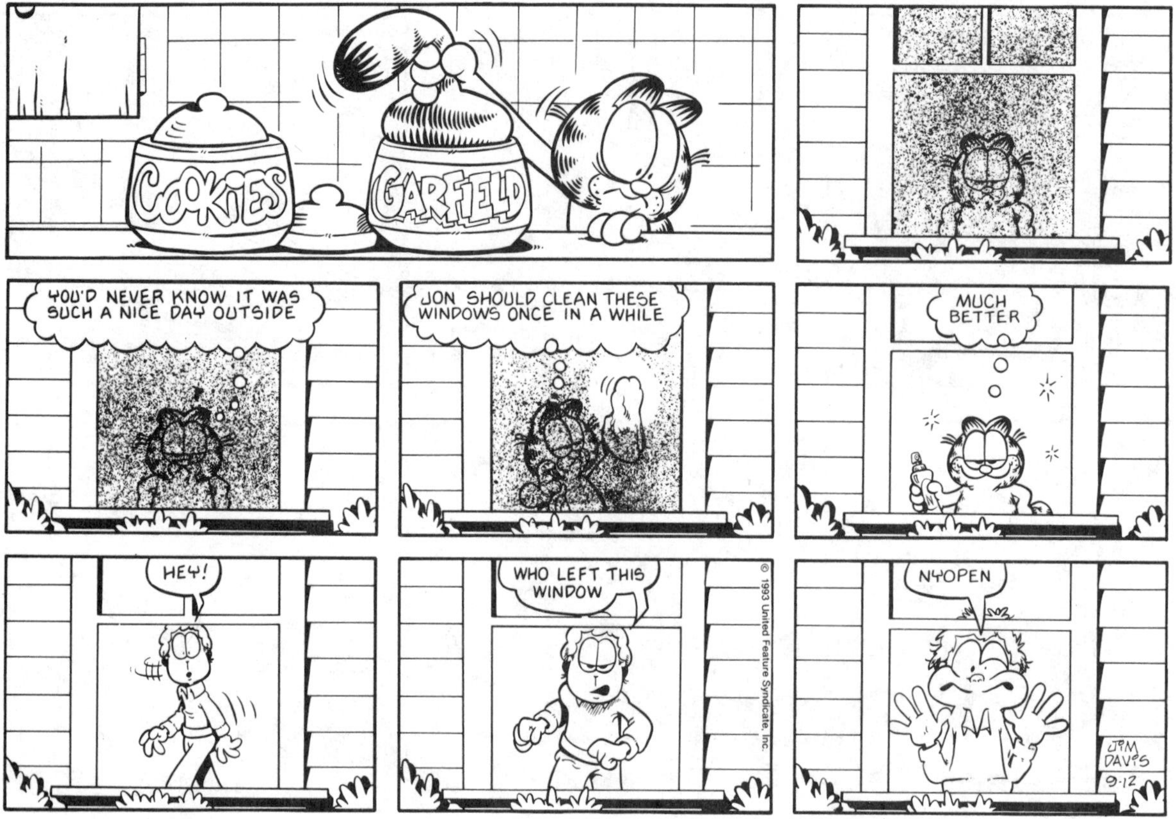
COOKIES
GARFIELD
YOU'D NEVER KNOW IT WAS SUCH A NICE DAY OUTSIDE
JON SHOULD CLEAN THESE WINDOWS ONCE IN A WHILE
MUCH BETTER
HEY!
WHO LEFT THIS WINDOW
NYOPEN
© 1993 United Feature Syndicate, Inc.
JIM DAVIS
9-12

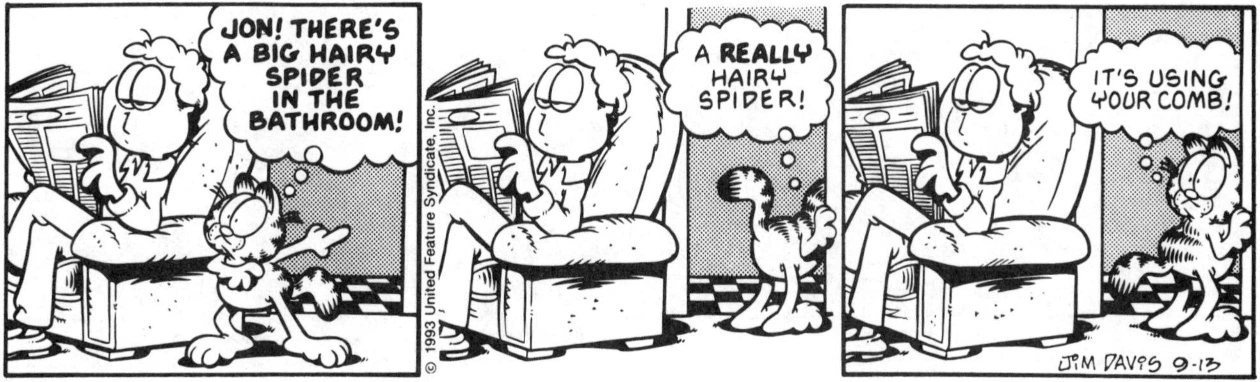
JON! THERE'S A BIG HAIRY SPIDER IN THE BATHROOM!
A REALLY HAIRY SPIDER!
IT'S USING YOUR COMB!
JIM DAVIS 9-13

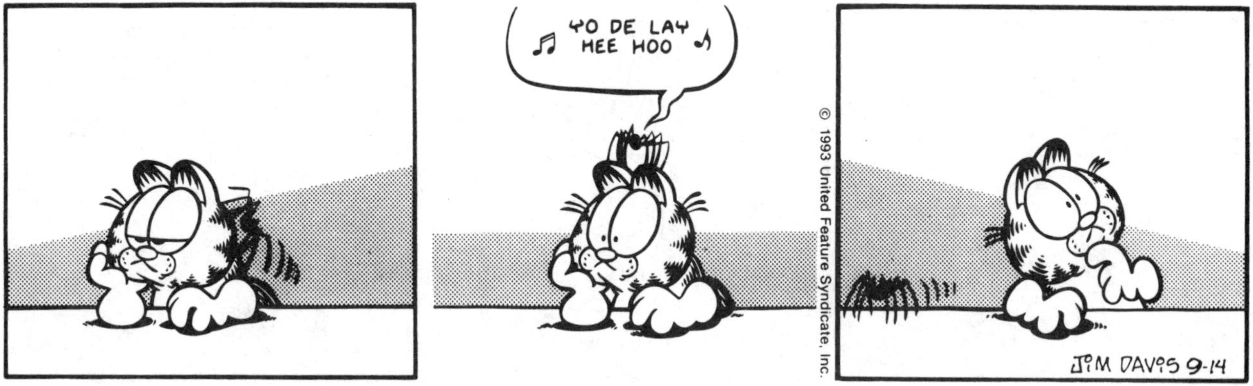
♫ YO DE LAY HEE HOO ♪
JIM DAVIS 9-14

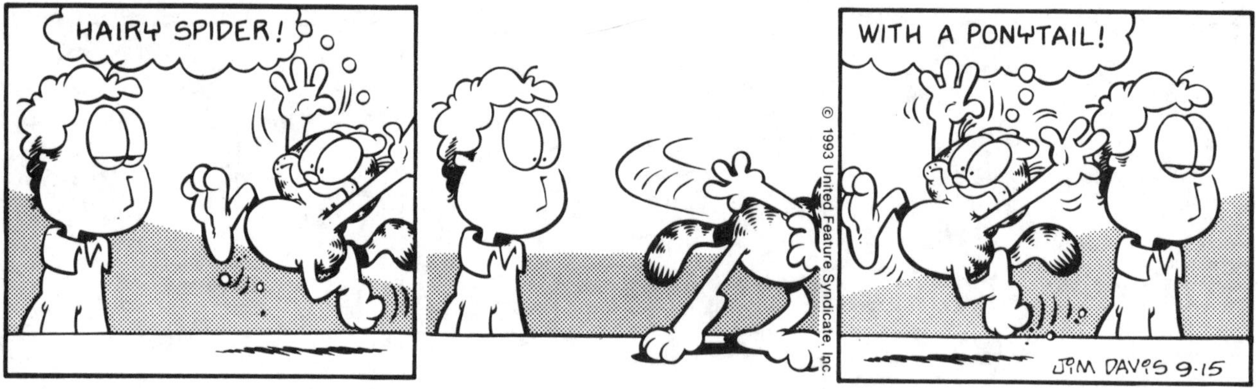
HAIRY SPIDER!
WITH A PONYTAIL!
JIM DAVIS 9-15
© 1993 United Feature Syndicate, Inc.

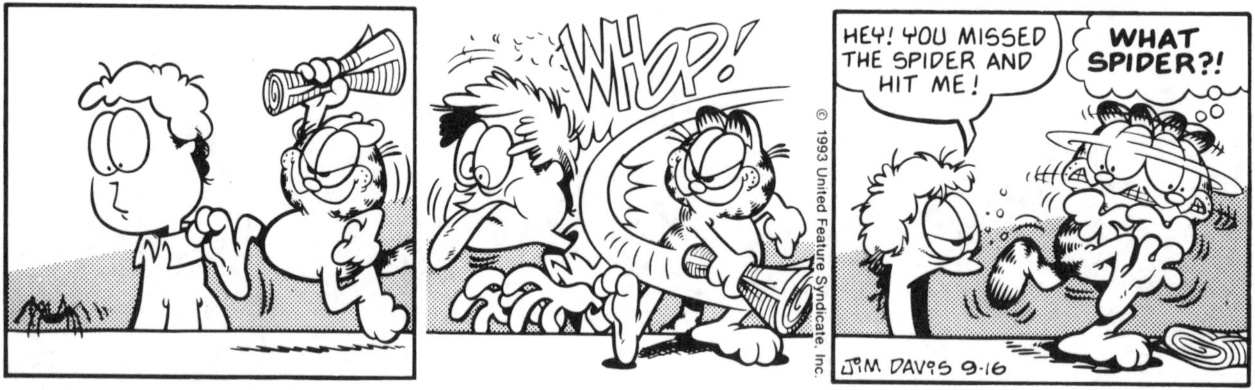
WHOP!
HEY! YOU MISSED THE SPIDER AND HIT ME!
WHAT SPIDER?!
JIM DAVIS 9-16
© 1993 United Feature Syndicate, Inc.

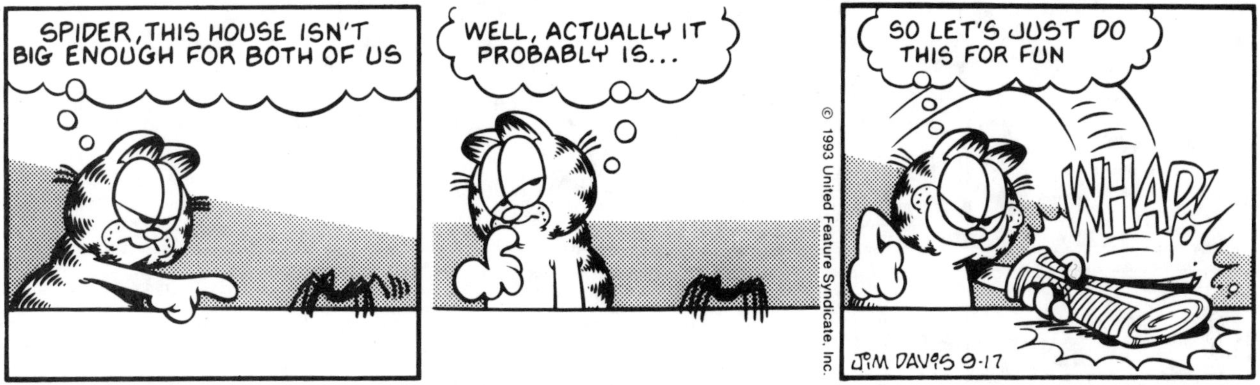
SPIDER, THIS HOUSE ISN'T BIG ENOUGH FOR BOTH OF US
WELL, ACTUALLY IT PROBABLY IS...
SO LET'S JUST DO THIS FOR FUN
WHAP!
© 1993 United Feature Syndicate, Inc.
JIM DAVIS 9-17

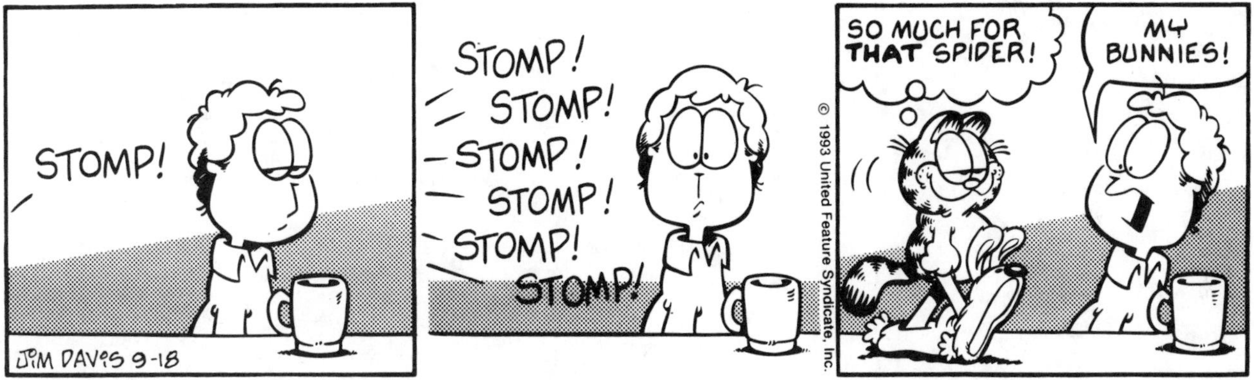
STOMP!
JIM DAVIS 9-18
STOMP! STOMP! STOMP! STOMP! STOMP! STOMP!
SO MUCH FOR **THAT** SPIDER!
MY BUNNIES!
© 1993 United Feature Syndicate, Inc.

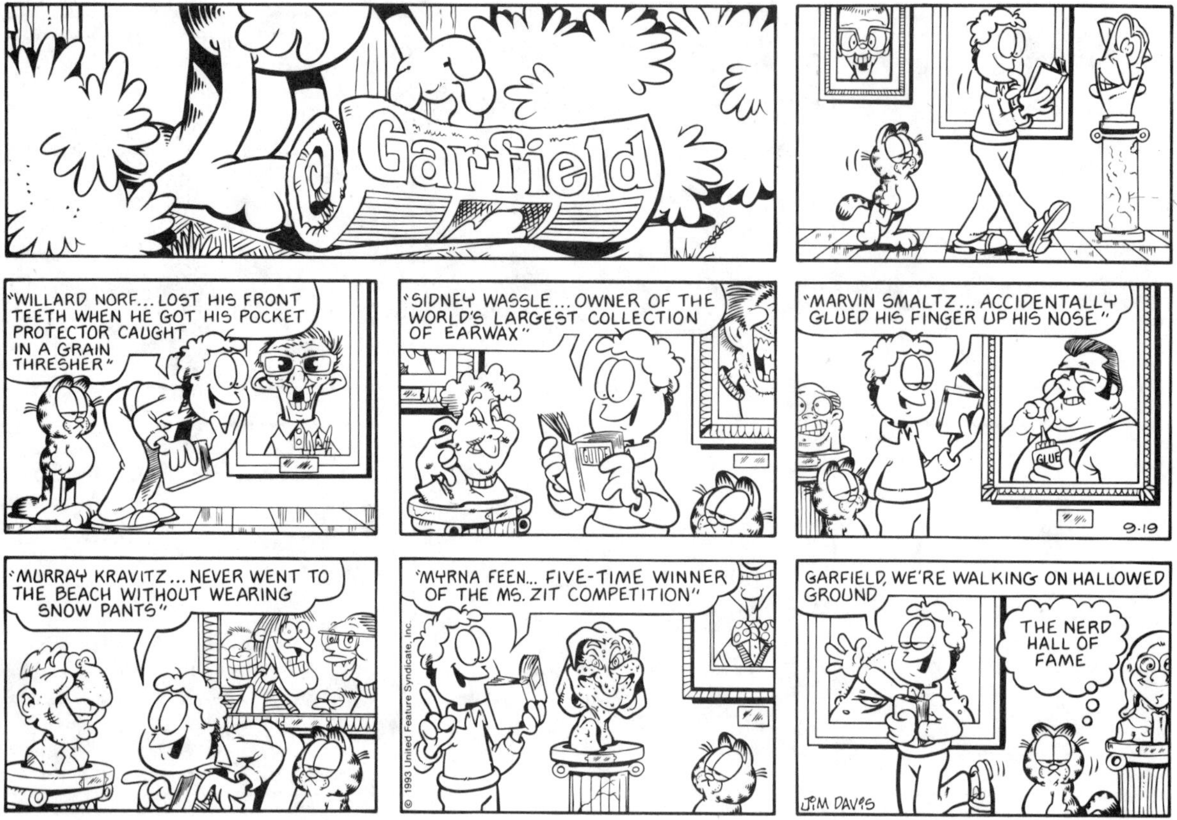
Garfield
"WILLARD NORF... LOST HIS FRONT TEETH WHEN HE GOT HIS POCKET PROTECTOR CAUGHT IN A GRAIN THRESHER"
"SIDNEY WASSLE... OWNER OF THE WORLD'S LARGEST COLLECTION OF EARWAX"
GUIDE
"MARVIN SMALTZ... ACCIDENTALLY GLUED HIS FINGER UP HIS NOSE"
GLUE
9-19
"MURRAY KRAVITZ... NEVER WENT TO THE BEACH WITHOUT WEARING SNOW PANTS"
"MYRNA FEEN... FIVE-TIME WINNER OF THE MS. ZIT COMPETITION"
© 1993 United Feature Syndicate, Inc.
GARFIELD, WE'RE WALKING ON HALLOWED GROUND
THE NERD HALL OF FAME
JIM DAVIS

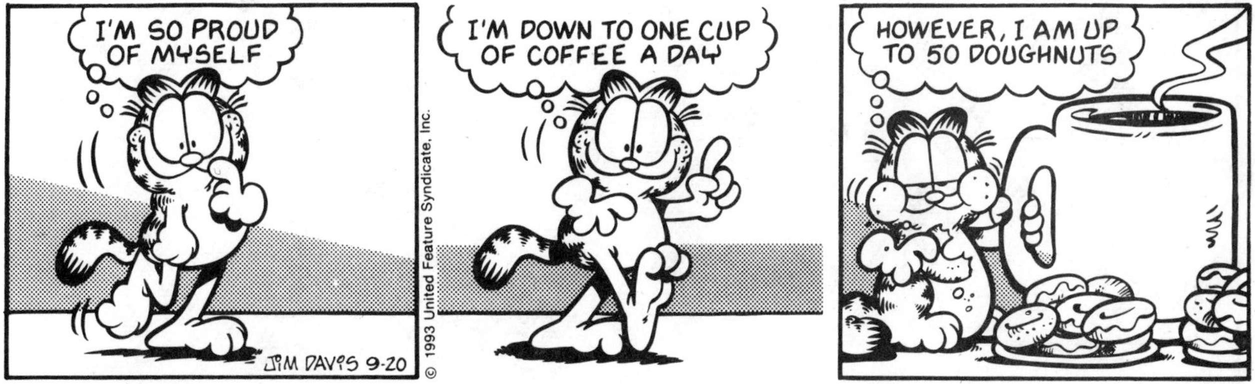
I'M SO PROUD OF MYSELF
JIM DAVIS 9-20
I'M DOWN TO ONE CUP OF COFFEE A DAY
HOWEVER, I AM UP TO 50 DOUGHNUTS

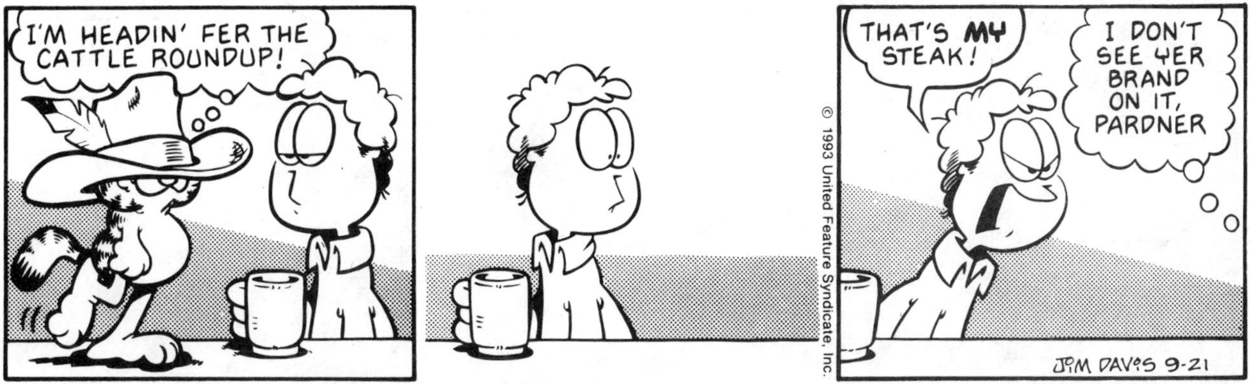
I'M HEADIN' FER THE CATTLE ROUNDUP!
THAT'S **MY** STEAK!
I DON'T SEE YER BRAND ON IT, PARDNER
JIM DAVIS 9-21

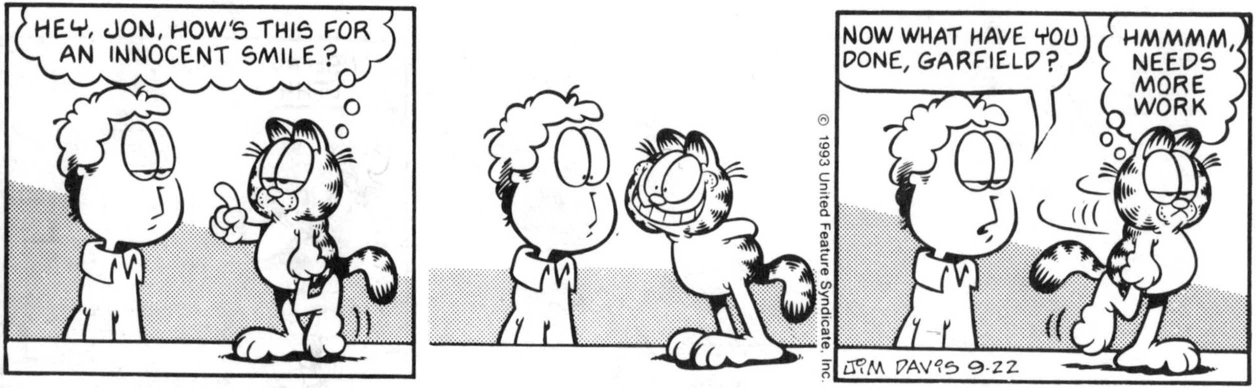
HEY, JON, HOW'S THIS FOR AN INNOCENT SMILE?
NOW WHAT HAVE YOU DONE, GARFIELD?
HMMMM, NEEDS MORE WORK
© 1993 United Feature Syndicate, Inc.
JIM DAVIS 9-22

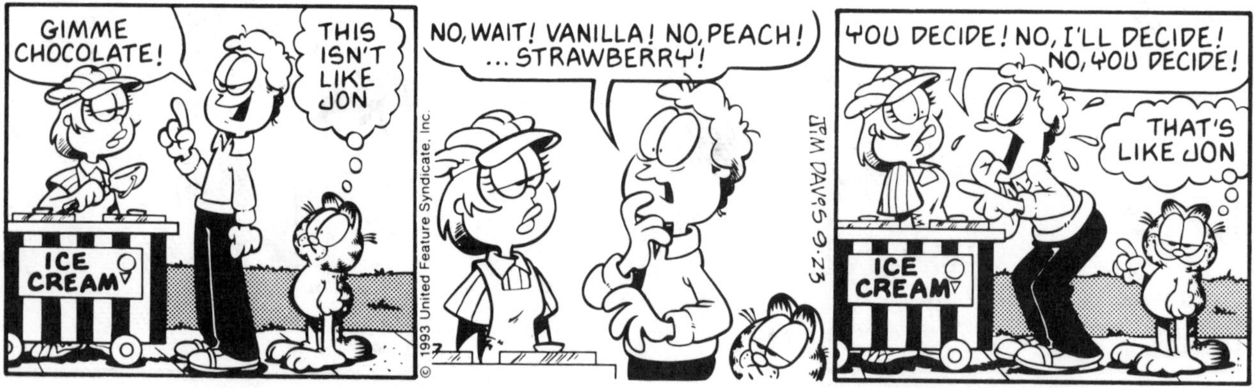
GIMME CHOCOLATE!
THIS ISN'T LIKE JON
© 1993 United Feature Syndicate, Inc.
NO, WAIT! VANILLA! NO, PEACH! ... STRAWBERRY!
JIM DAVIS 9-23
YOU DECIDE! NO, I'LL DECIDE! NO, YOU DECIDE!
THAT'S LIKE JON
ICE CREAM

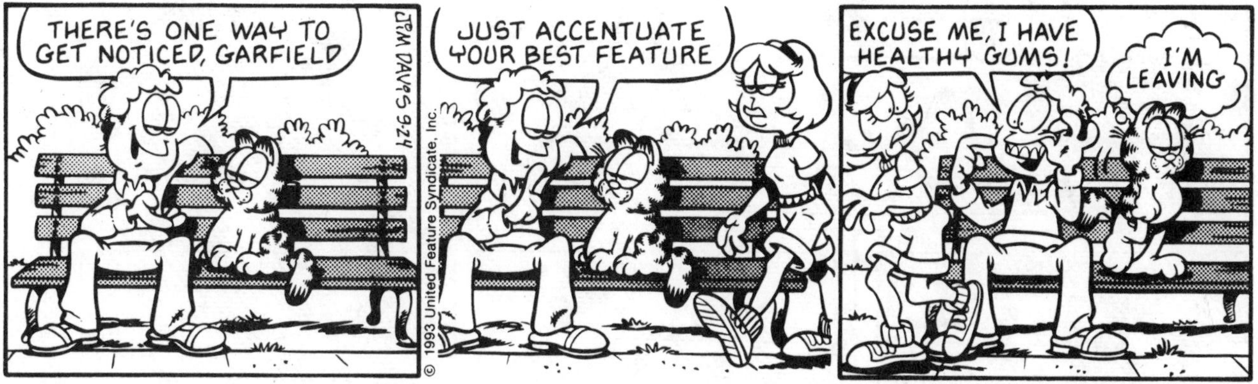
THERE'S ONE WAY TO GET NOTICED, GARFIELD
JIM DAVIS 9-24
JUST ACCENTUATE YOUR BEST FEATURE
© 1993 United Feature Syndicate, Inc.
EXCUSE ME, I HAVE HEALTHY GUMS!
I'M LEAVING

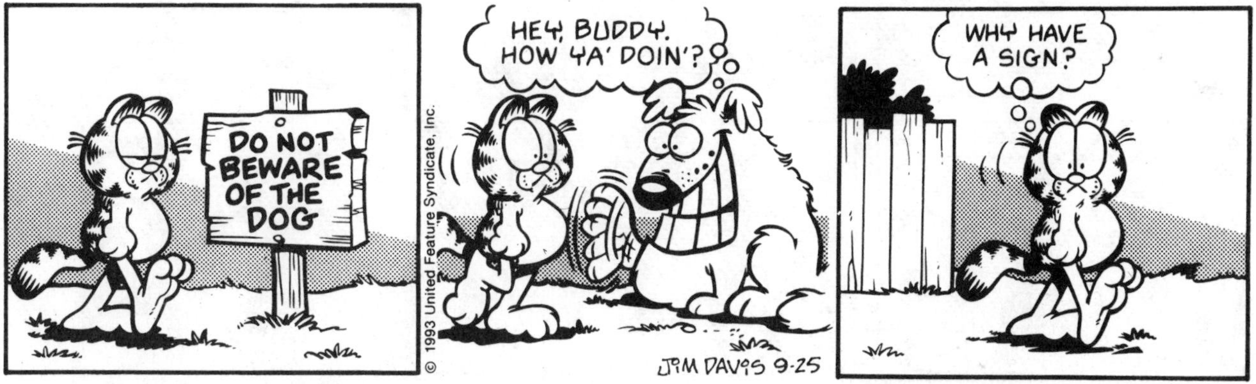
DO NOT BEWARE OF THE DOG
© 1993 United Feature Syndicate, Inc.
HEY, BUDDY. HOW YA' DOIN'?
JIM DAVIS 9-25
WHY HAVE A SIGN?

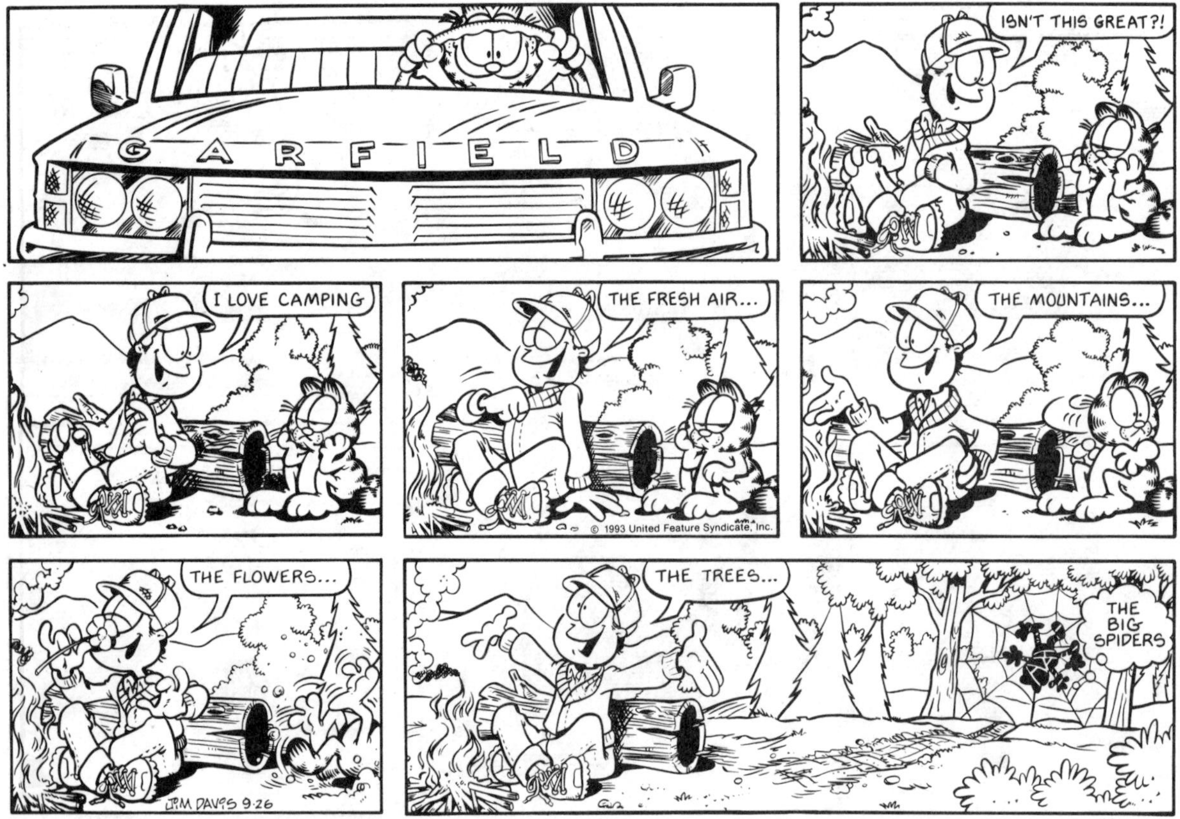
GARFIELD
ISN'T THIS GREAT?!
I LOVE CAMPING
THE FRESH AIR...
© 1993 United Feature Syndicate, Inc.
THE MOUNTAINS...
THE FLOWERS...
JIM DAVIS 9·26
THE TREES...
THE BIG SPIDERS

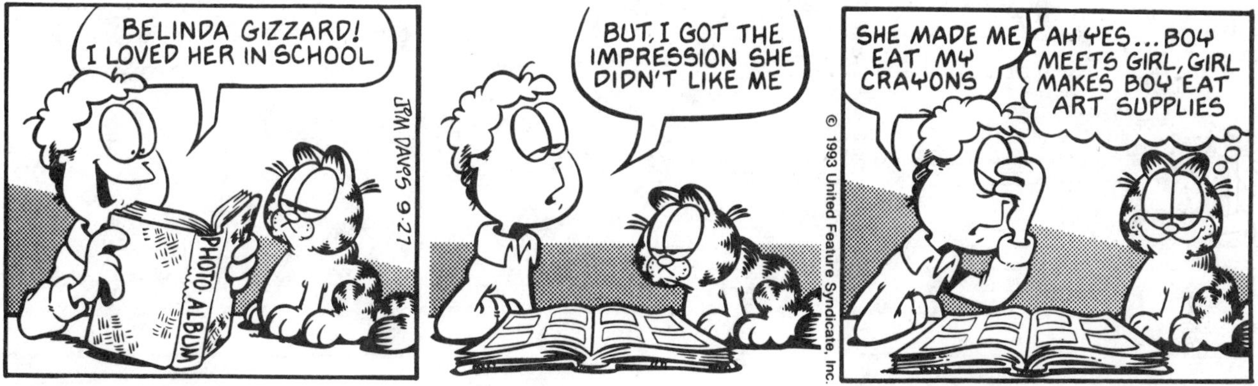
BELINDA GIZZARD! I LOVED HER IN SCHOOL
PHOTO · ALBUM
JIM DAVIS 9·27
BUT, I GOT THE IMPRESSION SHE DIDN'T LIKE ME
© 1993 United Feature Syndicate, Inc.
SHE MADE ME EAT MY CRAYONS
AH YES... BOY MEETS GIRL, GIRL MAKES BOY EAT ART SUPPLIES

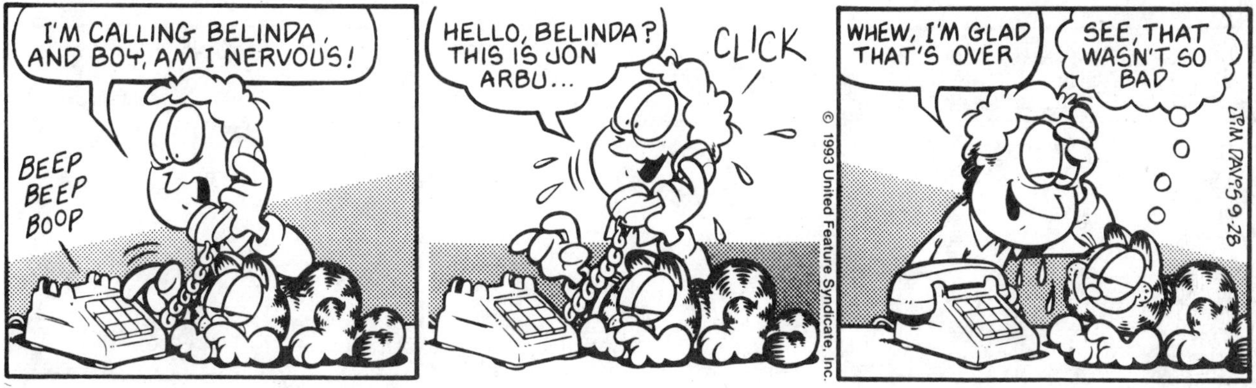
I'M CALLING BELINDA, AND BOY, AM I NERVOUS!
BEEP BEEP BOOP
HELLO, BELINDA? THIS IS JON ARBU...
CLICK
© 1993 United Feature Syndicate, Inc.
WHEW, I'M GLAD THAT'S OVER
SEE, THAT WASN'T SO BAD
JIM DAVIS 9·28

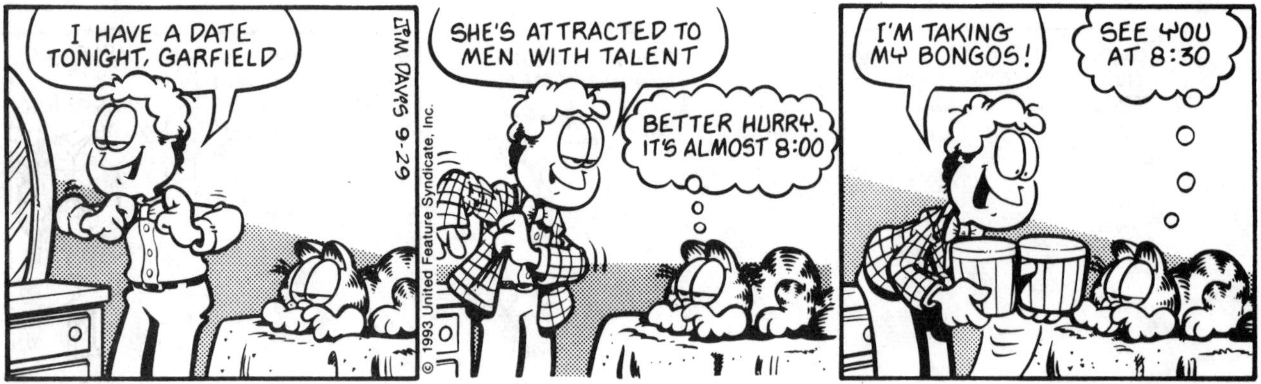

I HAVE A DATE TONIGHT, GARFIELD
JIM DAVIS 9-29
© 1993 United Feature Syndicate, Inc.
SHE'S ATTRACTED TO MEN WITH TALENT
BETTER HURRY. IT'S ALMOST 8:00
I'M TAKING MY BONGOS!
SEE YOU AT 8:30

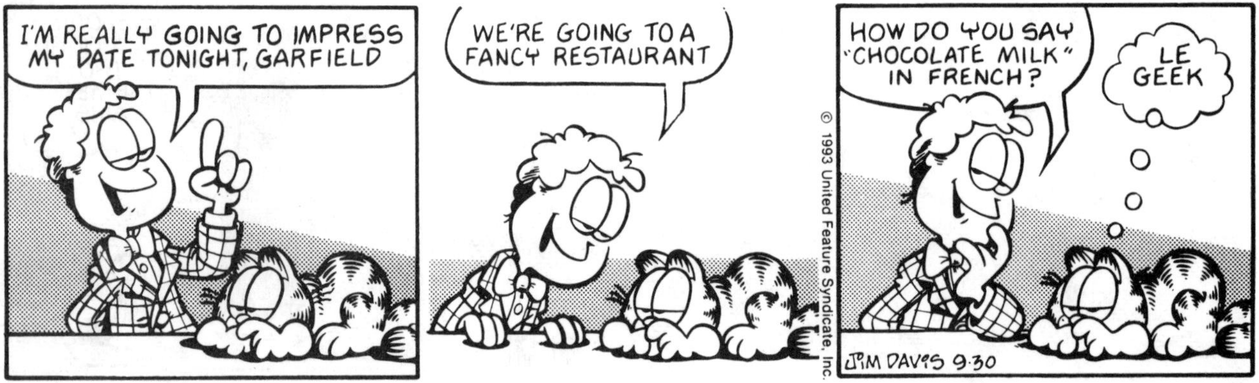

I'M REALLY GOING TO IMPRESS MY DATE TONIGHT, GARFIELD
WE'RE GOING TO A FANCY RESTAURANT
© 1993 United Feature Syndicate, Inc.
HOW DO YOU SAY "CHOCOLATE MILK" IN FRENCH?
LE GEEK
JIM DAVIS 9-30

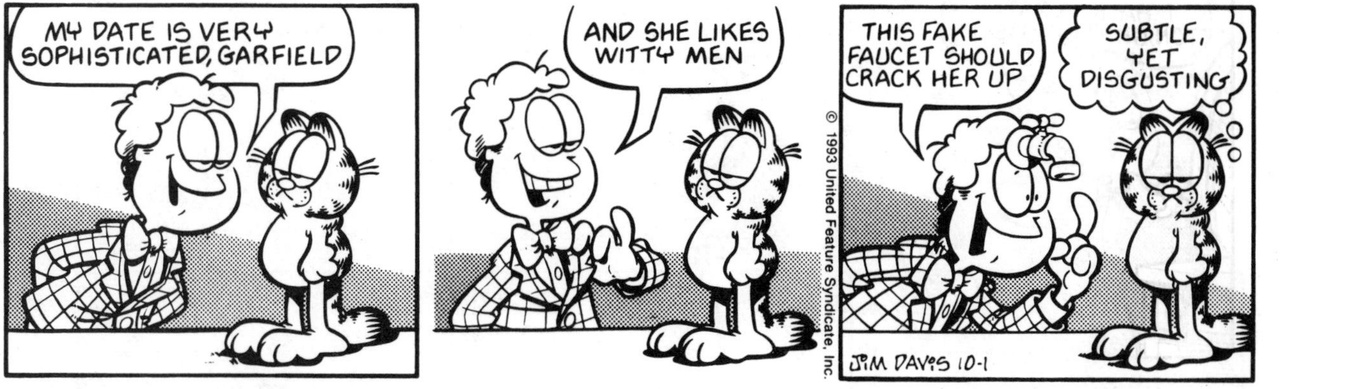
MY DATE IS VERY SOPHISTICATED, GARFIELD
AND SHE LIKES WITTY MEN
THIS FAKE FAUCET SHOULD CRACK HER UP
SUBTLE, YET DISGUSTING
© 1993 United Feature Syndicate, Inc.
JIM DAVIS 10-1

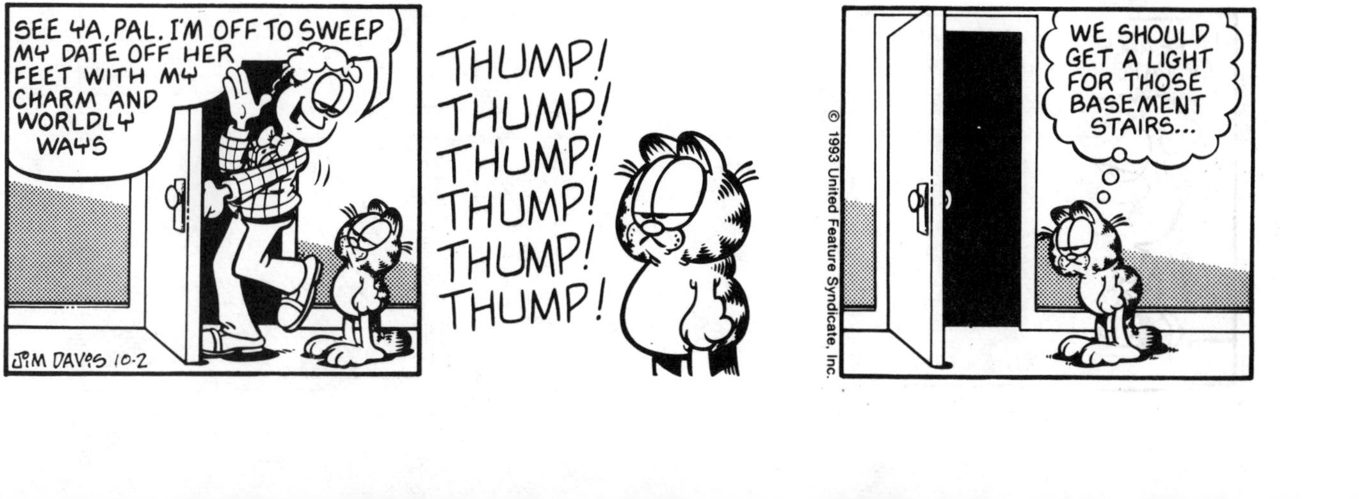
SEE YA, PAL. I'M OFF TO SWEEP MY DATE OFF HER FEET WITH MY CHARM AND WORLDLY WAYS
JIM DAVIS 10-2
THUMP! THUMP! THUMP! THUMP! THUMP! THUMP!
WE SHOULD GET A LIGHT FOR THOSE BASEMENT STAIRS...
© 1993 United Feature Syndicate, Inc.

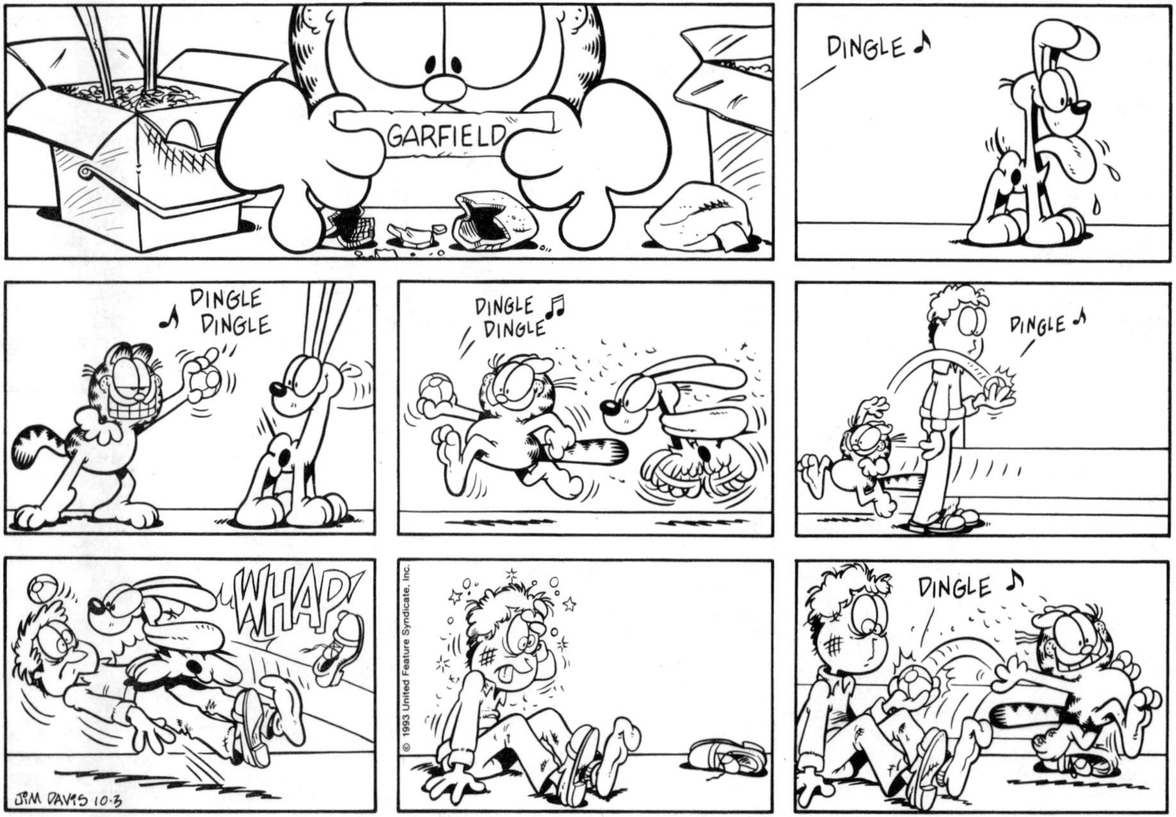
GARFIELD
DINGLE
DINGLE DINGLE
DINGLE DINGLE
DINGLE
WHAP!
JIM DAVIS 10-3
© 1993 United Feature Syndicate, Inc.
DINGLE

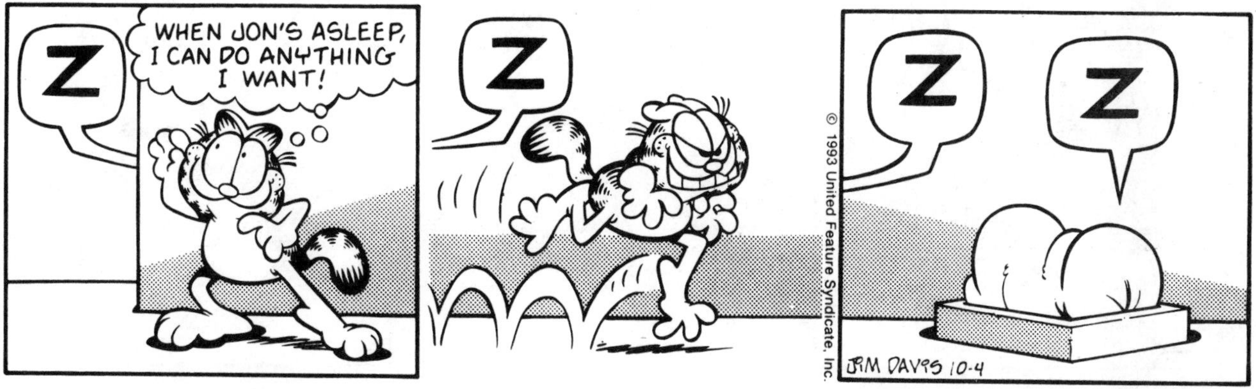
Z
WHEN JON'S ASLEEP, I CAN DO ANYTHING I WANT!
Z
Z
Z
© 1993 United Feature Syndicate, Inc.
JIM DAVIS 10-4

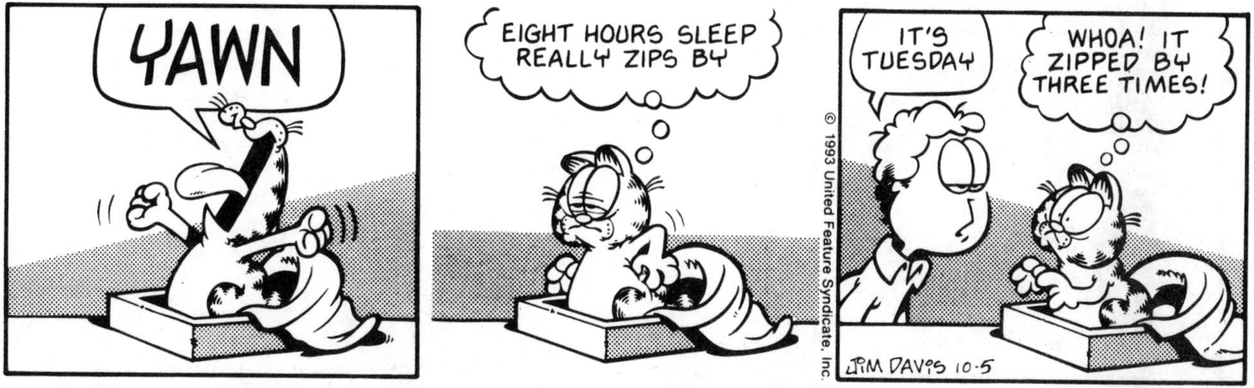
YAWN
EIGHT HOURS SLEEP REALLY ZIPS BY
IT'S TUESDAY
WHOA! IT ZIPPED BY THREE TIMES!
© 1993 United Feature Syndicate, Inc.
JIM DAVIS 10-5

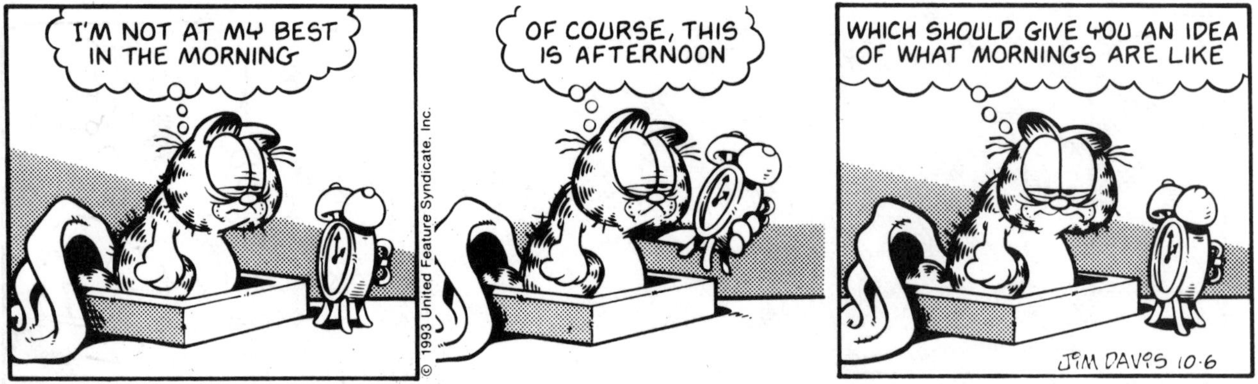
I'M NOT AT MY BEST IN THE MORNING
OF COURSE, THIS IS AFTERNOON
WHICH SHOULD GIVE YOU AN IDEA OF WHAT MORNINGS ARE LIKE
JIM DAVIS 10-6
© 1993 United Feature Syndicate, Inc.

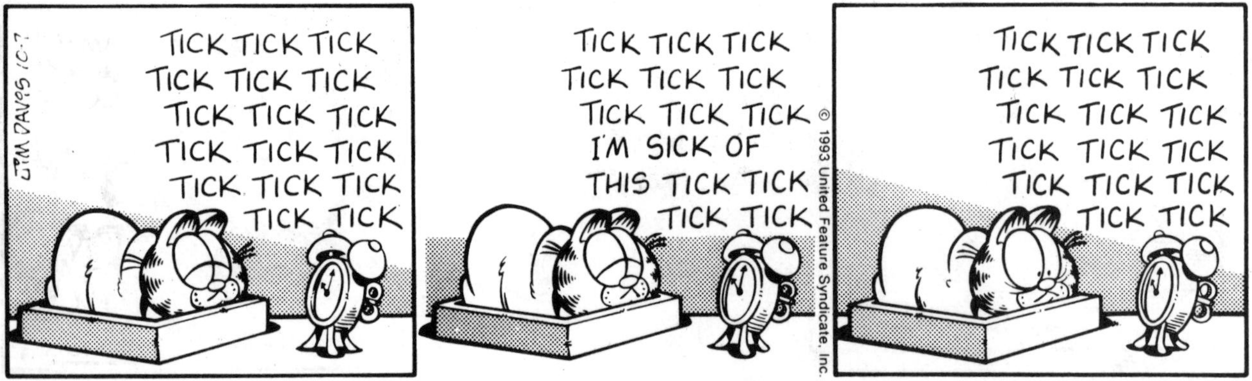
JIM DAVIS 10-7
TICK TICK TICK TICK TICK TICK TICK TICK TICK TICK TICK TICK TICK TICK TICK TICK TICK
TICK TICK TICK TICK TICK TICK TICK TICK TICK I'M SICK OF THIS TICK TICK TICK TICK
TICK TICK TICK TICK TICK TICK TICK TICK TICK TICK TICK TICK TICK TICK TICK TICK TICK
© 1993 United Feature Syndicate, Inc.

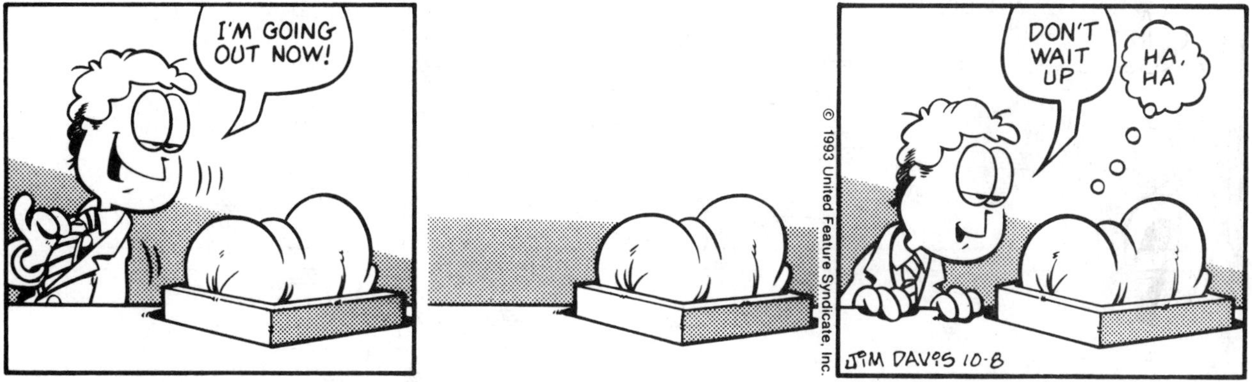
I'M GOING OUT NOW!
DON'T WAIT UP
HA, HA
© 1993 United Feature Syndicate, Inc.
JIM DAVIS 10-8

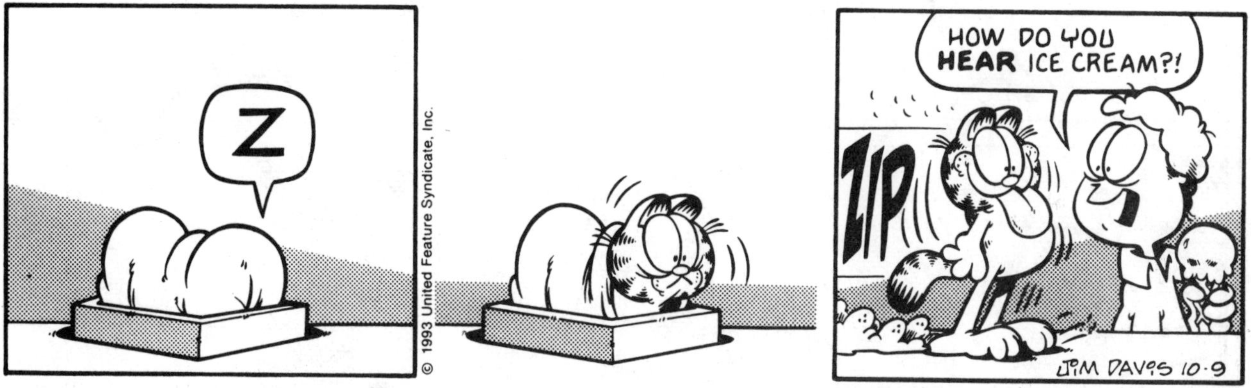
Z
© 1993 United Feature Syndicate, Inc.
ZIP
HOW DO YOU HEAR ICE CREAM?!
JIM DAVIS 10-9

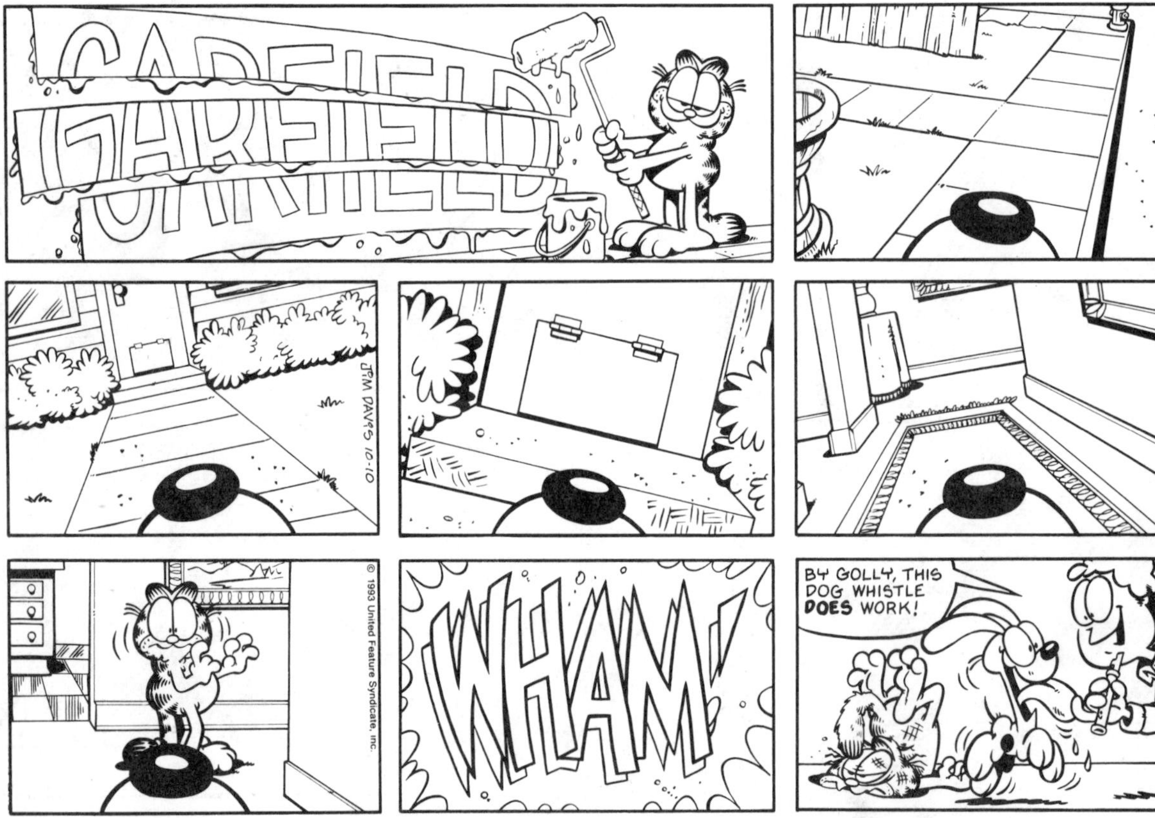
GARFIELD
GARFIELD
GARFIELD
JIM DAVIS 10-10
© 1993 United Feature Syndicate, Inc.
WHAM!
BY GOLLY, THIS DOG WHISTLE **DOES** WORK!

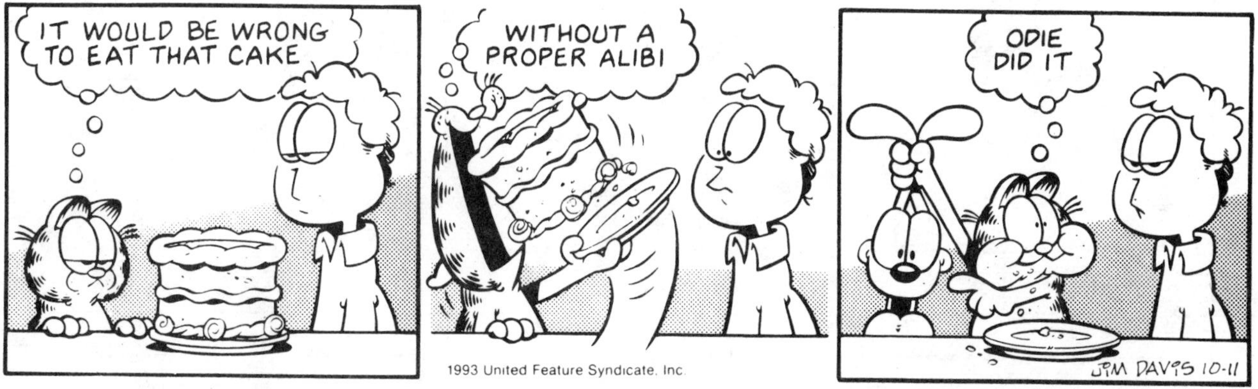
IT WOULD BE WRONG TO EAT THAT CAKE
WITHOUT A PROPER ALIBI
ODIE DID IT
1993 United Feature Syndicate, Inc.
JIM DAVIS 10-11

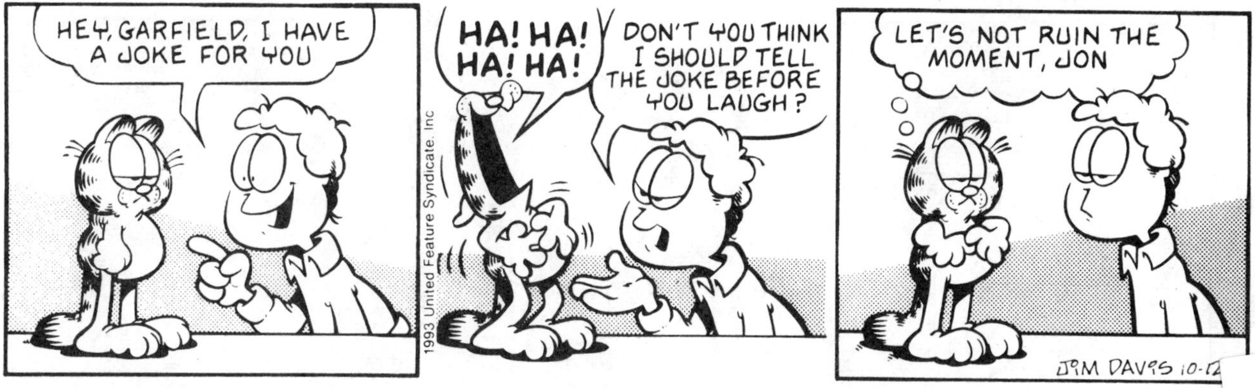
HEY, GARFIELD, I HAVE A JOKE FOR YOU
HA! HA! HA! HA!
DON'T YOU THINK I SHOULD TELL THE JOKE BEFORE YOU LAUGH?
LET'S NOT RUIN THE MOMENT, JON
1993 United Feature Syndicate, Inc.
JIM DAVIS 10-12

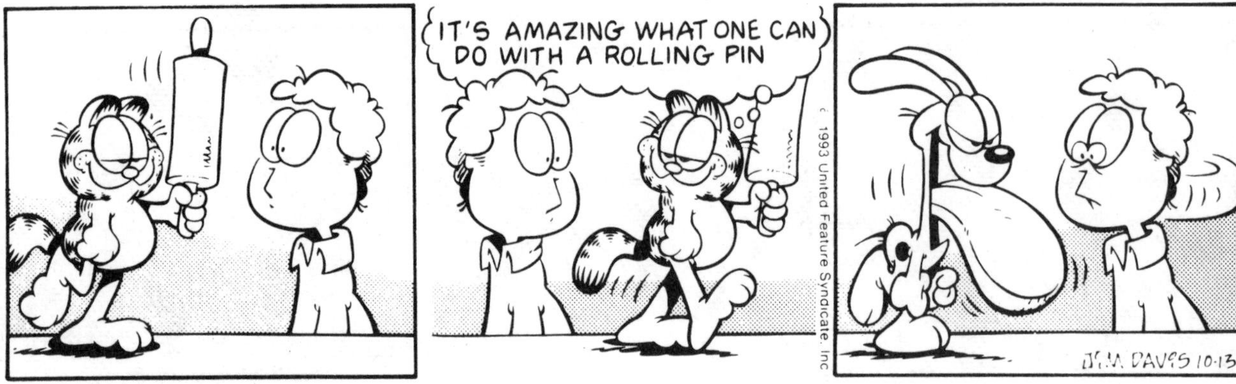
IT'S AMAZING WHAT ONE CAN DO WITH A ROLLING PIN
© 1993 United Feature Syndicate, Inc
JIM DAVIS 10-13

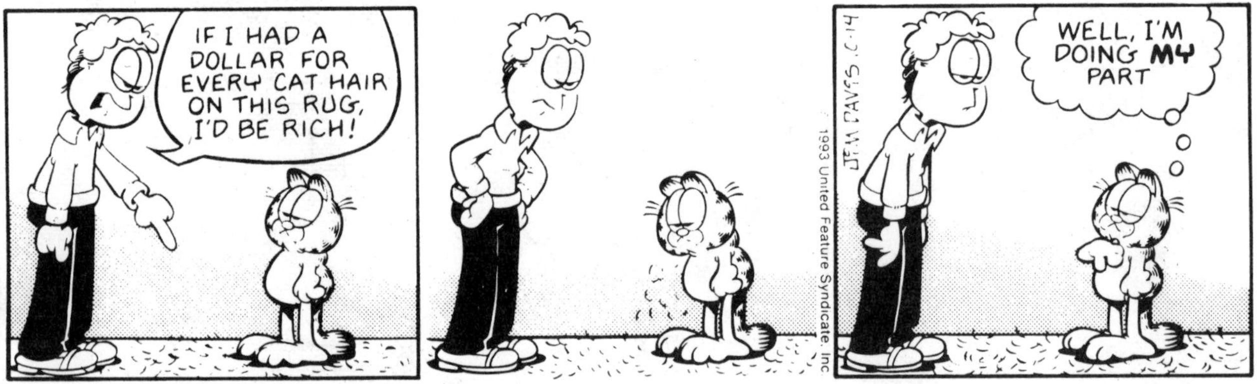
IF I HAD A DOLLAR FOR EVERY CAT HAIR ON THIS RUG, I'D BE RICH!
© 1993 United Feature Syndicate, Inc
JIM DAVIS 10-14
WELL, I'M DOING **MY** PART

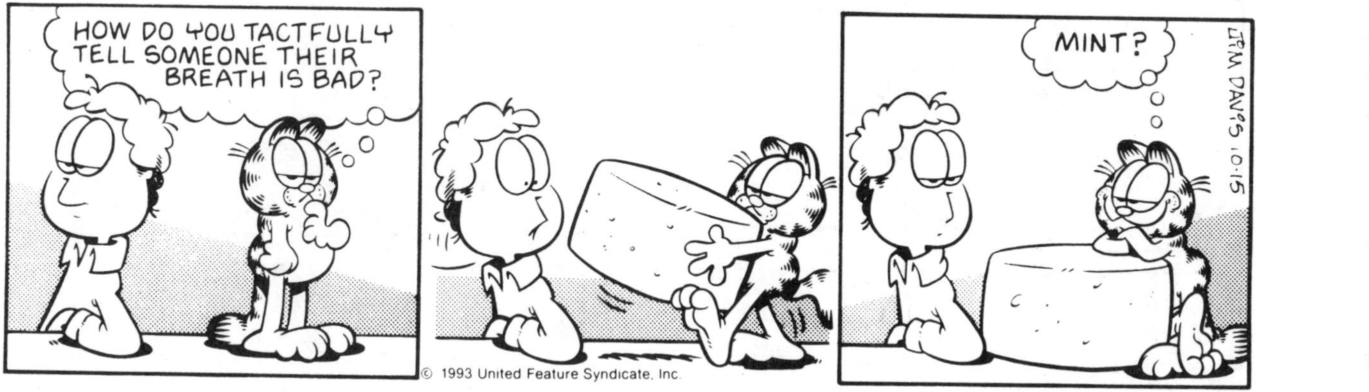
HOW DO YOU TACTFULLY TELL SOMEONE THEIR BREATH IS BAD?
MINT?
JPM DAVPS 10-15

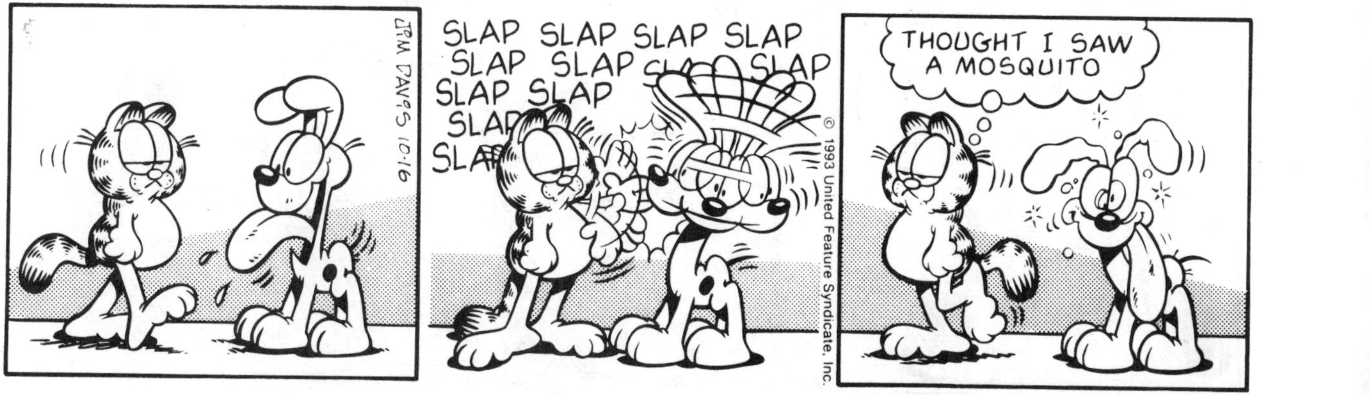
JPM DAVPS 10-16
SLAP SLAP SLAP SLAP
SLAP SLAP SLAP
SLAP SLAP
THOUGHT I SAW A MOSQUITO

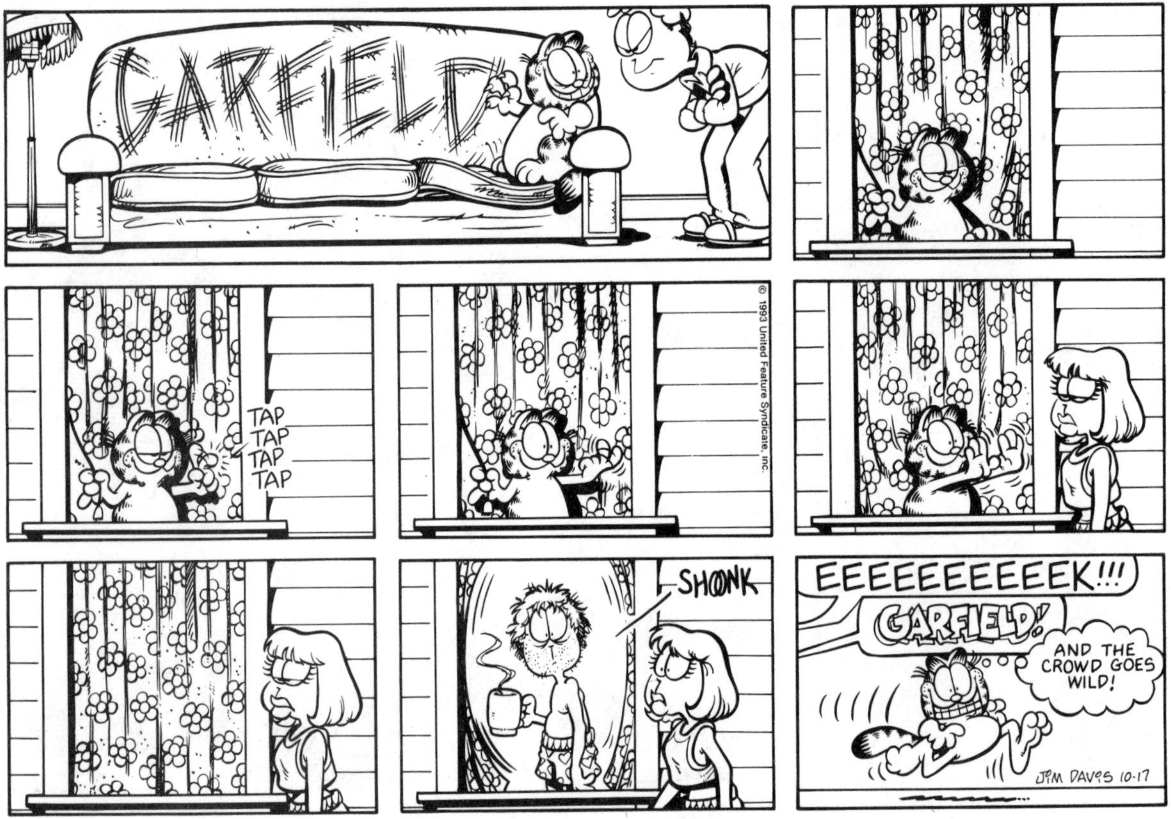
GARFIELD
© 1993 United Feature Syndicate, Inc.
TAP TAP TAP TAP
SHOONK
EEEEEEEEEEEK!!!
GARFIELD!
AND THE CROWD GOES WILD!
JIM DAVIS 10-17

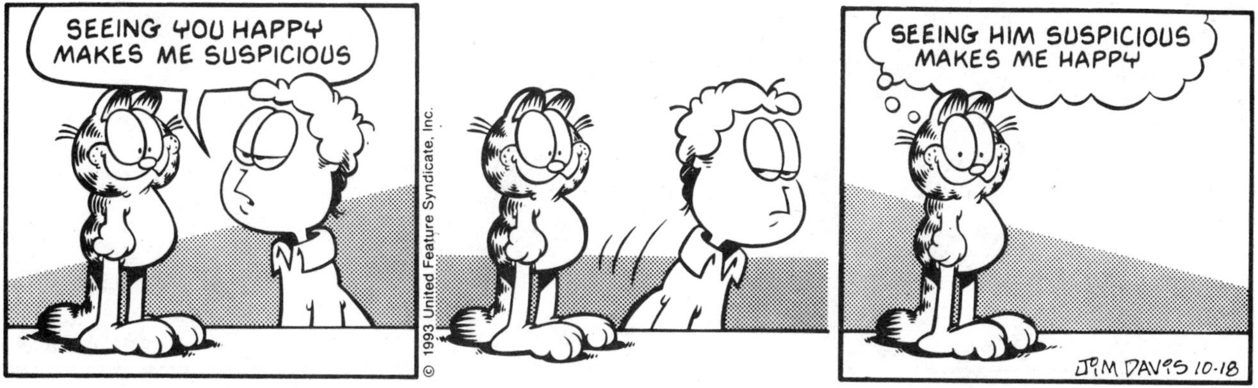
SEEING YOU HAPPY MAKES ME SUSPICIOUS
© 1993 United Feature Syndicate, Inc.
SEEING HIM SUSPICIOUS MAKES ME HAPPY
JIM DAVIS 10-18

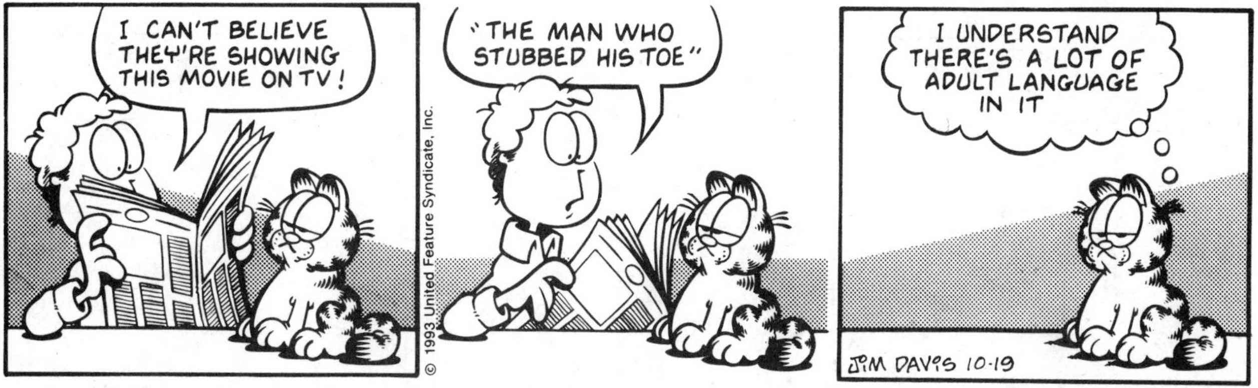
I CAN'T BELIEVE THEY'RE SHOWING THIS MOVIE ON TV!
© 1993 United Feature Syndicate, Inc.
"THE MAN WHO STUBBED HIS TOE"
I UNDERSTAND THERE'S A LOT OF ADULT LANGUAGE IN IT
JIM DAVIS 10-19

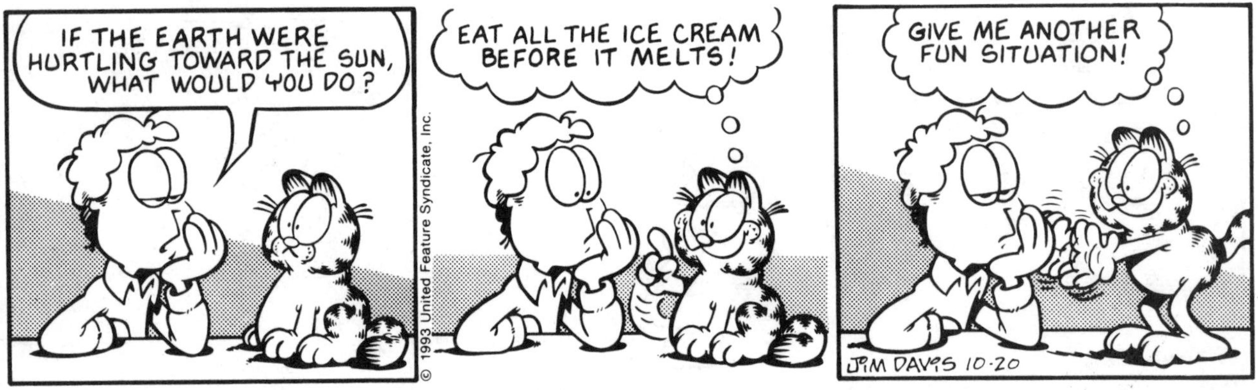
IF THE EARTH WERE HURTLING TOWARD THE SUN, WHAT WOULD YOU DO?
EAT ALL THE ICE CREAM BEFORE IT MELTS!
GIVE ME ANOTHER FUN SITUATION!
JIM DAVIS 10-20
© 1993 United Feature Syndicate, Inc.

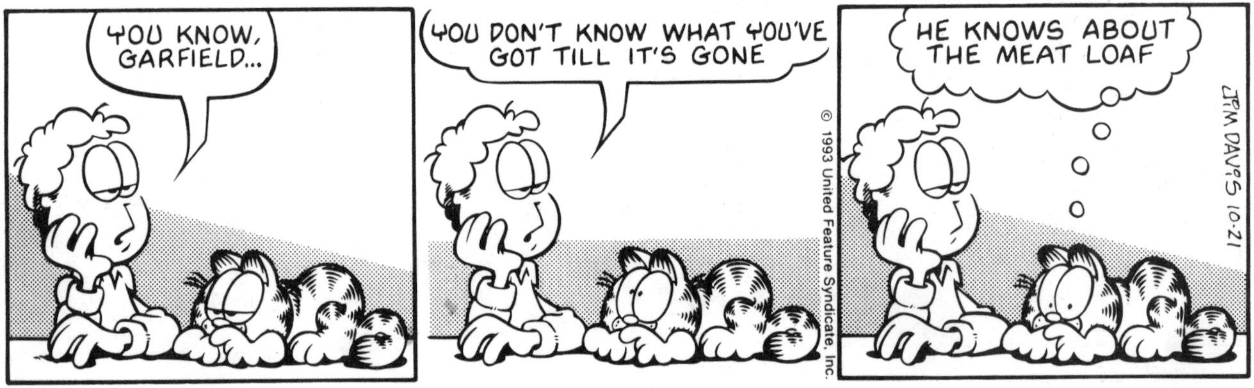
YOU KNOW, GARFIELD...
YOU DON'T KNOW WHAT YOU'VE GOT TILL IT'S GONE
HE KNOWS ABOUT THE MEAT LOAF
JIM DAVIS 10-21
© 1993 United Feature Syndicate, Inc.

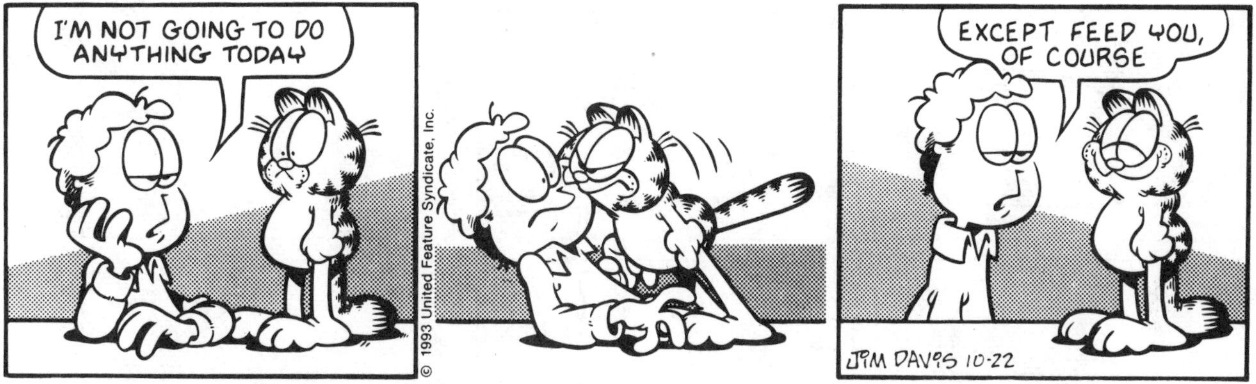
I'M NOT GOING TO DO ANYTHING TODAY
© 1993 United Feature Syndicate, Inc.
EXCEPT FEED YOU, OF COURSE
JIM DAVIS 10-22

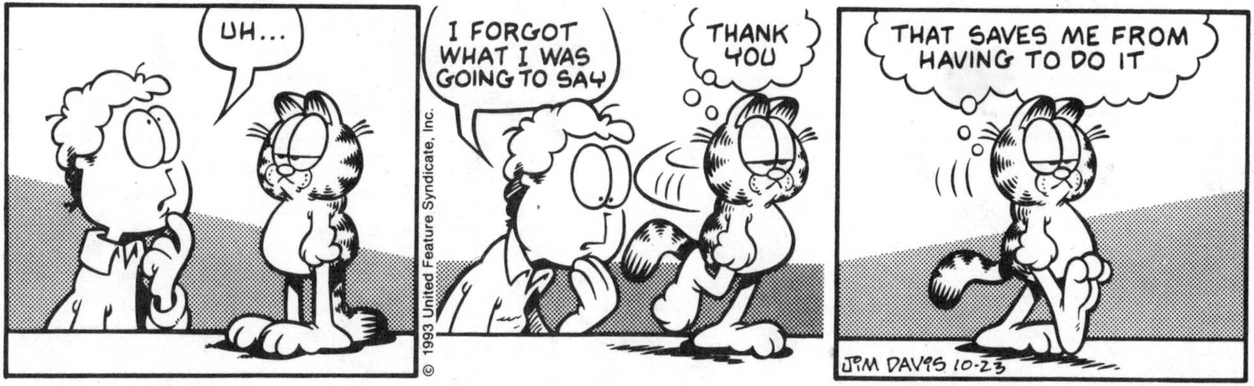
UH...
© 1993 United Feature Syndicate, Inc.
I FORGOT WHAT I WAS GOING TO SAY
THANK YOU
THAT SAVES ME FROM HAVING TO DO IT
JIM DAVIS 10-23

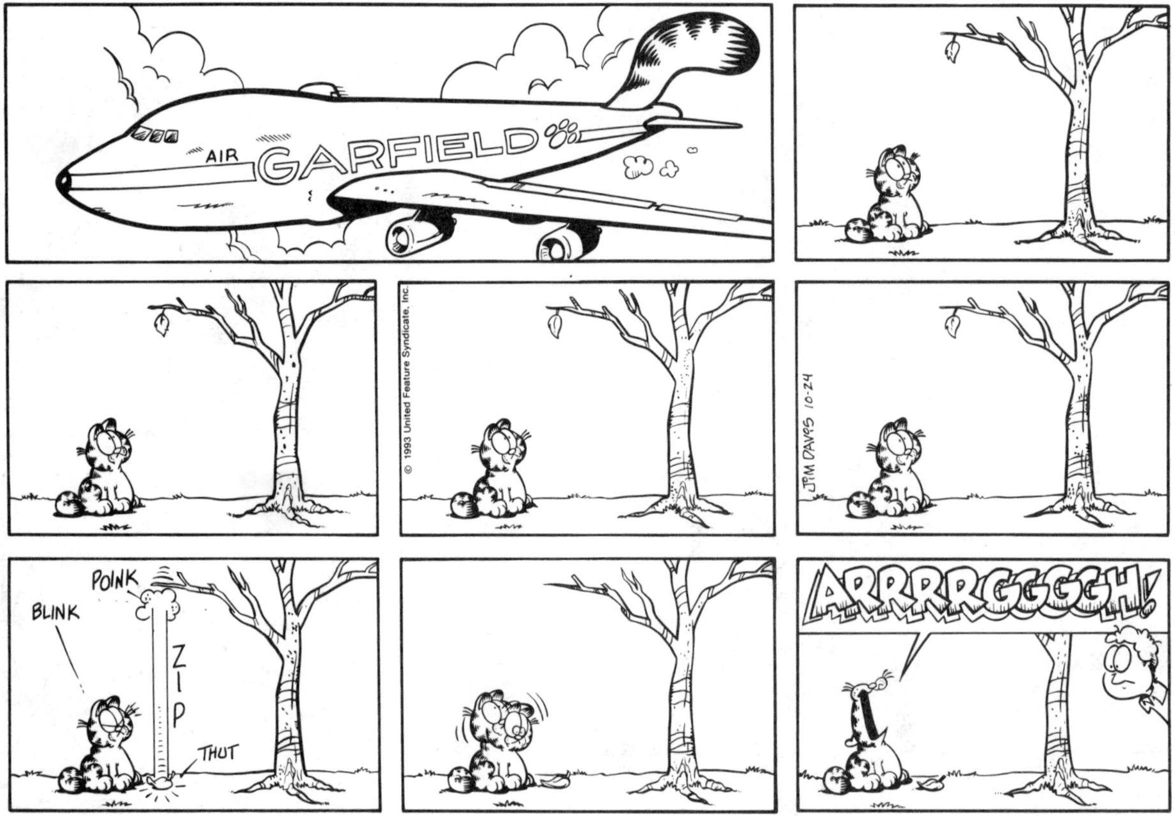
AIR GARFIELD
© 1993 United Feature Syndicate, Inc.
JIM DAVIS 10-24
POINK
BLINK
ZIP
THUT
ARRRRGGGGH!

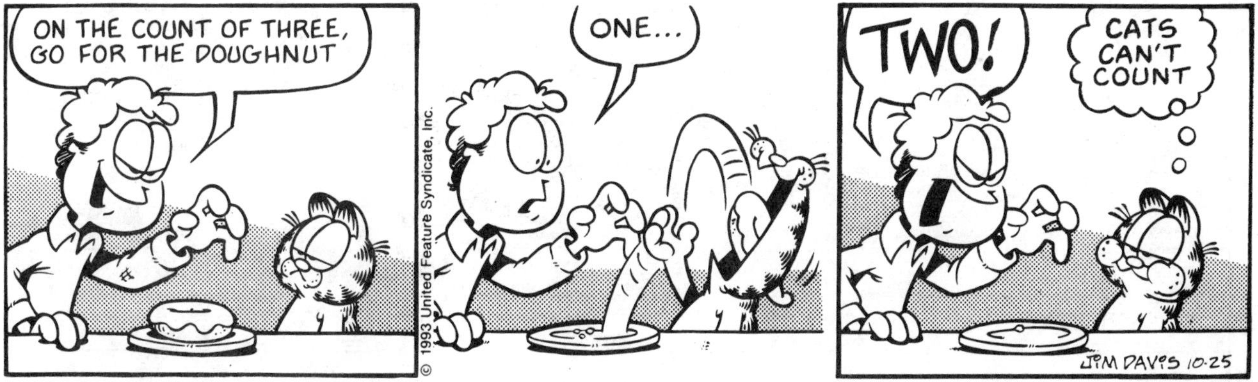
ON THE COUNT OF THREE, GO FOR THE DOUGHNUT
ONE...
TWO!
CATS CAN'T COUNT
© 1993 United Feature Syndicate, Inc.
JIM DAVIS 10-25

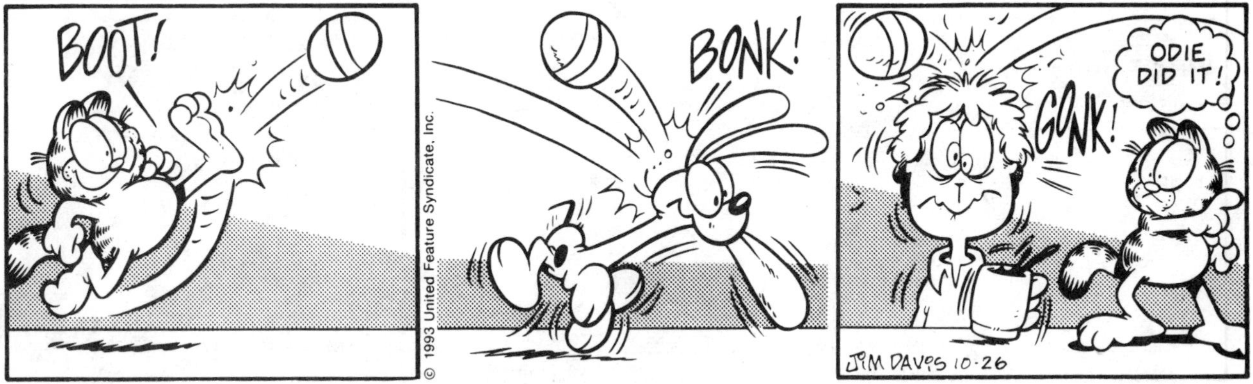
BOOT!
BONK!
GONK!
ODIE DID IT!
© 1993 United Feature Syndicate, Inc.
JIM DAVIS 10-26

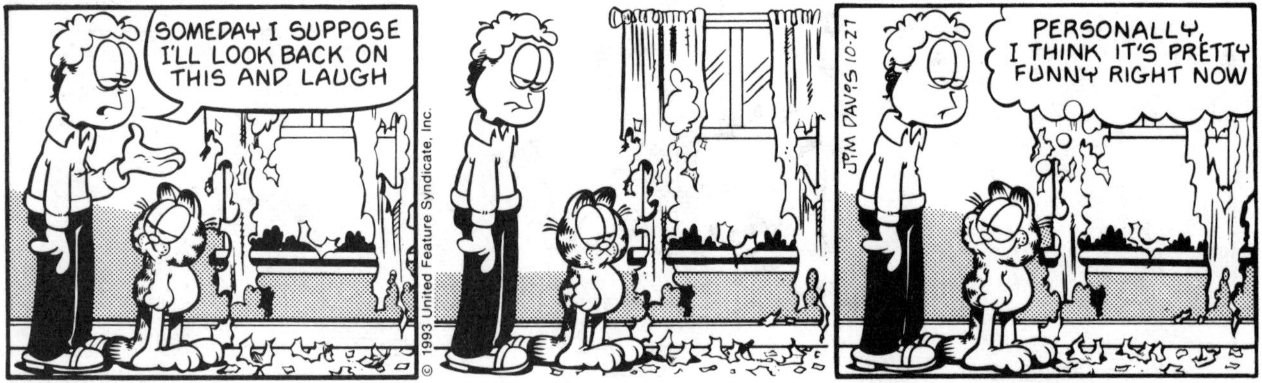
SOMEDAY I SUPPOSE I'LL LOOK BACK ON THIS AND LAUGH
PERSONALLY, I THINK IT'S PRETTY FUNNY RIGHT NOW
© 1993 United Feature Syndicate, Inc.
JIM DAVIS 10-27

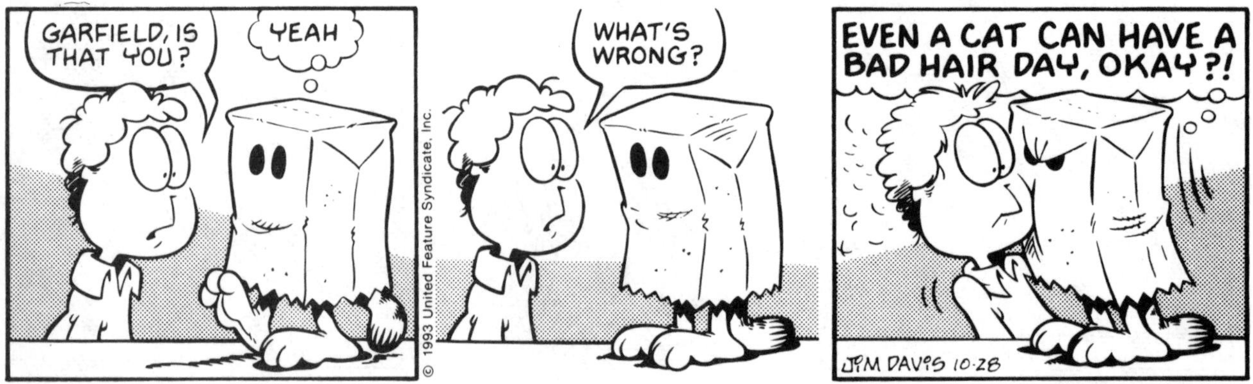
GARFIELD, IS THAT YOU?
YEAH
WHAT'S WRONG?
EVEN A CAT CAN HAVE A BAD HAIR DAY, OKAY?!
© 1993 United Feature Syndicate, Inc.
JIM DAVIS 10-28

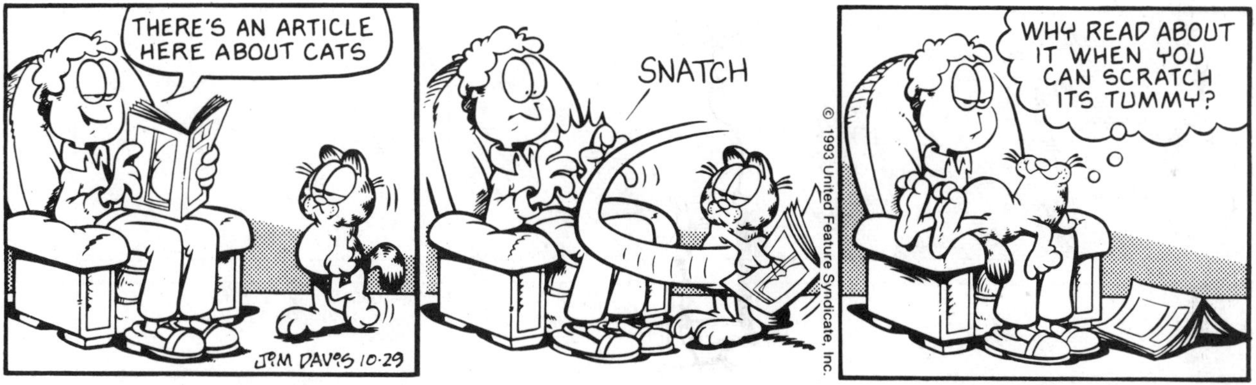
THERE'S AN ARTICLE HERE ABOUT CATS
JIM DAVIS 10-29
SNATCH
WHY READ ABOUT IT WHEN YOU CAN SCRATCH ITS TUMMY?

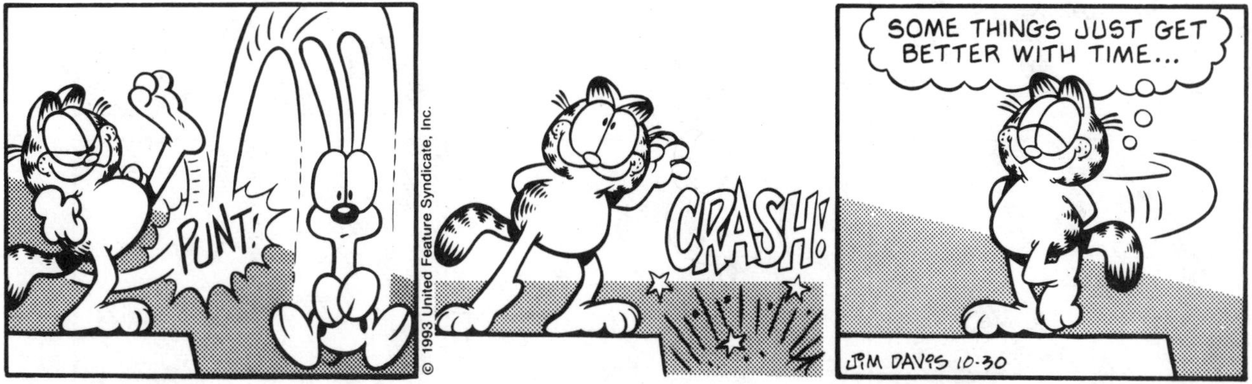
PUNT!
CRASH!
SOME THINGS JUST GET BETTER WITH TIME...
JIM DAVIS 10-30

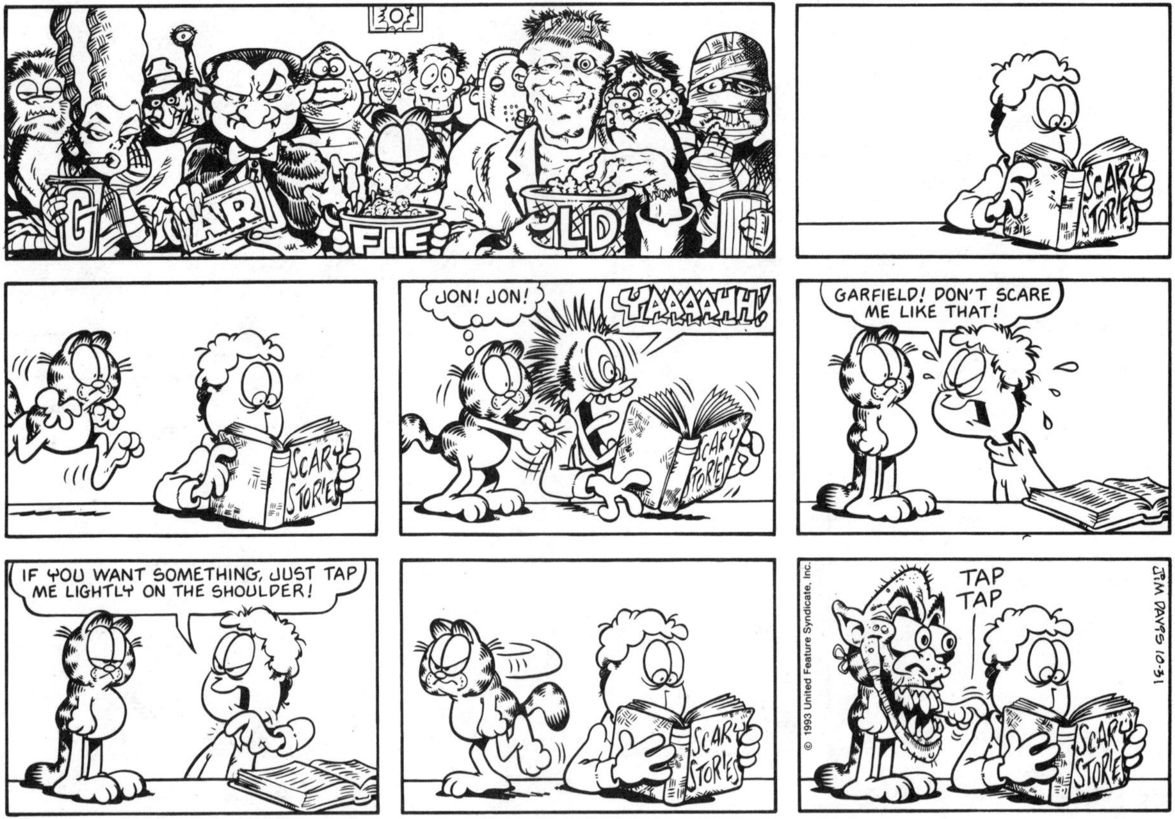
GARFIELD
SCARY STORIES
JON! JON!
YAAAAHH!
GARFIELD! DON'T SCARE ME LIKE THAT!
IF YOU WANT SOMETHING, JUST TAP ME LIGHTLY ON THE SHOULDER!
TAP TAP
JIM DAVIS 10-31
© 1993 United Feature Syndicate, Inc.

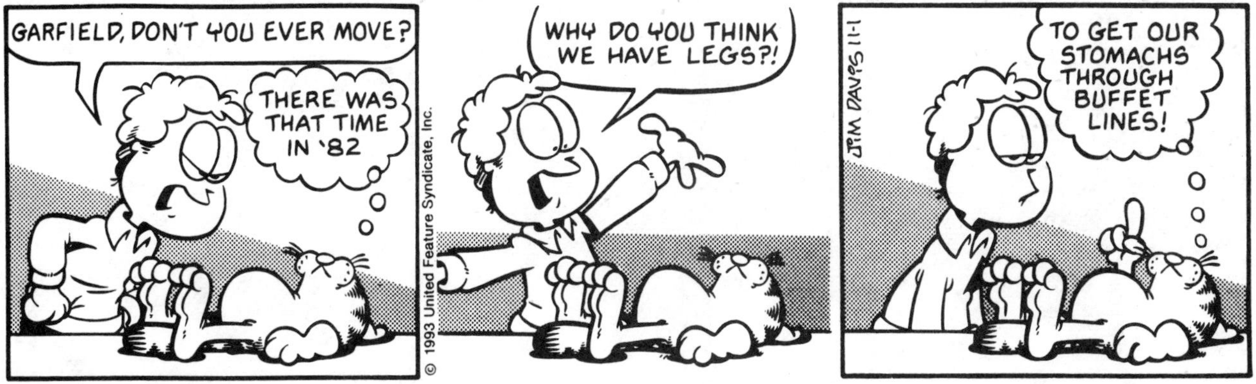
GARFIELD, DON'T YOU EVER MOVE?
THERE WAS THAT TIME IN '82
WHY DO YOU THINK WE HAVE LEGS?!
TO GET OUR STOMACHS THROUGH BUFFET LINES!
JIM DAVIS 11-1
© 1993 United Feature Syndicate, Inc.

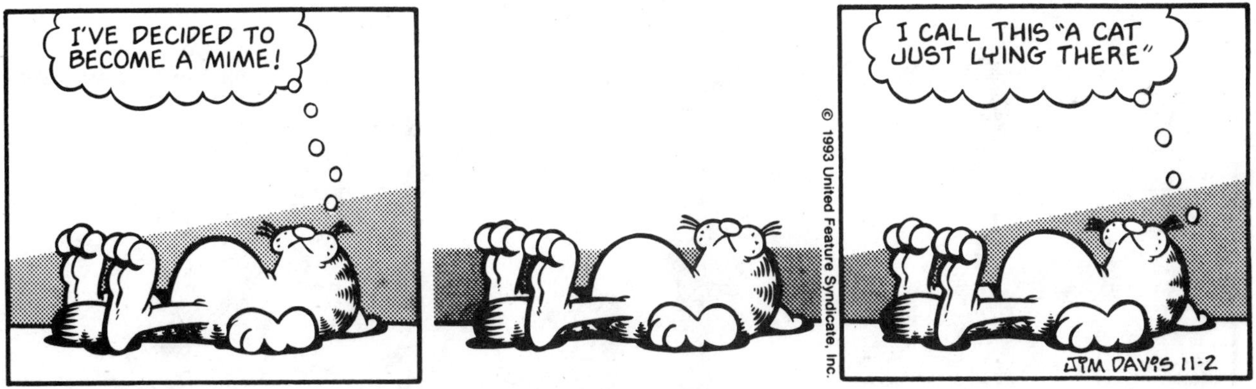
I'VE DECIDED TO BECOME A MIME!
I CALL THIS "A CAT JUST LYING THERE"
JIM DAVIS 11-2
© 1993 United Feature Syndicate, Inc.

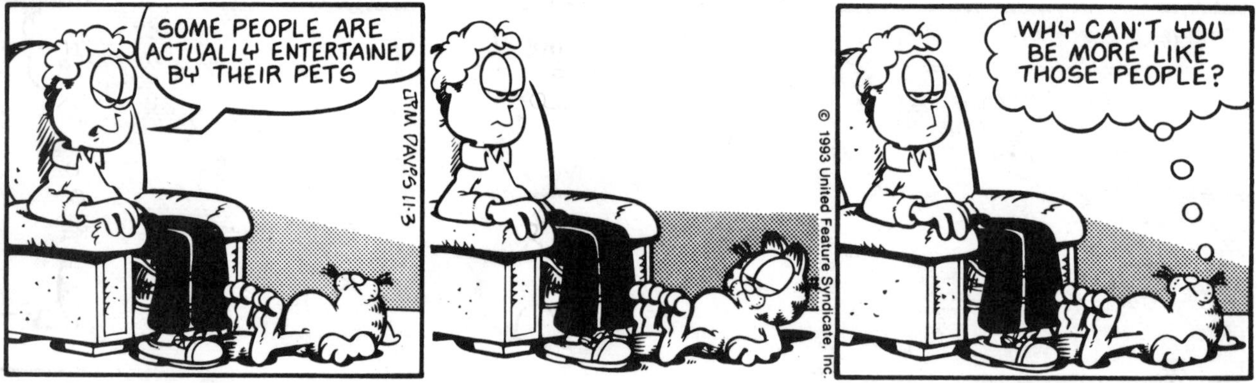
SOME PEOPLE ARE ACTUALLY ENTERTAINED BY THEIR PETS
JPM DAVPS 11-3
WHY CAN'T YOU BE MORE LIKE THOSE PEOPLE?
© 1993 United Feature Syndicate, Inc.

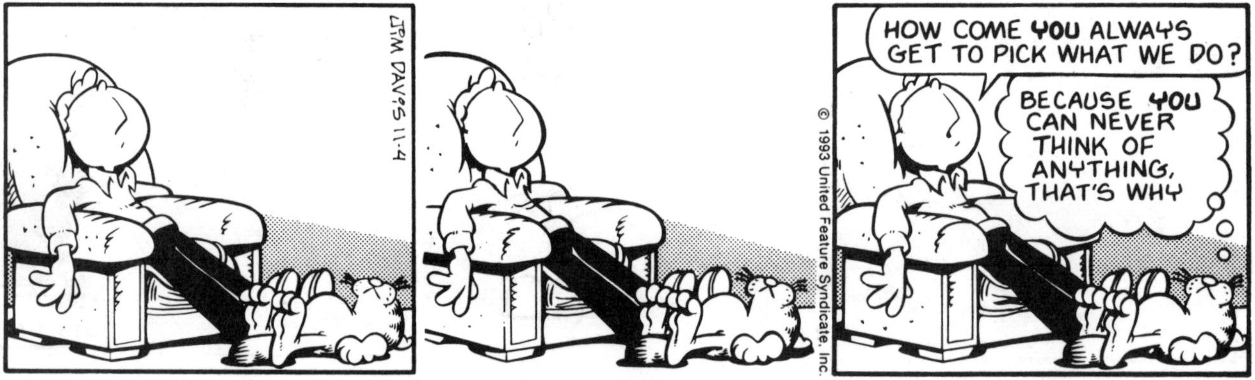
JPM DAVPS 11-4
HOW COME YOU ALWAYS GET TO PICK WHAT WE DO?
BECAUSE YOU CAN NEVER THINK OF ANYTHING, THAT'S WHY
© 1993 United Feature Syndicate, Inc.

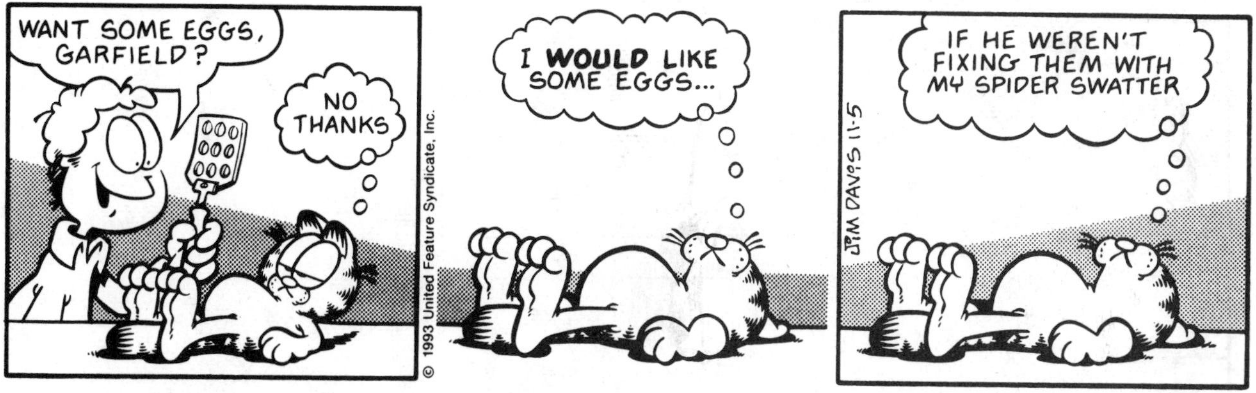
WANT SOME EGGS, GARFIELD?
NO THANKS
© 1993 United Feature Syndicate, Inc.
I **WOULD** LIKE SOME EGGS...
IF HE WEREN'T FIXING THEM WITH MY SPIDER SWATTER
JIM DAVIS 11-5

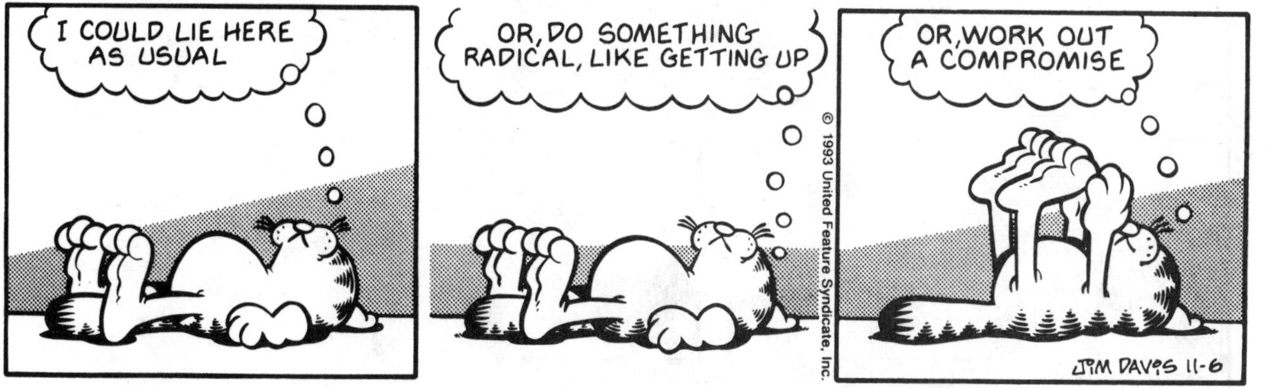
I COULD LIE HERE AS USUAL
OR, DO SOMETHING RADICAL, LIKE GETTING UP
© 1993 United Feature Syndicate, Inc.
OR, WORK OUT A COMPROMISE
JIM DAVIS 11-6

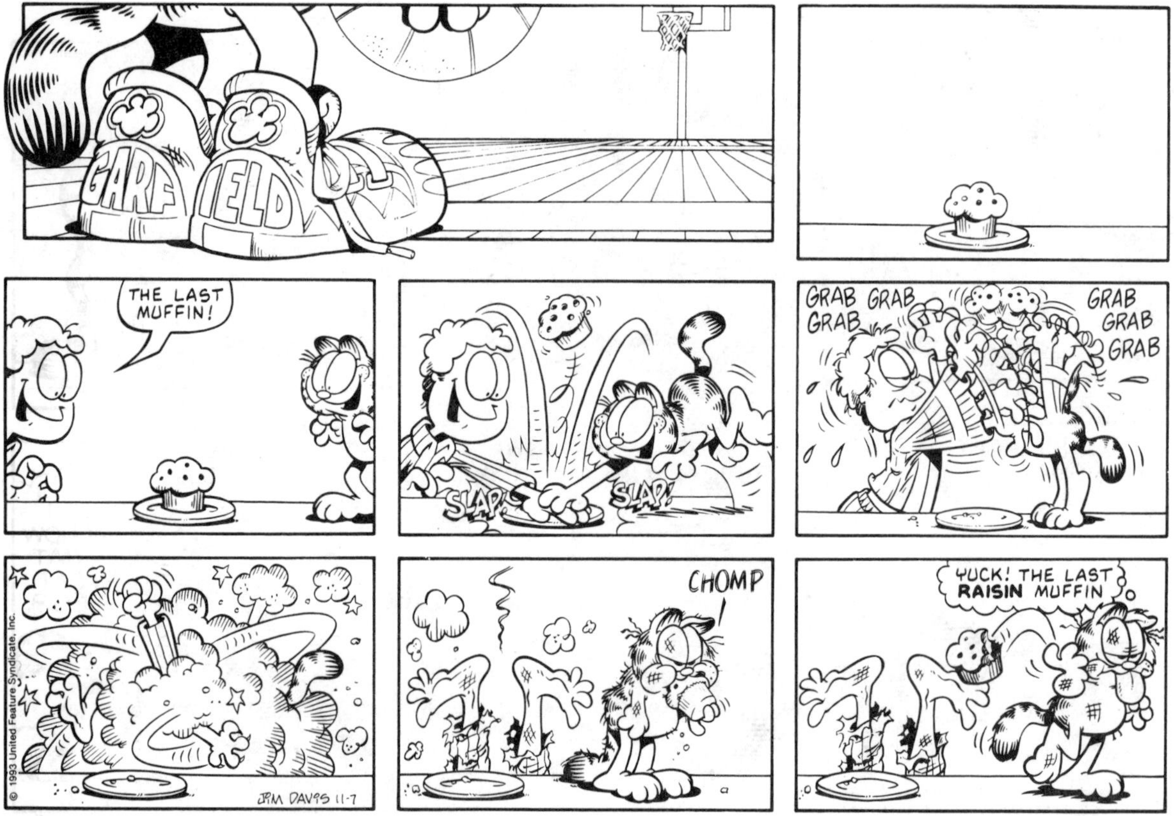
GARFIELD
THE LAST MUFFIN!
SLAP! SLAP!
GRAB GRAB GRAB
GRAB GRAB GRAB
© 1993 United Feature Syndicate, Inc.
JIM DAVIS 11-7
CHOMP!
YUCK! THE LAST RAISIN MUFFIN

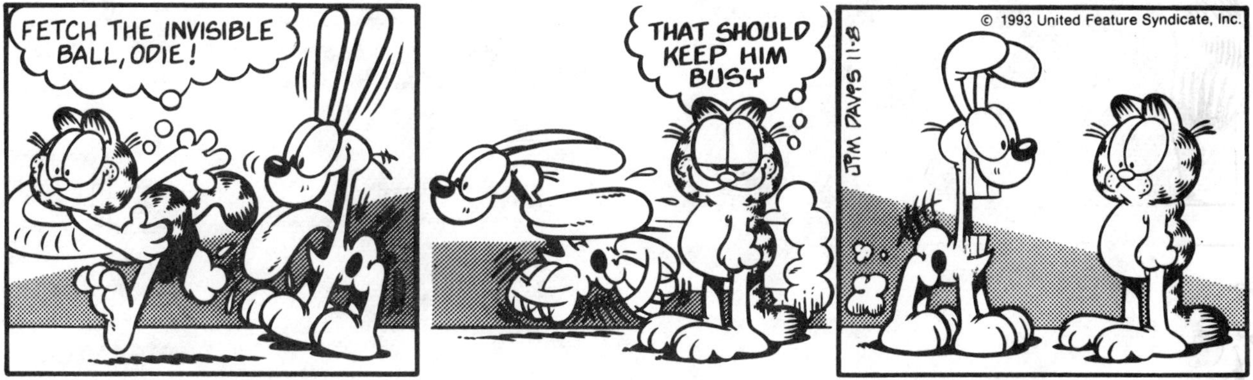
FETCH THE INVISIBLE BALL, ODIE!
THAT SHOULD KEEP HIM BUSY
JIM DAVIS 11-8
© 1993 United Feature Syndicate, Inc.

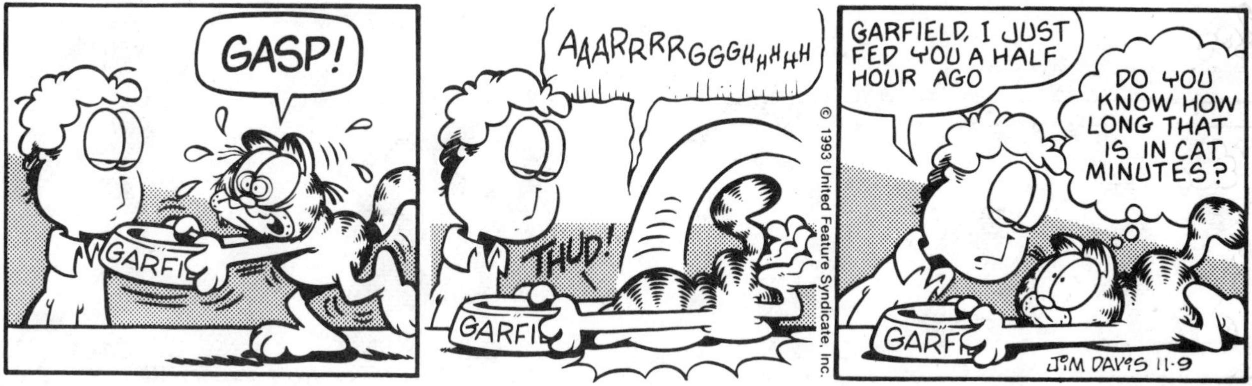
GASP!
GARFI
AAARRRRRGGGHHHHH
THUD!
GARFI
© 1993 United Feature Syndicate, Inc.
GARFIELD, I JUST FED YOU A HALF HOUR AGO
DO YOU KNOW HOW LONG THAT IS IN CAT MINUTES?
GARFI
JIM DAVIS 11-9

GARFIELD PRODUCTS YOU <u>WON'T</u> BE SEEING...

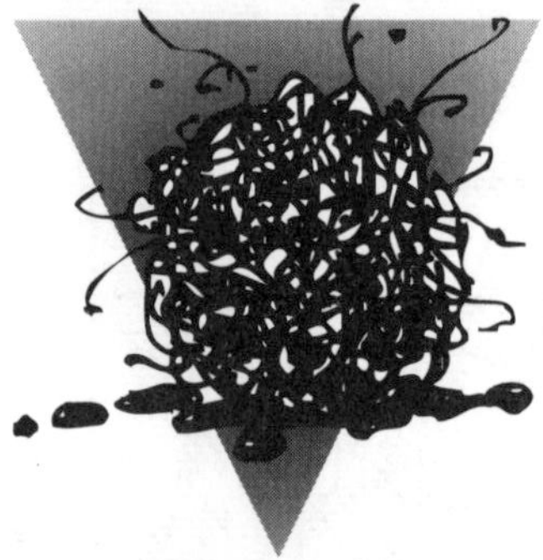

GARFIELD'S "HAIRBALL O' FUN"

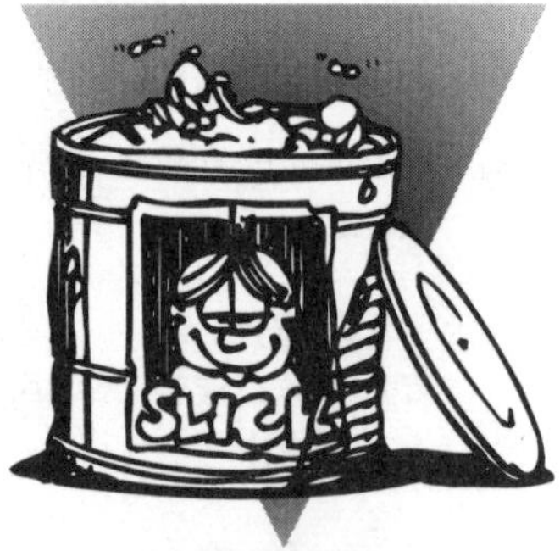
SLICK

GARFIELD'S STYLING LARD

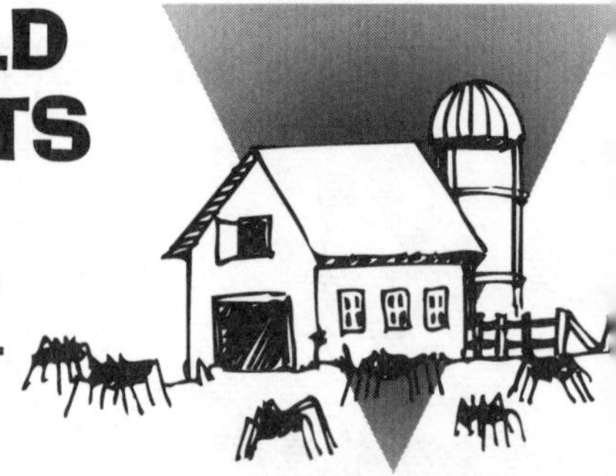

GARFIELD'S TARANTULA FARM

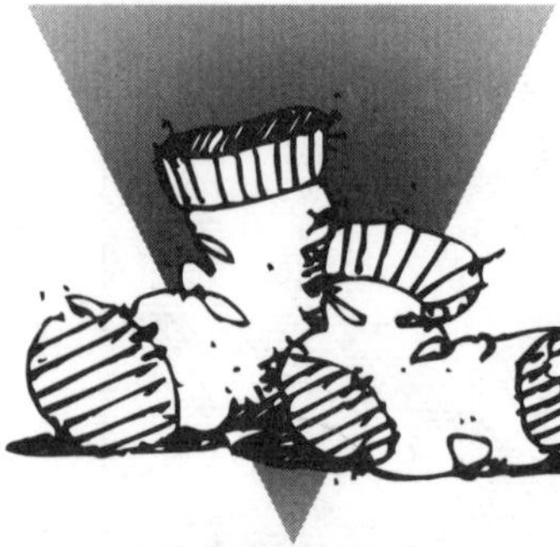

GARFIELD'S EDIBLE SWEAT SOCKS

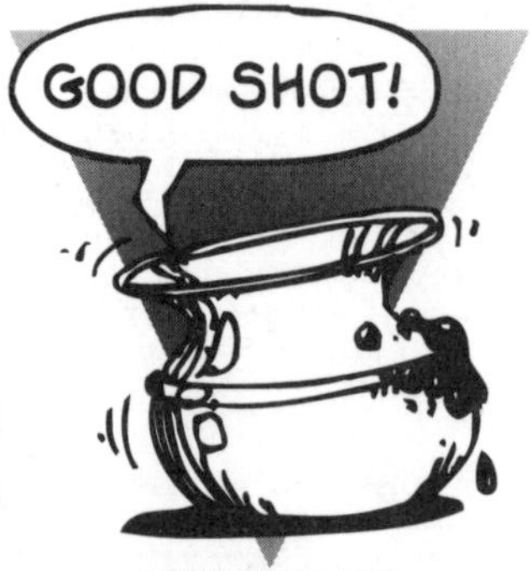
GOOD SHOT!

GARFIELD'S TALKING SPITTOON

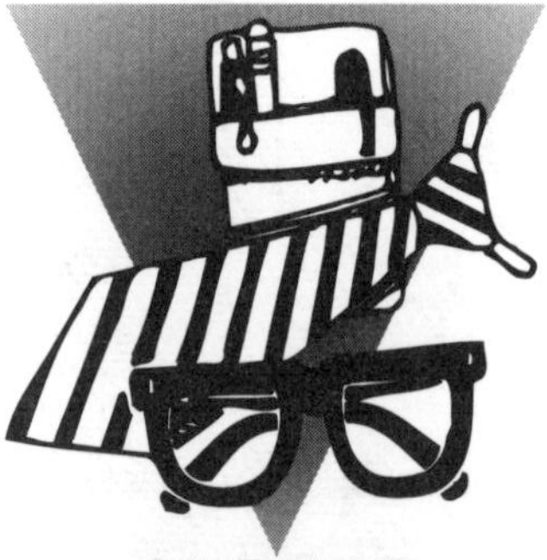

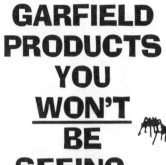

GARFIELD'S "JR. ACCOUNTANT" KIT

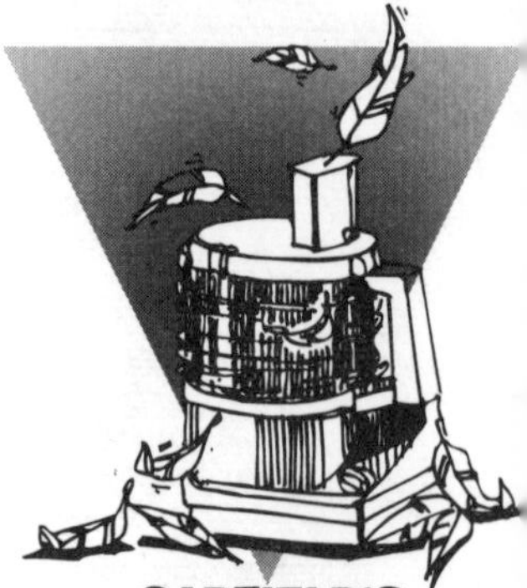

GARFIELD'S BIRD PROCESSOR

BIRTHDAYS, HOLIDAYS, OR ANY DAY . . .

Keep GARFIELD on your calendar all year 'round!

GARFIELD TV SPECIALS
__BABES & BULLETS   36339/$5.95
__GARFIELD GOES HOLLYWOOD   34580/$6.95
__GARFIELD'S HALLOWEEN ADVENTURE   33045/$6.95
  (formerly GARFIELD IN DISGUISE)
__GARFIELD'S FELINE FANTASY   36902/$6.95
__GARFIELD IN PARADISE   33796/$6.95
__GARFIELD IN THE ROUGH   32242/$6.95
__GARFIELD ON THE TOWN   31542/$6.95
__GARFIELD'S THANKSGIVING   35650/$6.95
__HERE COMES GARFIELD   32021/$6.95
__GARFIELD GETS A LIFE   37375/$6.95
__A GARFIELD CHRISTMAS   35368/$5.95

Please send me the BALLANTINE BOOKS I have checked above. I am enclosing $_____. (Please add $2.00 for the first book and $.50 for each additional book for postage and handling and include the appropriate state sales tax.) Send check or money order (no cash or C.O.D.'s) to Ballantine Mail Sales Dept. TA, 400 Hahn Road, Westminster, MD 21157.

To order by phone, call 1-800-733-3000 and use your major credit card.

Prices and numbers are subject to change without notice. Valid in the U.S. only. All orders are subject to availability.

GREETINGS FROM GARFIELD!
GARFIELD POSTCARD BOOKS FOR ALL OCCASIONS.
__GARFIELD THINKING OF YOU   36516/$6.95
__GARFIELD WORDS TO LIVE BY   36679/$6.95
__GARFIELD BIRTHDAY GREETINGS   36771/$7.95
__GARFIELD BE MY VALENTINE   37121/$7.95
__GARFIELD SEASON'S GREETINGS   37435/$8.95
__GARFIELD VACATION GREETINGS   37774/$10.00
__GARFIELD'S THANK YOU POSTCARD BOOK   37893/$10.00
ALSO FROM GARFIELD:
__GARFIELD: HIS NINE LIVES   32061/$9.95
__THE GARFIELD BOOK OF CAT NAMES   35082/$5.95
__THE GARFIELD TRIVIA BOOK   33771/$6.95
__THE UNABRIDGED UNCENSORED
  UNBELIEVABLE GARFIELD   33772/$5.95
__GARFIELD: THE ME BOOK   36545/$7.95
__GARFIELD'S JUDGMENT DAY   36755/$6.95
__THE TRUTH ABOUT CATS   37226/$6.95

Name_____

Address_____

City_____ State_____ Zip_____
30   Allow at least 4 weeks for delivery   7/93 TA-267

STRIPS, SPECIALS OR BESTSELLING BOOKS . . .
GARFIELD'S ON EVERYONE'S MENU
Don't miss even one episode in the Tubby Tabby's hilarious series!

__GARFIELD AT LARGE (#1)   32013/$6.95
__GARFIELD GAINS WEIGHT (#2)   32008/$6.95
__GARFIELD BIGGER THAN LIFE (#3)   32007/$6.95
__GARFIELD WEIGHS IN (#4)   32010/$6.95
__GARFIELD TAKES THE CAKE (#5)   32009/$6.95
__GARFIELD EATS HIS HEART OUT (#6)   32018/$6.95
__GARFIELD SITS AROUND THE HOUSE (#7)   32011/$6.95
__GARFIELD TIPS THE SCALES (#8)   33580/$6.95
__GARFIELD LOSES HIS FEET (#9)   31805/$6.95
__GARFIELD MAKES IT BIG (#10)   31928/$6.95
__GARFIELD ROLLS ON (#11)   32634/$6.95
__GARFIELD OUT TO LUNCH (#12)   33118/$6.95
__GARFIELD FOOD FOR THOUGHT (#13)   34129/$6.95

__GARFIELD SWALLOWS HIS PRIDE (#14)   34725/$6.95
__GARFIELD WORLDWIDE (#15)   35158/$6.95
__GARFIELD ROUNDS OUT (#16)   35388/$6.95
__GARFIELD CHEWS THE FAT (#17)   35956/$6.95
__GARFIELD GOES TO WAIST (#18)   36430/$6.95
__GARFIELD HANGS OUT (#19)   36835/$6.95
__GARFIELD TAKES UP SPACE (#20)   37029/$6.95
__GARFIELD SAYS A MOUTHFUL (#21)   37368/$6.95
__GARFIELD BY THE POUND (#22)   37579/$6.95
__GARFIELD KEEPS HIS CHINS UP (#23)   37959/$6.95
__GARFIELD TAKES HIS LICKS (#24)   38170/$6.95
__GARFIELD HITS THE BIG TIME (#25)   38332/$6.95

GARFIELD AT HIS SUNDAY BEST!
__GARFIELD TREASURY   32106/$11.95
__THE SECOND GARFIELD TREASURY   33276/$10.95
__THE THIRD GARFIELD TREASURY   32635/$11.00
__THE FOURTH GARFIELD TREASURY   34726/$10.95
__THE FIFTH GARFIELD TREASURY   36268/$12.00
__THE SIXTH GARFIELD TREASURY   37367/$10.95
__THE SEVENTH GARFIELD TREASURY   38427/$10.95

Please send me the BALLANTINE BOOKS I have checked above. I am
enclosing $_____. (Please add $2.00 for the first book and $.50
for each additional book for postage and handling and include the appropriate
state sales tax.) Send check or money order (no cash or C.O.D.'s) to
Ballantine Mail Sales Dept. TA, 400 Hahn Road, Westminster, MD 21157.

To order by phone, call 1-800-733-3000 and use your major credit card.

Prices and numbers are subject to change without notice. Valid in the U.S.
only. All orders are subject to availability.

Name_____

Address_____

City_____ State_____ Zip_____
30   Allow at least 4 weeks for delivery   7/93